Josefina de Vasconcellos

Also by Margaret Lewis

Ngaio Marsh: A Life
Edith Pargeter: Ellis Peters

Josefina de Vasconcellos

HER LIFE AND ART

Margaret Lewis

First published in Great Britain in 2002 by Flambard Press
Stable Cottage, East Fourstones, Hexham NE47 5DX.
Reprinted 2004

Typeset and cover design by Gainford Design Associates.
Printed in Great Britain by Cromwell Press, Trowbridge.

A CIP catalogue record for this book
is available from the British Library.

ISBN 1 873226 56 X

Flambard Press wishes to thank Northern Arts
for its financial support.

CONTENTS

Chapter 1   The Early Years   1

Chapter 2   Growth of a Sculptor: The 1920s   19

Chapter 3   A Challenging Decade: The 1930s   51

Chapter 4   Safe Haven in the Langdales: The 1940s   72

Chapter 5   New Artistic Horizons: The 1950s   96

Chapter 6   Sculpture and Vision: The 1960s   122

Chapter 7   Working for Others: The 1970s   143

Chapter 8   A New Beginning: The 1980s   156

Chapter 9   International Acclaim: The 1990s   173

Chapter 10   The New Century   199

Notes   214

Bibliography   217

Representation in major exhibitions   219

Acknowledgements   220

Index   222

If I am here, to work in this great place,
Let me from small designs avert my face.
With strong desire, for all lost years atone,
Transformed by love, empowered by faith alone
Give Vision a new form, serene in stone;
Or strike a bronze, in rugged shapes to cry –
'This is love's sign!' – against a flaming sky.

J de V

CHAPTER ONE

The Early Years

What makes a sculptor? Frankly; I don't know.

What made me, at the age of three, dig under the grass at the edge of the lawn and find clay... and model a bird's nest?

Why there? There was no clay anywhere else – why dig with bare fingers as though it were urgent? – (quite difficult – a vivid memory) – and I still don't know.

I ask myself, Imagine an unborn soul somewhere or nowhere – waiting to be born – how does it know it is – or is it only God that knows? No light nor dark – no here nor there – but it is. Only through entering into MATTER can one know anything or relate to anything – even to oneself! It is all beyond knowing.

J de V

Josefina de Vasconcellos, the child in the garden, responding intensely to the sounds and sensations of a world that she knew, even then, to be the source of life's truths – the child in the garden, escaping from an abrasive adult world that she did not understand – the child watching parents who were both protective and curiously blind to her unique perceptions – the child that would become a sculptor, creating works that have moved people profoundly in countries around the world.

What does make a sculptor? What is the special combination of artistry and practicality; of sheer physical strength and inspiration? Does it begin in childhood, or is it discovered through careful teaching? Many small children play in the sand or clay in the garden, as Josefina did, making shapes of birds or animals. It is a natural thing to do. But very few go on to devote their lives to sculpture and for Josefina de Vasconcellos it has been a very long life indeed.

From earliest times, individuals have worked with stone or wood, carving with traditional tools to commemorate their dead, to celebrate their gods, to produce a personal but recognisable image of man or nature. Sculptors in the twentieth century have travelled down so many different paths that now it is difficult to define exactly what sculpture is. For Josefina de Vasconcellos, whose work spanned the twentieth century, communication has been at the heart of her endeavour and she has steadfastly held to that path, producing work that offers beauty and spiritual refreshment to those who view it.

She is one of the tiny group of twentieth century British women sculptors, including Barbara Hepworth and Elizabeth Frink, who have managed to make and retain an international reputation. Hepworth is still admired today but the originality and power of Elizabeth Frink is, regrettably, often overlooked. De Vasconcellos, too, would no doubt have drifted into obscurity had it not been for her longevity and a fiery artistic energy that enabled her, in her eighties, to effect a renaissance that brought her back into the public eye.

Josefina Alys Hermes de Vasconcellos was born to a handsome, outgoing Brazilian father and a captivating English mother on 26 October 1904, in Molesey on Thames, near London. Already the marriage, only ten months old, was suffering from the tensions of too many opposites and too many barriers that could not be overcome. Josefina's parents had met in the heady atmosphere of *fin-de-siècle* London: Hippolyto de Vasconcellos, an aristocratic Brazilian government official, star-struck in a theatre audience; Freda Coleman, the object of his fascination, acting and singing on stage.

He asked her to dine with him, but despite the Zola-esque situation, there was no hint of impropriety in his approaches to Freda; this was no King Cophetua and the Beggar Maid. Freda

Coleman came from a prosperous and respectable Quaker family and her father, Alfred Coleman, was an esteemed medical doctor and dentist. Soon Hippolyto was being invited to the Colemans' comfortable home in Streatham, South London, where he met other members of the extensive Coleman family and was brought into a lively and cultivated environment.

Hippolyto came from the founding family of the Brazilian republic. He was born in 1872, the oldest of six children, two of whom died in infancy. His great-grandmother, Dona Rosa da Fonseca (1802–1873), a poet, was known as the mother of heroes because of the sacrifice of her sons in the bitter 1865–70 Paraguayan war. Slavery finally ended in Brazil in 1888, but the abolition was fiercely resisted by the slavocrats who depended on slave labour in the coffee and rubber plantations. A military uprising followed by a bloodless coup on 15 November 1889 ended the monarchy of Emperor Dom Pedro II. Heading the forces who surrounded the Palace on that day was Generalissimo Manuel Deodoro da Fonseca (1827–1892), Hippolyto's uncle. Supported by the army, Deodoro informed the nation that 'The people, the army, and the navy, in perfect harmony of sentiment with our fellow citizens resident in the provinces, have just decreed the dethronement of the imperial dynasty, and consequently the extinction of the representational monarchical system of government.'[1] He immediately became chief of state and was elected President of the Republic in 1891.

A powerful figure, Deodoro rigorously controlled the often volatile political situation and secured international recognition for the new republic. One of his first acts was to separate the powers of church and state, but although a new constitution was drafted along American lines he did very little to establish a liberal regime, and in fact acted as a military dictator. He soon clashed with the congress, who refused to vote him funds, and, threatened by a revolt from the navy, resigned at the end of 1891. He died the following year. Although he had maintained a regime that was much more directed by military power than political subtlety, his discipline kept the country from descending into anarchy at a critical time, and his contribution as the founder of the new nation of Brazil was fully recognised in years to come.

Hippolyto's father, Josefina's Brazilian grandfather, Amarilio Olinade de Vasconcellos (1845–1929), was not a politician, but an engineer. He surveyed much of Brazil for the new railway lines that were so important for the economic growth of the developing nation. His first wife, Josefina Rosa da Fonseca Hermes, died young, leaving him with four surviving children, but this did not prevent him from placing his fifteen-year-old son Hippolyto in charge of the family and the estate when he went on an urgent mission to survey a new railway line to reach the famine-struck interior. Hippolyto was given his father's cheque book and told to look after the servants, the slaves and his siblings. Not only that, he also had to supervise the construction of a new house being built for the family.

Hippolyto was introduced to more dubious adult pleasures when his debonair uncle Tio Manuel felt it his duty to take him to sample the brothels of Rio. Manuel was a poor example for the teenage boy, and encouraged him to take promiscuity for granted. This marked him for the rest of his life and would ultimately destroy his marriage. He had several illegitimate children in Brazil.

After his schooling Hippolyto attended a Military Academy in Rio de Janiero, as was usual for his social class, and was briefly imprisoned because of his political activities, having led a rising in the army against his uncle Hermes. Possibly as a result of this, and with a maturity beyond his years, Hippolyto decided that all his siblings should be educated overseas and he brought them to Europe to attend school. Amarilio was sent to a college in Germany, became a doctor and was involved in early work on combating malaria. Heraclito, the youngest, went to Stoneyhurst and became a diplomat. Alice, who as the only girl was used to being the centre of attention and rather spoiled, was sent to the Convent of the Sacred Heart in London, where she upset the nuns by pouring ink into the Holy Water Font. They were terrified that the devil had left his mark on their foreheads and indeed a certain devil had, but she was soon persuaded to improve her conduct, and was happy at her new school. After completing her education she stayed in England, married Afonso Deodora d'Alincourt Fonseca in 1909, and had nine children. Her second-born daughter, Lucilia, was born in London in 1911 and was to become Josefina's closest connection with her father's family.

Although the family were all sent to Roman Catholic schools, Hippolyto was a firm atheist, and this was not unusual in Brazil at that time. According to the historian Fred G. Sturm of the University of New Mexico, 'the liberated church of the 1890s was extremely weak, with reference to both the political elite and to the society at large. The intellectual elite of the late nineteenth century had rejected the faith as popularly practiced, viewing it as largely irrelevant superstition, and Brazil's high culture had become increasingly secular.'[2] Hippolyto's views were to have a profound effect on the development of his daughter in years to come.

With his brothers and sister established in school and university, Hippolyto returned to Brazil and undertook his first expedition into the Amazon for the Ministry of Agriculture, mapping rivers and surveying for rubber and minerals. Having heard of another explorer who had nearly gone mad from toothache while deep in the jungle, and had been reduced to banging his head against trees with pain, he decided to have all his excellent teeth pulled out so that he would not be troubled. His travels into the interior continued over many years, even when he was posted to Inquitos in Peru in the early 1920s, but he had fallen in love with England and was happy to be sent back there.

The spirit of rebellion and independence that was clearly part of Hippolyto's family was mirrored, to a lesser extent, in the Colemans. Josefina's grandfather, Alfred Coleman, FRCS, was a distinguished member of the medical profession. He was a distant cousin of Joseph Lister (1827–1912), later Lord Lister, who brought great benefits to all by his development of antiseptic surgical techniques.

Alfred Coleman came from an old Quaker family where his maiden aunts still wore Quaker dress and used 'thee' and thou' in speech. Although he should have followed in the family footsteps by entering Lloyds, the financial house, he rebelled against his family, first by joining the army, which was strictly against Quaker thinking, and then by deciding to study Dentistry at a time when it was regarded with little respect.

In 1864 he married Fanny Butler from the wealthy Butler family of 'Hollywood', Wimbledon and they had thirteen children. Freda was one of the youngest, born in 1882, with three more girls to follow.

Dr Coleman did a great deal to raise the standing of Dentistry in the second half of the nineteenth century and was active in founding the British Dental Association in 1880. His early work on the use of anaesthetics allowed considerable progress to be made in dental techniques, and he invented several instruments, including a device, the Coleman Gag, designed to keep the mouth open during the administration of anaesthetic. His well-known textbook *Dental Surgery and Pathology* was published in 1882 and was used for years in Dental Schools. As well as being a practising dentist, he lectured at a number of Dental Schools and was very interested in dental research. His grand-daughter, Josefina, would inherit his ability as an inventor; in her case, devising useful aids to improve the lives of disabled people.

Coleman retired to Nelson, New Zealand in 1884 for reasons of health, bringing the entire family with servants and furniture, including a grand piano and chandeliers. The chandeliers proved to be particularly useful as they tinkled to give early warning of an earthquake, and the whole family would race out of doors. Fanny must certainly have been resilient because as soon as they arrived in New Zealand all the servants deserted and promptly got married, leaving her and Ethel, the eldest daughter, to run the household. The boys went to the famous public school in Wellington, and the rest of the family, released from the restrictions of Victorian England, thrived. Alfred did not practise in New Zealand, but he did accept the honorary appointment of Surgeon to the Defence Forces. Eventually, missing England and with his health improved, Alfred Coleman returned to London in 1890.

It is possible that the ship bearing the Coleman family back from New Zealand docked at Rio de Janiero while the youthful and politically-minded Hippolyto was in jail overlooking the harbour, not knowing that on board was the young girl who was to become his wife. Freda would have been about eight years old at that time. Certainly the ship's entry into the great harbour at Rio, with the Sugar Loaf mountain behind, must have impressed everyone, and Fanny still remembered it nearly forty years later when she wrote to her daughter Freda that 'Rio is a magnificent place. I shall never forget my one day there.' But she added pragmatically, 'You cannot live on scenery alone... no better place for living in than England, on the whole.' She was clearly glad to be home.

On his return to London, Dr Coleman became a Governor of St Bartholemew's Hospital, 'Barts', and an Almoner in 1894. His Quaker principles led him to decline a knighthood, but he remained in contact with members of his Association, and his tolerant and wise counsel was greatly valued by his fellow practitioners. Much of his collection of early dental instruments was presented to the Hunterian Museum, in which he took a great interest in his later days. His son Frank followed in his footsteps and became a highly regarded dentist in London.

The Colemans were clearly a stylish family and they all loved the theatre. When Freda's brother Maurice was married in October 1900, the whole wedding party went off to the Duchess Theatre, Balham after the reception. For the ceremony the six bridesmaids had worn white Liberty silk and black velvet hats with black ostrich plumes; not, one would suspect, a commonplace choice of dress. Wedding presents included a Bechstein piano and a great deal of antique silver and china.

Josefina's grandmother, Fanny Butler, was of Irish ancestry, and daughter of a London wine merchant, James Butler. Through his marriage to Frances Mary Hedges in 1839 he joined a very profitable business, later to be known as Hedges and Butler, the Bond Street wine merchants.

Like the Colemans, the Butlers were another old Quaker family. Fanny was one of a family of fifteen children, all but one of whom survived into adulthood, quite an unusual situation for a time when many children died young. From all accounts she was unconventional, lively and full of ideas, and she gave her children much more freedom than was usual at that period. Josefina remembers that 'Even as a child I found my aunts far more lively and fun than any other grown-ups, but about some things, like manners, Granny could be very strict.' When Fanny returned to London after her stay in New Zealand, she enjoyed the artistic and intellectual life of London and joined Madame Blavatsky's fashionable Theosophist circle.

Fanny's brother, Josefina's great-uncle Frank Hedges Butler, became a very prosperous wine merchant indeed, and a partner in

Hedges and Butler. He was a dashing Edwardian gentleman who flew his own hot-air balloon, *Dolce far Niente*, and drove the very latest Mercedes Benz and Panhard motor cars. In 1901, with his daughter Vera, who often flew with him, and the Honourable C S Rolls, he founded the Royal Aero Club. This group of pioneer airmen was to form the basis of the new Flying Corps that served with such gallantry in the First World War.

Despite his unremarkable appearance, dressed as any businessman would be in a three-piece suit and bowler hat and with a flourishing moustache, Frank Butler was a man of considerable courage, having flown with Wilbur Wright in a biplane as early as 1908. He was remarkably far-seeing in his confident views on the future of aviation, and even predicted in a 1910 edition of *The Motor* that helicopters, 'by which an aviator will rise immediately into the air, like a lark', would be available within a very short space of time.

Frank Butler took Josefina's mother, Freda, up in his balloon for a ride, and she found it a very peaceful experience, though not very exciting. Perhaps the experience of sailing to New Zealand and back had made her blasé. Photographs taken at that time show a wealthy and well-connected family, very much integrated into their comfortable suburban houses and gardens, and always near the stabilising figures of their parents, Alfred and Fanny.

But although the Colemans may have been liberal in outlook, they were not inclined to welcome a foreigner like the Brazilian Hippolyto de Vasconcellos, no matter how well connected, into the family. Alfred Coleman had recently died in 1902 and only Freda's mother, Fanny, was tolerant towards the match. The marriage between Freda and Hippolyto took place against the wishes of the family on 24 December 1903, and Josefina (her pet name was always Fifina) was born the following October. Soon afterwards Hippolyto returned to Brazil, on an assignment from the government to explore and survey the Amazon. Ten years older than Freda, his character was already formed at the age of fifteen and could not change. He was infinitely more versed in the ways of the world than she was, and they were never able to live happily together.

After his trip into the Amazon Basin, Hippolyto joined the Brazilian Diplomatic Service and returned to his wife and child in England. They lived first in Ravenscroft Park in London, next in Wallington, and then in Southampton, where he was Consul. From 1911 until the outbreak of hostilities in the First World War they lived at 7 Westwood Road, Southampton, a large and comfortable house with a garden that bordered the Common, on the edge of the New Forest. As the War escalated, Hippolyto thought there was a chance of Southampton being attacked, so the family moved to Bournemouth. They remained there even when Hippolyto became Consul-General in London from 1916 to 1920.

The marriage between Hippolyto and Freda was full of disappointment for them both. He was a lover of women, popular, strong and handsome, and felt no particular loyalty towards his wife. Even in the early days of their marriage he was unfaithful. Although looking to Hippolyto for glamour and romance, Freda had also expected a conventional marriage and home life. She found herself deeply frustrated and unhappy. Having married against the advice of her family, she kept her misery to herself. She knew that among her family there would be little sympathy for her situation.

As a very small child, Josefina was conscious of the tension between her parents. She remembers saying from her high chair, 'Don't take any notice of him, Mummy,' during a fraught breakfast when her mother was being bullied and in tears. 'They looked at me in absolute silence as if to say "How dare she!" Then my father got up and very slowly left the room.'

Happy first memories are of the presence of light and feeding the birds from her pram in the park; less happy ones are of her father's deep voice and threatening gesture with his slipper raised in the air, when she was still in her cot. 'Ai, Ai!' he would say, Brazilian for 'Look out!' She was made to feel that her parents were always ready to punish her for being naughty in ways that she could not understand.

Hippolyto had a fierce temper and in the early days of the marriage was wildly jealous of anyone who even looked at his wife or daughter. Josefina, who was an exceptionally pretty child with rich brown curls and unusual green eyes, remembers his rage when a kindly gentleman smiled at her in a railway carriage. She had to pretend to be asleep along with her mother until they reached the station because they were afraid of Hippolyto's anger. He was immensely strong, and once stopped a moving hansom cab by reaching out and holding the wheel.

He had wanted a son, and gave Josefina a man's name (Hermes), perhaps because she bore the birthmark that all male members of the family shared. He may have found his daughter disappointing, but she was anxious to please him. He made the best of the situation by giving her a magnifying glass to look at plants and by taking her for long walks in the forest to tell her about the trees and wildlife. Like his daughter he loved the world of nature: 'animals came to him and loved his deep voice,' said Josefina. He managed to calm a wild and ferocious Brazilian jaguar at London Zoo, to the amazement of keepers who had been too frightened to go into the cage, as he did. Even so, it was Freda, with her Quaker background, who confiscated the small gun that he gave his daughter, and it was never seen again, although Josefina had enjoyed exploring its mechanism, and trying target practice in the garden.

Josefina loved her father to tell her about his adventures in the Amazon jungle, such as the story of a huge tarantula that had to be trapped beneath a washing-bowl as her father lay quietly in his hammock reading Shakespeare by the light of a single candle stuck in a tree. He had to put his heavy boots on top of the basin to keep the spider from escaping. It was so big that he later had it stuffed. Or the unforgettable sight of a young and beautiful Indian man paddling a canoe along the Amazon in the early morning, clad only in a head-dress of white feathers. His knowledge of the Amazon led to him being made a Fellow of the Royal Geographical Society in 1917.

Hippolyto had a high regard for education and he abandoned his strict atheist principles sufficiently to enrol his daughter in the Convent of the Sacred Heart in Southampton because the academic results were the best in the area, although he insisted to the Mother Superior that Josefina was not to receive any religious education. Freda did not object to this, because as a child herself she had been horrified by a religious studies teacher at school who said that all non-baptised babies went to Hell, and her mother removed her from these classes from then on. Both parents seemed to feel that if the child wanted religion she could seek it out as an adult instead of having it forced upon her, but Josefina had a clear sense that she was being deprived of comfort and inspiration that other children were offered. She had music lessons instead of religious instruction with the other girls and this contributed to her sense of being outside the group, although she found that their secrets and chatter were of little interest to her. It was, she realised later, good training for other rebuffs in later life.

Like many other only children Josefina took refuge with the maids and the cook in 'the big homely kitchen' where she found affection and fun. They were 'real and natural' and allowed her to play games hopping around the cupboards and playing with a tame robin that came in to sit on the dresser. She had a kitten who comforted her at night and in the garden there was a pet lizard and a toad. The flowers and birds in the garden were a constant source of joy. While very young she started to shape birds and animals from clay and her parents encouraged her artistic leanings, although they were very strict in other ways.

Forbidden to get out of bed before her parents in the morning, Josefina would listen to the birds in the tall trees at the end of the garden, feeling that somehow she was transported to be with them. This sense of being taken out of herself, of belonging somewhere else, of escape, has stayed with her throughout her life – she has been described as 'a natural mystic' by one cleric; someone whose understanding of people and nature goes much deeper than the tangible surface.

From her earliest memories, the presence of light was comforting; a candle, a window, the stars in the night sky: 'the morning sunlight, held in a wet, gleaming lawn, sparked off darts of pure prismic colour... sometimes also seen in my own tears – trembling between eyelashes before dropping off – so sudden and near that one forgot what it was that one had been naughty about, or sad.'

Her early childhood was full of fears that no one helped her to alleviate: 'At about the age of eight or nine, my father's atheistic pronouncements about there being no God and no such thing as life after death produced long hours of wakeful thinkings in the dark after I'd been sent to bed, followed by horrible nightmares.' Then there was the terrible nightmare of 'The Humming Cubes' which even today is as vivid to her as it was at the time:

> First there was a greyish blanket everywhere, and the sound
> of distant humming on one note... (like wasps, only softer
> and more even) and with it a feeling of a sort of paralysis, as
> though velvet were being smoothly moved all over my skin.
>
> Then, out of the grey distance, advanced an army of small
> white cubes.
>
> As they came slowly nearer, they increased in size, and the
> humming increased in volume... larger and louder until the
> humming was a siren scream, and the cubes arrived huge,
> and crushed me.
>
> I awakened in terror, the whole of my body cramped with
> vibrations, as though stuck to an electric wire... the humming
> still heard in the distance... and it took some time to wear off.
> I knew the cubes were EVIL – and was a terrified little girl.[3]

She was desperately afraid of the empty house across the road
that was considered to be haunted, and at night she would bite her
arms to try to stop crying out. In the morning she would dress
quickly before her mother could see the marks. She knew that her
mother would dismiss these fears of evil spirits as stupidity, and she
only overcame them when she had a comforting and healing dream
that she later interpreted in Christian terms. Her father's robust
dismissal of any form of the afterlife – 'when you die, you just die,
like a donkey' – had terrified Josefina, and she lay in bed imagining
her body gradually stiffening up and being unable to move.

A great deal of her mother's misery and resentment against her
husband found its way to the child. Josefina resembled Hippolyto,
with her intense response to nature, her silences, and her penetrating
stare. 'My mother wanted me to chatter, like the children in school,
but I couldn't,' said Josefina. Little wonder, seeing such unhappiness
in her parents, that Josefina knocked on the door of the morning
room one day, having been forbidden ever to disturb her mother at
that time, and told her that she did not want to grow up. What was the
point, when adults could not do what they wanted or find happiness?
But her mother had little understanding of the troubled child, and
she never asked why Josefina had come to her, or tried to explain.
Yet from the earliest age Josefina knew that her mother was unhappy.

Few children, apart from her cousins, were allowed to make contact with the lonely girl. One good friend was her cousin Doris, daughter of Freda's sister Norah, and they were able to play in the garden, enjoying the usual games of hide and seek and imaginary adventures. Josefina wrote plays for them to perform to the adults, but it was a very adult world that she inhabited. The son of a friend was banished when Hippolyto discovered how happily they had been playing outside. Dancing lessons stopped immediately when he discovered that Josefina enjoyed dancing with one particular boy. She was never allowed to have a birthday party, because that would have meant having other children to the house. Although she had started to attend Miss Allnut's School in Southampton, she was taken away and a series of governesses educated her at home. Religious material of any kind was forbidden, and if any members of the Coleman family gave her a Bible or other religious books they were confiscated. Apparently Freda had no desire to go against her husband's wishes in this. Josefina grew up with her spiritual hunger unsatisfied, and it remained so until she met her husband, Delmar Banner.

The sense of being an outsider was always with her. She remembers being locked in a dark cupboard by the other children on her first day at Miss Allnut's, and soon afterwards she remembers fighting a group of children who had imprisoned a butterfly in a matchbox. Josefina set it free from the upstairs window and watched it fly out of sight in the summer air: 'I turned back to the empty room and suddenly felt very lonely,' she said. On another occasion she was invited to a tea-party and offered the one remaining cream bun left on the plate. It was a joke bun, made of rubber, the sort of thing she had never seen before, and everyone roared with laughter. But no one offered her a real bun and the joke was burned into her memory as yet another way in which she was separate from the rest. Her mother's offer to buy her a cream bun next day did nothing to heal her hurt feelings and sense of being apart.

This feeling of isolation remained as she grew older and went to secondary school. Her foreign name, her strictly controlled life, her passionate response to art, music and nature made her different from the other girls. When the family moved to Bournemouth she attended Bournemouth High School and was allowed to take lessons at Bournemouth Art School on Saturdays. The High School was exceptionally well run and Josefina's love of literature was nurtured by her teacher, Miss Broad. But abruptly her parents decided that she had little more to gain from school, and took her away, although she was only fourteen, and happy there. They felt that the subjects she was best at – Art, French, Nature Study and Literature – she could do better at home, and she was told to go off and buy whatever books she wanted to study on her own. A school notebook for her final term in the spring of 1919 reveals superb drawings from nature and careful work that was praised by teachers.

Several years later Hippolyto wrote to Josefina about his regrets at cutting her education short. When he was Consul in Manchester in 1925 she sent him some essays to read, and he replied in his perfect but very formal English that although she was gifted by nature, 'the practical and theoretical basis so indispensable for the perfection of all productions in life are lacking, I may say, due to my neglect in your early years to provide you with the groundwork that you so much need now. This point, though a subject apart, to be fought between myself and my conscience, I mention solely for the purpose of inspiring you with the energy to supplement now, while it is time, that which was not adequately and proportionately given you.'

Academic learning was never easy for Josefina, and mathematics was so stressful for her at the High School that she was excused the classes, although she clearly had an intuitive understanding of shape and form. Throughout her childhood her most ardent response was to the sounds and sensations that came from the natural world. This was where she found happiness, feeling the smooth cool feathers of ducks brushing against her legs as she waded into a pond to feed them, hearing the sound of a pine tree singing in the wind as she held its trunk, gazing back at the steady green eye of a cat beyond the garden shed, feeling at one with the old oak tree where she perched. When Josefina was allowed to take her lessons outside she was content. 'Nature,' she said 'was the comfort and support and companionship of my life.' She was building up a bank of references that would be drawn on later as her mastery of shape, form and movement emerged through sculpture.

The end of the First World War in 1918 meant that the following summer the family could travel safely to Brazil to meet Hippolyto's relations. Brazil had initially been a neutral country during the early years of the war, but attacks on Brazilian shipping by the German Navy brought them into the war on the side of the Allies in October 1917, the only South American country to do so. This decision enhanced Brazil's international status after the war and brought substantial dividends in terms of trade and diplomatic prestige.

When the Vasconcellos family travelled to Brazil it meant a long passage on a White Star Liner, the *Andes*, but it was a great adventure for Josefina, who was then fourteen. She wrote many poems on the voyage and some dramatic prose pieces describing storms at sea. These were carefully written into a notebook and eventually typed up. The poems are restless, romantic, overly decorative and always close to descriptions of the natural world: birds, trees, seas and storms feature prominently and the human presence is often destructive. Yet for a fourteen-year-old girl they have the seeds of an unusually profound outlook on life and an unconscious pantheism in her outlook. A prose fragment called 'The Meadow' shows this clearly: 'When wandering by the almost silent stream, the senses drowsy with the sunny air, you suddenly awake, and looking down, feel your soul's secrets understood, laid bare before the sweet blue eyes of the forget-me-not.' Like Wordsworth in his poem 'Nutting' – 'there is a spirit in the woods' – this fragment describes finding a moral force in the natural world to which Josefina responded.

They stayed for over a year in Brazil, taking ship once more in July 1920. Although Josefina loved meeting her Brazilian relatives, learning to ride horses and play the guitar, the strained relations between her parents was always in the background. 'She would have left him,' said Josefina, 'but she was afraid that he would take me from her.'

There was also a strange tension that Josefina could not understand, when some members of the family appeared to resent her presence and others did not. She was startled and upset when she was momentarily left unattended at a railway station and a woman rushed up to her and said, 'You have a brother!' Many years later Josefina understood that she had a number of illegitimate half brothers and sisters in Brazil, although she never met any of them.

Freda could not have been unaware of the situation, and her misery deepened. She became more and more depressed. She gave up her singing and playing the violin and increasingly lived her life through her daughter. Freda was unable to accept Hippolyto's unfaithfulness and this blinded her to the more positive aspects of his character: his kindness to others and his fierce sense of justice. The romance and glamour of Brazil had come to her, but by then the relationship with her husband had been irrevocably destroyed.

For Josefina, however, the visit to Brazil had transformed her life: 'It was like going from a black and white film to 3D colour.' The company of her lively cousins, the street calls of Rio de Janiero, the music, the tropical flowers and trees opened up a whole new world that would give redolence to her life from then on. She took some lessons in painting and sculpture from the respected Bernardelli brothers in Rio, and a decade later, on her next trip to Brazil, she would exhibit her own work beside her teacher, Rodolpho Bernardelli. She was also writing with increasing sophistication.

Poems written on the return voyage to England aboard the *Demarara* reveal a more mature young woman, and perhaps a sadder one. 'Ravings' is a poem about someone who looks out to sea from a ship and is drawn to throw himself into the waves. But she also wrote amusing verses about playing deck tennis and overhearing her mother playing Patience. On her return one of her poems, 'Thoughts', was published in the *Bournemouth Graphic* newspaper, and it demonstrates that, for a sixteen-year-old, Josefina was already establishing a philosophy of life that would manifest itself in many different artistic endeavours in the years ahead.

> Our thoughts, like columns of different hue,
> Are born in our souls, and, if they are true,
> Right glorious thoughts, they speed to the sun,
> As they always have since life begun.
>
> If our thoughts are kindly, gentle and bright,
> They go to the stars to lighten the night.
> For the weary Traveller, who, timid and poor,
> Is too frightened to knock at the Inn's closed door.

> So go our thoughts to different spheres,
> Some to rouse courage, some to calm fears;
> But all to do work that will help mankind
> To lose what is bad and the good to find.

These were unusual thoughts for a young girl, and suggest that at that time Josefina's considerable creative powers were being directed towards words, as well as towards fine art, and expressing herself in poetry was a way of trying to cope with uncertainties in her personal life.

Not long after the family returned to England in 1920, Josefina remembers walking along a canal in Manchester, where her father had taken up the post of Consul-General. The three of them walked along the dreary towpath, where according to Josefina 'even the weeds looked depressed'. Her parents asked her what they should do. Should they stay together or part? Josefina, not surprisingly, did not know what to say. They walked on, each full of unhappy thoughts. Eventually Josefina suggested that they try living apart, and that is what they did. The marriage was not dissolved, but they did not live together again. Hippolyto continued his career in South America and became Consul-General in Inquitos, Peru, and Montevideo. He later returned to Europe and served with distinction in consulates in Genoa, Manchester and Liverpool.

Although distanced from his wife and child, Hippolyto was a great believer in Josefina's natural gifts and he was still able to influence her development as a sculptor. The Manchester School of Art was able to provide Josefina with very little to advance her career. The staff offered no tuition in stone-carving, and suggested, quite seriously, that she might like to learn how to paint wood to look like marble. Clearly, this was not going to lead anywhere, so Hippolyto very wisely took his daughter to a stonemason who gave her two pieces of Portland Stone and a handful of tools worn very short. He said, 'Have these. They are what my father taught me with when I was a lad. You'll find out by using them how to carve stone.' Nothing could have fitted her more effectively for the art school training to follow.

Shortly afterwards, in the autumn of 1920, Josefina and her mother left Manchester for London, and Josefina was enrolled at the

Regent Street Polytechnic for a course in Fine Art, specialising in Sculpture. She and her mother took rooms in a house overlooking Regent's Park, and every morning Freda would walk with Josefina across the park to the door of the College, and would collect her again in the evening. Josefina had been so protected that she had never lit a gas stove or used a sharp knife. She rarely handled money and her mother still bought all her clothes. When asked to boil up some glue during a lesson at College, she had to confess that she was not allowed to light a gas flame. But the Poly opened up a new world to Josefina, and despite the protective presence of her mother, she began to find new friends, new happiness and success in her artistic achievements.

CHAPTER TWO

Growth of a Sculptor

THE 1920s

Inspiration is a driving force coming from outside, like a letter through a letterbox – like a voice or command straight into the mind, into the receptive part of one – you don't have to question it. Then you begin to work and you are putting inspiration into material and then your own imagination starts working on it as well. Operating with that is the intellect and technology and they all work together indivisibly.

J de V

Josefina was particularly drawn to sculpting in stone, which was not taught in art schools at that time, as she had discovered in Manchester. It was something of a pariah pursuit as far as the fine art community was concerned, since the true artist was supposed to draw a design or make a model and hire an artisan to execute the work. Carving in stone and wood did not become part of the official syllabus of the Royal College of Art until 1927, and both Henry Moore (1898–1986) and Barbara Hepworth (1903–1975) were taught outside the syllabus by Barry Hart. According to Penelope Curtis, writing in her book *Sculpture 1900–1940* (2000), 'carving flourished among those students who either cared little for the status brought about by an academic training, or who had indeed received their training within the craft and vocational sections of art schools.'[1] The Regent Street Polytechnic was such a place.

An academic of that period, Herbert Maryon, Master of Sculpture at Armstrong College (now the University of Newcastle upon Tyne), wrote in his book *Modern Sculpture* (1933) that 'the most notable development within the realm of sculpture in recent years is the remarkable interest, on the part of sculptors, critics and public alike, in the actual carving of stone, marble and wood.'[2] He noted that in the closing years of the nineteenth century 'the number of sculptors who carved with their own hands was few indeed.'[3] As attitudes changed, the concept of 'truth to materials' became fashionable and the driving force behind the more progressive sculptors such as Jacob Epstein (1880–1959), Hepworth and Moore.

This change of attitude was fortunate for Josefina, and like them she found herself looking back in time for inspiration. On her visits to the British Museum she was drawn to the ancient Chinese stone carvings which evoked massive emotion and strength. With her large, strong hands she wanted the physical and emotional satisfaction of cutting away the stone to release the form contained within it. All her life she used hand tools, like the old masters.

Gradually she came to know the qualities of different stone and how these attributes could be used to help the artist's vision. Marble was a superb medium to work with, but had cold shadows and needed to be carved deeper than stone. Slate was difficult but rewarding; Hoptonwood stone was not only beautiful but also satisfying to work. Wood offered its own unique challenges:

> Wood is alive. The shape of the wood suggests something and very delicately you remove the bark and parts that interfere with the main design. As you go forward and begin to see the flow of the grain, you see where the wood is leading you and from then on it is a partnership between your idea and the life and poetry provided by the material.
>
> With stone, you don't feel the life as in wood. You feel the sinking away into the ages. You are drawn back and back to the time when it was all under the pressure of the sea. Sometimes when a large portion was knocked off in the roughing out period, one could find, gleaming sharply in the sunlight, the perfect form of a minute shell. The extraordinary feeling that this was the first time that little shell had seen the sunlight for

thousands of years seemed to give me a very deep experience. Carving with stone you give yourself into the character of the material and with luck you get led aright. Carving stone is really what I enjoy most. It has a kind of weight of perfect satisfaction. Carving wood is more like playing a violin.

The scholar and sculptor Philip Rawson discusses the particular qualities of stone and wood in his book *Sculpture* (1997), and echoes some of Josefina's experience:

Stone and wood have special symbolic values of their own. Stone is dug from the quarry or found as a boulder, in both cases viewed as being a part of the eternal earth. One of the purposes of carving images in stone is to externalize them, displaying their unchanging value and timeless significance...

Wood evokes the nature of the forest and is a substance still containing evidence of life in its grain. It is not surprising that it was the natural choice of carving material for peoples whose own life was closely bound up with forests, for example in Africa, Oceania, and medieval Germany.[4]

Rawson also reminds us that sculpture has a serious place in society and sees 'an active force working through the sculptural expression':

Earlier ages identified this force with a transpersonal energy: not exactly communal but present and acting to create and change the world from somewhere beyond the control of either person or community. The best general word for it is *spirit*, which implies air moving invisibly. Spirit works through sexual activity to create children; it animates the environment of earth, sky, forest and sea.[5]

Rawson speaks here after a lifetime studying art and sculpture, particularly from the East. Josefina was to reach a similar awareness as she worked and learned, imbuing every piece with her own unique spirit and philosophy of life. Watching her as a very old craftsman run her hands over a huge lump of rough stone in a stonemason's yard, feeling its texture, excited by its golden-grey colour, one could clearly see that, for Josefina, carving stone was no academic exercise.

She was moved by its nature: 'the very bones of the world – why stop at apes? The stones are our ancestors.'

Josefina was still to reach these insights as a mature artist, and as a young student at the Poly, she was making friends and having fun for the first time since she left Brazil. After a lonely childhood, beset with fears conjured up by an acute imagination and the tensions caused by unhappy parents, and after the widening horizons of the year in Brazil, she was at last beginning to bloom.

The Regent Street Polytechnic was founded in 1882 as the Youth's Christian Institute and had been enormously successful in what it aimed to do: 'every reasonable facility shall be offered for the formation of a steadfast character and true friendships, for training the intellect and for leading an upright and useful life.'[6] By 1920 the Polytechnic was recovering its momentum after the restrictions of the First World War and over 25,000 students were registered. Fees were low and there were no entrance requirements.

Josefina registered as a student of sculpture, but because so much was on offer, she attended classes in drama and dance as well. 'It was such a sensible art school,' said Josefina, 'they showed you all the basic things that you had to know, technical things, architecture, anatomy and all the things that you do for sculpture. They were very strict on all that, drawing from the antique and drawing from life, but when it came to doing your own thing, you were free. That was ideal. We were all very happy. We were all very different characters and had fun and worked harder than anybody.' None of the sculpture students was particularly wealthy, and this cut across the idea at the time that women sculptors were often high society dabblers with little talent who could afford to use expensive materials.

There were only about seven students in the advanced class, working in a large room divided from the beginners by a green baize curtain. Howard Brownsword, the Master of Sculpture, was highly regarded at the time. Natural dancing was taught by Annea Spong, and Josefina loved these classes. She would have liked to have been a dancer but her parents were totally against it. She would wait many years to reclaim this talent, but she did, in old age, to the amazement of many.

It was through the drama class that Josefina met Margery Allingham (1904–1966), an exact contemporary in age, who was destined to become a well-known writer of detective fiction.

I think one's first impression of Margery would be of a generous friendliness – exuberant body and brain activity – large glowing deep well-water eyes. She used to write plays in which we all took part, with roles that suited our own characters. We used to go out and do them for charity in small theatres on the perimeter of London. We did quite a lot of that. Enormously enjoyable. It was a good training. Great jokes, hard work. Experiencing different sides of life that you didn't get in the sculpture. The natural dancing was by someone who came from Norway. It mixed in very naturally with the drama.

The Art School Christmas Show of 1921 saw Josefina acting in a short play called 'The Silence of Sime' and also composing the music for the performance. Her fellow student P H Morgan wrote the play and designed the programme, and Josefina made a portrait sculpture of him. Although an early work, this portrait is one of her most dynamic and unusual pieces, with clean, modernist lines. She also took part in one of Margery Allingham's most ambitious writing projects, her five-act blank-verse drama, 'Dido and Aeneas', and in the spring of 1922 the formidable Miss Bagley, who was in charge of drama studies at the Polytechnic, was sufficiently impressed to allow the group to give performances outside the college. Margery played Dido and Josefina played Cleon in the production.

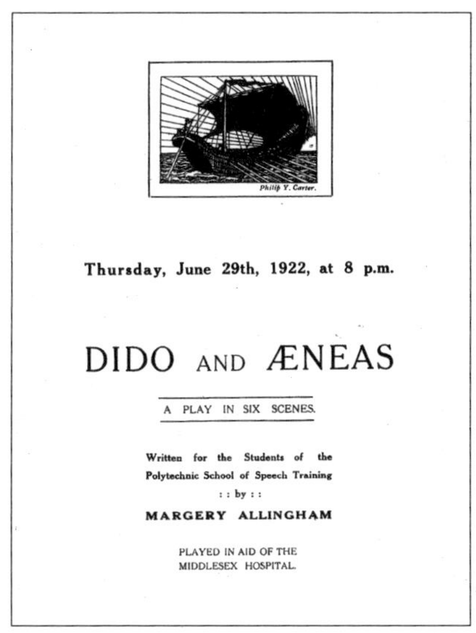

Drama and music continued to share a place with sculpture in her life and in January 1923 Josefina took part in a costume recital of dramatic monologues called 'Through the Windows of Legend', again written by Margery Allingham. Philip Youngman Carter (Pip), who later became Allingham's husband, designed the programme. With her bobbed hair under a heraldic red wig and her tiny frame, Josefina was well suited for her role as the Player's Boy: 'I was impudent, telling secrets, introducing, linking, making farewells, suggesting magic, cocky, confidential.' Her boyish charm did not go unnoticed.

Two weeks later she played Pallas Athene in 'The Trojan Women' (Margery Allingham played Andromache) and she continued to take part in performances for the next two years if she was available. Occasionally in concerts she would sing Brazilian songs and accompany herself on the guitar. Even after leaving the Poly she was still playing boyish roles in a Poetry Revue staged in the Polytechnic Hall in February 1926, when she played a Porter and a Gentleman Thief in two sketches, as well as taking part in folk dances. Sometimes she performed her own compositions and she became sufficiently professional as a composer to have a volume of eight short piano pieces for children called 'Nursery Folk' published by Paxton of London in 1926.

The relationships within the group at the Polytechnic were explored in 1924 when Allingham wrote 'Green Corn', a novel, still unpublished, which deals with art and drama students at a college called the Straker; in reality, the Regent Street Polytechnic. 'Green Corn' is too close to the personal experience of Margery Allingham to function successfully as a novel, and a publisher's reader very clearly rejected it: 'The tale concerns a number of bright young persons, and we are given an appalling amount of their bright young conversation about all their bright young thoughts. There is little more in it than that.'

The students were indeed a confident and energetic group and Josefina's many talents, in acting, music, dance and poetry, were at last being creatively used in hard work and fun. They all valued the education and training that they were given at the Poly, and in 'Green Corn' Margery Allingham wrote definitively about the ethos of the school:

> The Straker students had their high-brow moments but underneath it all they had the sound conviction that once you can part with your handiwork to a complete stranger for money and feel perfectly sure that neither you nor he is under the impression that he has been cheated, then you have a definite right to be called the tailor, the artist or the actor which your heart has acclaimed of you all along, and you may then continue to work out your life and your ambitions without being afraid that no one but yourself believes that you have chosen the right occupation... craftsmen it could make them, if they would be more they must find their own road to it afterwards, but craftsmen they must be first.[7]

This clear-sighted approach was one that Josefina shared with her friends, and one that her father would have accepted as well.

Hippolyto had now returned to Brazil, and in 1922 was posted to Inquitos in Peru, a town sited on the upper reaches of the navigable Amazon River. It must have been a huge contrast to his life in England, with the greatest excitement being the regular arrival of the river steamer. He wrote amusingly to Josefina and Freda about his life there, playing cards, drinking whisky and dining occasionally with the General of the local regiment. There was some excitement, however, when an airplane in difficulties managed to land near Inquitos and the plane itself was transported in sections to the consulate building to be repaired. To Hippolyto's relief the pilot gave up his plan to fly deeper into the wilderness, having seen the dangers involved, and the plane was transported back to the nearest port on the river steamer.

Hippolyto had a deep love and respect for the Amazon rain-forests. He was disappointed at not being able to explore up the rivers 'to rough it and to recover youth'. But the Vice-Consul was going on six-months' leave, and Hippolyto was required to stay at his post for the next few months. Philosophically he wrote to Josefina and Freda that 'I make it a rule to consider every 24 hours a life time and every fresh day a new life,' but he also revealed his attachment to them both by adding, rather poignantly, 'I read and reread the minute descriptions in your letters regarding the daily events of your lives, with earnest interest and pleasure.'

He went on to describe his new friend Punch, 'a vagabond terrier, a runaway from a British ship, who has made his home in Inquitos in the good old fashioned way of a conquistador or a pirate.' Whether or not Hippolyto succeeded in his plan to give Punch a bath is not noted: 'He must have guessed it, because he has not yet made his morning call. Perhaps he is busy, on his rounds, annoying the other dogs. Good old Punch, you would love him, the ruffian!' In another letter he urges them to 'be happy and continue to be the good friends you have always been.'

On a previous visit to Inquitos, Hippolyto had discovered a leper colony deep in the jungle, surrounded by a high stockade. He was puzzled by this high fence and found an overhanging tree to climb to the other side. There he found people abandoned, with no medical care of any kind, and only the occasional sack of food thrown over the stockade. They crowded round him and embraced him, having not seen anyone from the outside world for many years. Furious at this neglect he returned to his Consulate at Inquitos and demanded that doctors and medicines be sent out to them, and ensured that better facilities were provided. During his 1922 posting he lectured on this topic to the ladies of Inquitos, and instead of organising festivities to celebrate the centenary of Brazilian Independence he took up a collection to improve the local hospital and the leprosarium. Conditions among the Indians of his district were very bad at the time, with many tribes starving, and Hippolyto felt very angry at government expenditure on celebrations and exhibitions when the money could have been better spent. He maintained his interest in the leper colony even when he was back in England.

He did manage to escape from the Inquitos Consulate for a day in July, travelling by canoe up a tributary of the Amazon, and he wrote to Josefina about his deep love of the region:

> The attraction of this wild country becomes incomprehensible; its magnetism is irresistible to the extent of binding one to its soil, permanently, even in suffering, as it is to be seen everywhere, without the energy to seek more promising lands or the aspiration for a better fate. It is a mysterious unknown where dangers and freedom have no limitations.

This aspect of her father was the one that Josefina loved and admired, and she could easily understand his feelings. He probably came to understand his daughter through her poetry, because at this time Freda regularly sent Hippolyto copies of Josefina's latest poems and these were carefully retained by him. Every letter written to his wife and daughter from Inquitos during that posting ends with heartfelt wishes 'that you will continue to devote yourselves to each other with the same love and affection of the present.'

And at this time, Josefina and her mother were indeed devoted to each other. It was the happiest time for Freda, although she continued to be entirely focused on her daughter, with little life of her own to support her. She bought her daughter's clothes, and Josefina made her mother's hats. At weekends they would walk up to Hampstead Heath and watch the birds on the ponds. They took holidays together in St Ives, Cornwall, a favourite spot with artists, where Josefina painted.

'We were always poor,' said Josefina, 'because although Daddy had a good salary he was always giving it away to poor people or to his relatives. But we were quite happy being poor.' When her fellow students asked why she allowed her mother to be so protective, and told Josefina that she was like a child, she simply replied: 'If it pleases my mother, I'll do it.' Her nickname was 'The Goose Girl' because of her long skirts, a style that Josefina has always favoured.

Although Josefina maintained that she was content, her poetry at the time reveals considerable desire to escape from what must have been an intense and sometimes claustrophobic relationship with her mother. 'Poetry', written in 1922, encapsulates both her desire for freedom and her intuitive response to the natural world. The poem begins:

> As soon as I die and my happy soul is free
> I shall dance to the music of the wind and the sea.
> I shall be a leaf on a wind-tossed tree
> And flutter in the sun! How glad I shall be!

Another poem written in 1922 is also concerned with death, and begins with the sentence, 'You are for ever asking, What is Death!' It ends with the lines:

> You'll fling your arms to Heaven, its little roof
> And shudder... lest, by chance, you hear the truth.

She had never forgotten her father telling her as a little girl that 'when you die you die like a donkey, that's all,' and despite her outward happiness and zest for life, these fears had never left her.

Although most of Josefina's poems revealed her spiritual qualities, she was also quite capable of writing verses that were satirical and reminiscent of Rudyard Kipling in style. A poem called 'The Scarf', one of two labelled 'Depressed Arias', shows this side of her writing, a side that surfaces unexpectedly throughout her writing career:

> We were up at the old game of 'Get you a taxi, sir?'
> Outside the 'Ruddy Kitty' in the middle of the night.
> There was business on the taxi ranks and things were pretty
>   bright
> In the scrum of toppers and little bits of fur,
> When a fellow came out with his girl and gave me half
>   a glance.

Well, I'd got a taxi waiting, with my hand out for the tips,
While he fumbled for his pocket; it had been a gala dance –
When down fell his crimson scarf, as bloody as her lips;
And I thought of little Billy, when his guts fell out in France,
And I curst his dirty money, and I curst his dirty hen,
And I wished I'd died in Flanders, I wished I'd died then!

An awareness of the victims of war and oppression was never going to be far from Josefina's thinking, no matter how much she was involved with the busy life of an art student in London, and how sheltered her mother tried to keep her.

The happiness that Freda experienced during Josefina's time at the Poly was soon to be shaken when Delmar Banner became interested in her daughter. Josefina remembers that 'My relationship with my mother received a terrible shock because right from the first she knew there was something funny about Delmar. She disliked him. There were a lot of things to dislike. He was very idealistic, very academic. Overly academic. But from my point of view that was a good thing. The more he was the more I liked it. She knew there was something. She couldn't stand him. It wasn't just because she was jealous. It was agonising for her. It tore me me apart.'

Delmar Harmood Banner was studying painting at the Regent Street Poly, having already graduated in History from Magdalen College, Oxford after school at Cheltenham College. He was born on 28 January 1896, in Freiburg-im-Breisgau, Germany, where his grandfather, George Banner, a Church of England minister, was chaplain to the English community. George Banner's father founded the Liverpool Orphanage for which Josefina would later carve a lunette over the door in the north porch. The family motto, which Delmar never forgot, was *Nil Sine Numine*, 'Nothing Without God's Will'.

Delmar's great-grandfather, the Austrian violinist Zeugheer Herrmann, was the conductor of the Liverpool Philharmonic Orchestra from 1843 until his death in 1865. Born in Zurich in 1805, and then called Jakob Zeugheer, he had come to England with his own string quartet in 1829, and played for the Prince Regent at the Royal Pavilion in Brighton. At this stage of his career Herrmann was credited with introducing English audiences to the Beethoven String

Quartets. After touring England and Ireland he settled in Liverpool, married, and raised a large family. His daughter Josefine married into the Banner family.

Herrmann was clearly energetic and determined, and as a conductor in Liverpool undertook an ambitious programme of orchestral and choral works. Contemporary accounts of the concerts reveal that all the usual artistic squabbles took place, with the orchestra occasionally plotting revenge on the conductor by playing too fast, as in a famous rendition of the 'William Tell' Overture which left Herrmann breathless. Battles with the Chorus, on the other hand, could instigate the opposite response, and once caused a full-scale revolt with singers dawdling at half speed. But Herrmann rose above it all, and in 1849 he shared the podium with the pianist Julius Benedict at the inaugural concert of the magnificent new 2,100 seat Philharmonic Hall in Hope Street, Liverpool. Mendelssohn had been commissioned to write a new work for the event and to be guest conductor, but he died before the opening concert took place. The Philharmonic, then as now, was a source of great civic pride to Liverpool, and continued to flourish under the baton of Sir Charles Hallé in the latter years of the century.

The Harmood Banners were much involved with public life in Liverpool. Delmar's uncle, Sir John Harmood Banner, who was a partner in the family firm of accountants in Liverpool, served as MP for Everton from 1905 to 1924, and became Lord Mayor of Liverpool in 1913. He was made a Baronet in 1924 but the title became extinct with his death. His country house, Ingmire Hall, near Sedbergh, burned down in 1928.

Delmar's father Wilfrid had been an engineer, but he married a wealthy and socially conscious woman, Emily Tiffin, who did not think that men in her circle should demean themselves with work, so she made him give up his profession. Delmar grew up both suffocated and starved of parental love.

Patrician and handsome in a rarified way, with swept-back hair and a Roman nose, he strode through the room where Josefina and her class were all drawing from the antique, and Josefina decided at that moment that he was the man she was going to marry. Unlike all the other students in their paint-spattered overalls, he always wore a pure white overall, and Josefina's nickname for him was 'the holy ghost'.

'It was very strange,' said Josefina. 'There was no falling in love at all. It just seemed quite natural. It was just as though saying it's Thursday today, without the slightest feeling of anything. Very strange. I admired him. And of course everyone was amused by him because he was eccentric.'

She was fascinated by Delmar, and the fascination grew. He courted her with his intellect; she interested him because of her talent. But Josefina still had her career as a sculptor to pursue, and the relationship did not develop for several years. After completing her studies under Howard Brownsword at the Poly in 1923, and winning the Bronze Medal for Design in Sculpture, Josefina, like all art students, was keen to see the treasures of Europe. In October 1924 she and her mother travelled to Florence where they stayed for several months in a small *pensione* on the banks of the Arno, quite near the Ponte Vecchio. It is interesting to note that Henry Moore and Barbara Hepworth, quite independent of each other, were also in Italy about this time, each taking from the great works of the past what they needed to develop their own vision of sculpture.

Josefina studied for some time with Guido Calore, whom she found a very rewarding teacher: 'he helped you to do what you wanted, only better.' It was here that she sculpted *The Repentance of St Hubert*, an attractive curving sculpture of the saint with a gazelle. The fascination of the legend of St Hubert for Josefina says a great deal about the way her mind was to develop in the years ahead. The story of the prince who irreverently hunted on Easter Day, whose horse and hounds refused to move forward to kill a stag at bay in a forest clearing, and who saw a vision of the crucified Christ between the antlers of the stag at the moment he lifted his dagger for the kill, had enormous significance. Most obvious was her love of animals. But more profound was the recognition of repentance and redemption that came to the saint. The idea of redemption was to become very important to Josefina in years to come as she met modern saints, like Mario Borrelli of Naples and others who worked to create new hope for people who had none. In her practical work for approved-school boys and in much of her sculpture the theme of redemption is seldom far away.

During this visit to Florence, Josefina visited the Monastery of San Marco and saw for the first time the bronze figure of the mythical

Chimera. It was to prove a truly stimulating experience that would lead, twenty years later, to one of her finest pieces of sculpture. Her visit to San Marco was vividly remembered:

> My mother and I emerged into the cloister where an ancient tree and loved plants seemed suffused in honey-gold sunlight. From there we went as though in a waking dream, from cell to cell in each of which Fra Angelico had painted in fresco the loves of his soul for the joy and comfort of the Brothers.
>
> Lastly we came to the large room in which there are mostly those small bronzes of archaic warriors, bristling with strength and purpose. And there! – about 51 x 41, a glorious and unique Chimera in shiny bronze as perfect as when just made... How could such a tortured little monster be beautiful? This is one of the great mysteries of art.

On their way back to England in the spring of 1925 they stayed in Paris, and Freda, always anxious to further her daughter's prospects, arranged for them to visit the Académie de la Grande Chaumière, the famous art school established by the sculptor Emile-Antoine Bourdelle (1861–1929). The Académie was in Montparnasse, on the Left Bank, located near the Luxembourg Gardens. Bourdelle had started to work in the ground floor studios of the Impasse du Maine when he moved to Paris in 1884. He remained in the same studios for forty-five years, and they were obviously ideal for their purpose. John Milner describes them in *The Studios of Paris*:

> The ground floor studios of the Impasse du Maine are perfect for sculpture with maximum daylight and doors opening into the courtyard allowing heavy materials to be brought in and sculpture to be taken out from the courtyard to the street. The open-air space would allow the sculptors also to work on large-scale projects. There were balconies and cupboards for the storage of drawings and maquettes and a suite of rooms for living accommodation. The dust of plaster, stone and clay was easily swept out and water could be used in a manner problematic in any studios above ground level or opening into a central Parisian street.[8]

1 *The marriage of Josefina's English grandparents, Alfred Coleman and Fanny Butler, at the Butler family home in Wimbledon, 1864.*

2 *Freda Coleman, Josefina's mother.*

3 *Dr Alfred Coleman, FRCS, a distinguished doctor, pioneer dentist and inventor.*

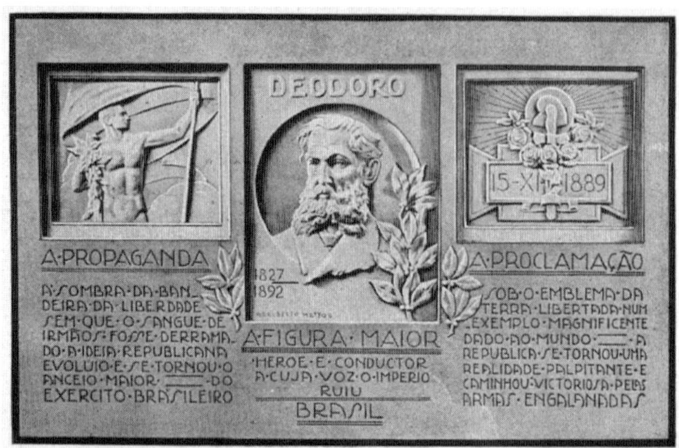

4 A public memorial, carved in stone, honouring Josefina's great-uncle Deodoro da Fonseca, founder of the modern republic of Brazil.

5 Hippolyto de Vasconcellos, Josefina's father, as a small boy with his family in Brazil.

6 Hippolyto de Vasconcellos, while Brazilian Consul-General to England.

7 Josefina with her father in Buttermere, shortly before his fatal accident in 1936.

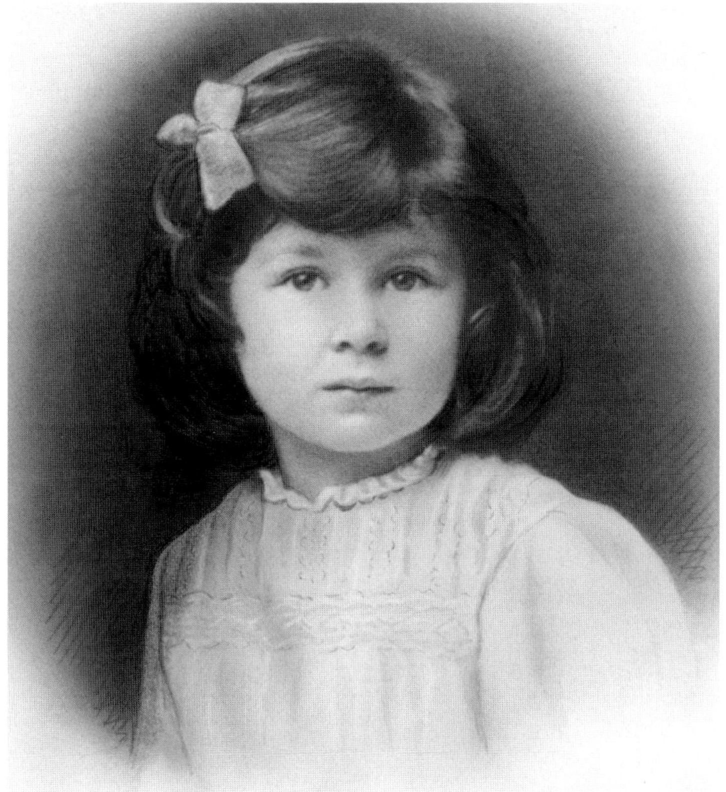

8

9

10

8 *Josefina as a young child.*
9 *With Freda, her mother.*
10 *Josefina aged 14, riding in Brazil.*

11

12

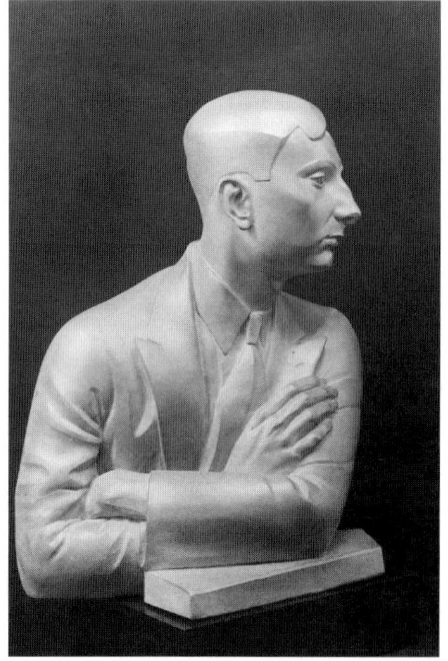

13

14

11,12 *At the Regent Street Poly, Josefina performed regularly in student shows, singing, dancing and acting. She is pictured left, dancing, and right in a comic spoof about sculpture.*

13,14 *Josefina sculpted the heads of fellow students at the Poly: P H Morgan, 1923 (left) and Constance West, 1924 (right).*

15

16

17

18

*15 Andreotti's studio in Florence, where Josefina worked on the full-sized clay model of
St Valerie (seen left foreground) for the church in Varengeville.*

16,17 Josefina at the Lido, Venice, in 1925.

18 Josefina (centre) skiing in the Dolomites with fellow student Giovanni Delago (right).

19 Church of St Valerie at Varengeville, Normandy, where Josefina executed her first major commission.

20 The crucifix designed and made by Josefina for the altar.

21

22

21 *Josefina in Normandy while working at St Valerie.*
22 *'The Repentance of St Hubert' was exhibited in Paris and in the Royal Academy in 1926.*

23 Delmar Banner with his mother, Emily Tiffin.
24 Josefina and Delmar were married in London on 28 April 1930.

25

26

25 *Josefina wearing her wedding dress, painted by Delmar in 1932.*
26 *Delmar's painting of his mother (centre) and his wife.*

27

28

29

27, 28, 29 Interiors of The Bield, Little Langdale.

30

31

30 *In the porch at The Bield, 1939.*
31 *Billy and Brian, the adopted boys, at home on the Fells.*

32 'Scafell from Hardnott', an oil painting typical of Delmar's visionary work in the 1940s.
33 Delmar at his painting desk.

34

35

*34 During the Second World War the Royal College of Art was evacuated to Ambleside.
Professor E W Tristram, Head of the School of Design, and his family visited The Bield when
transport allowed. Josefina is on the right, sitting beside Dorothy Nevinson, her friend and helper.*

35 'The Last Chimera' was exhibited by Josefina at the Royal Academy in 1946.

36

37

36 *'Boys Wrestling',
Cumbrian style, a popular
sculpture modelled on
Brian and Billy, was first
exhibited at the Royal
Academy in 1948.*

37 *With Brian, while he
was a schoolboy at St Bees.*

38

39

38 *'The Spirit of Man':
Josefina working in her
studio at The Bield.*

39 *Josefina with 'The
Hand', carved in slate, a
War Memorial at St Bees
School.*

40

41

40 In 1950, 'Christ the Judge' was placed as the centrepiece of the National Memorial in Aldershot to the air heroes of the Battle of Britain and the people of the blitzed cities and towns.

41 Transporting large sculptures was not an easy job.

The Grand Chaumière was run, rather improbably, by two stern English ladies. They thought that Josefina was a little young to join the other students, but did accept her to work under the dramatic direction of le Maître Antoine Bourdelle. She and her mother lived not far away in an old-fashioned *pension* near the Luxembourg Gardens, and Josefina thrived in an atmosphere where art was taken with high seriousness. And to be an artist in Paris in the 1920s was to become part of a great heritage. John Milner observes:

> Paris, the common factor of artists famous then but now forgotten, and of those whom subsequent history has lifted from obscurity, had a pull that was scarcely to be resisted. The resulting network of ambitions and talents had a structure which selected the successful, providing frameworks for tuition and subsequent advancement or failure. The relationship between Paris and its artists is visible in its geography, in whole streets devoted to studios, in the distinct areas they favoured, in its monuments, its collections and its art.[9]

Josefina was fortunate in having the opportunity to study with Bourdelle. He was held in high esteem in the Parisian art world and was vice-president of the Salon de Tuileries, an annual exhibition where many artists, including his favourite students, could show their works. Josefina would, in due course, be one of them.

Bourdelle was a friend of the sculptor Aristide Maillot (1861–1944) whose influence can be seen in some of Josefina's early works. Like her, he looked to primitive and archaic works of art for inspiration. His sculpture *Female Wrestlers* (1900), which Josefina must have seen, is echoed in her *Boys Wrestling* which she made in the late 1940s. The serenity and massive strength of his female forms can be found in several of her student pieces. Another sculptor who excited Josefina and her fellow students was Ivan Mestrovic, who was working in Paris but had exhibited in London and was admired for his powerful wood carvings of religious figures.

The Grand Chaumière was strict and adventurous at the same time and highly regarded across Europe. One of Josefina's fellow-students was the Italian sculptor Alberto Giacometti (1901–1966), whom Josefina loathed and whose bad temper made him very unpopular within the group. According to his biographer James Lord, Giacometti was intolerant of models who wanted to rest and would shout out rudely, 'Hold the pose please!', insisting that they stayed still even if they had cramp.[10]

Most of the students were much older and much more sophisticated than Josefina and included two Russians, who distributed Communist propaganda in their spare time; a beautiful Polish girl who owned only one dress, a black velvet evening gown; a cheerful Greek; a Chinese who invited the whole group to share a beautiful golden fish on his birthday, and made them stand waiting while he painted it before they ate it; a Scandinavian; and an American dressed as a cowboy, complete with four pistols. This wildly assorted group of people got on well although it was not always a peaceable kingdom; on Josefina's first day there was a fight that might have been serious had not the elder Russian separated the contestants.

They worked hard, with Bourdelle looking in weekly to inspire them with his presence or simply to read them a poem. He was interested in Josefina's work, and Freda recorded in her notebook that on one occasion he said that a sculpture of hers 'was philosophy, not sculpture.' Bourdelle had been marble carver and helper to Auguste Rodin (1840–1917) for fifteen years and his sculpture reflects that massive style. Josefina admired the strength and elemental qualities of Bourdelle's work, and responded particularly to his advice to work out of doors and be responsive to the play of light and shade: *le soleil est votre meilleur critique.*' Many years later, in her studio in Langdale, Josefina would work in this way, with a room that opened straight out on to the constantly changing light of the Lake District Fells.

The rather more shabby studios of the Grand Chaumière provided Josefina with practical experience, of life as well as of art. The many models who waited patiently on a bench outside, hoping to be called and to earn a few francs, were obviously desperately poor. Nudity was taken for granted, and when the man selling grapes arrived outside with his cart piled high, all the students would come out to buy, as would the models, who did not bother to don clothes if the weather was warm. Young girls were bought and sold; drugs were available; drink was often a refuge from despair. Josefina talked to her mother about her progress in her work, but said little about the side of Paris that she discovered through these artists and their friends. But despite the hardships that many artists endured, Paris was still the only place to be: 'none doubted that Montparnasse was the hub of the universe,' according to John Milner.[11]

The seriousness at the Grande Chaumière was not so high that mischievous Josefina could not produce an elaborate practical joke. The students were exhibiting at a Salon at the Porte Maillot and an extra exhibitor's ticket had been sent to the school. Josefina thought that a joint effort, 'A Portrait of Madame X', would be fun to do, so they put a piece of clay on a stand and each student modelled for two minutes before they turned it round for the next person. They pooled resources to have the head fired in terracotta and submitted it to the exhibition under a false name made up from the initials of all who had taken part. When they arrived at the exhibition they were dumbfounded and rather annoyed to see 'A Portrait of Madame X' given pride of place in the exhibition, with the critics gathered round it admiringly, ignoring the genuine works of the group. It was not the first or the last time that students have managed to fool critics with a spoof effort.

Josefina's work was gaining in confidence and power. Two of her pieces were exhibited at the Salon de Tuileries in Paris, a portrait relief in bronze and a terracotta head. Her sculptures from this time are impressive in their strength and simplicity. She did many portraits of fellow students and friends and these display not only a refined neo-classicism but also a modernist approach. Her bust of P H Morgan (1923) and the head of Constance West (1924), made while she was still at the Regent Street Poly, demonstrate an interesting blend of abstraction and naturalism in the portraiture.

After finishing her spell at the Grande Chaumière in 1925, Josefina and her mother travelled through France and Belgium and south again to Italy, with Josefina filling many sketch-books with drawings of churches, sculptures and occasionally people.

While staying in a *pensione* in Florence they made friends with a Huguenot family from Normandy, the Malletts, who invited them to visit their home at Varengeville sur Mer. This chance meeting was to open up unexpected opportunities for a young sculptor on the brink of her career, and Josefina regarded the ancient church at Varengeville as 'the source of some of the greatest experiences of my life in France and Italy.' Josefina loved the church and the village, and wrote in a poem at that time, 'this spot is sweet forever.'

She was not alone in her response. The pretty village of Varengeville was favoured by several Post-Impressionist and modern painters: both Claude Monet and Georges Braque lived and painted there at various times. Monet painted the church and the custom house in 1882 and many visitors today come to see the source of his inspiration. More recently, in 1954, Georges Braque designed stained glass windows for the church and was buried in the graveyard when he died in 1963.

The Malletts' residence, 'Le Bois des Moutiers', is an exquisite house, high on the cliffs next to L'église de Sainte Valerie on the Normandy coast near Dieppe. In 1898 Guillaume Mallett, a wealthy banker, and his wife commissioned the English architect Edwin Lutyens to rebuild their old Norman manor house that stood on a spectacular site overlooking the sea. Lutyens was already in France to design the British Pavilion for the 1900 Paris Exhibition, so he was able to undertake the work. Even more convenient was his collaboration with the famous garden designer Gertrude Jekyll in creating the grounds to surround the house. Beyond the garden, rhododendrons gave way to pine trees and grassland along the clifftops. When Josefina and Freda came to stay in the summer of 1925 the house was furnished in the 'Arts and Crafts Movement' style, with tapestries by Burne-Jones in the central hall, and an organ. There were art treasures everywhere.

The Malletts had a piece of stone left over from building the house available for Josefina to carve, and she set about this very happily, working outside under the loggia which made 'a lovely open studio, with a wonderful view and often good music on the piano or the organ being played by M. Mallett in the room above – an ideal place to work on a Madonna and Child.' Her friends were delighted with the sculpture and at a special ceremony it was presented to the church. A little later Josefina's sculpture *The Repentance of St Hubert* was placed in a niche inside the church, and at the dedication service to celebrate the repentance of the saint, the congregation sang, the organ played, bells rang, huntsmen sounded their horns and their hounds ran all over the churchyard.

M. l'Abbé Hochard, who conducted the dedication, referred to the sculpture as 'the special expression of a pure and charming spirit,' and suggested that Mademoiselle de Vasconcellos be invited to present a proposal to replace the old wooden altar of the church with one carved in stone. The antiquity of the church required that various committees of venerable authorities had to approve the work, including the Société pour la Préservation de Monuments Antiques, the Beaux Arts as well as the Church Commissioners. Josefina's design was unusual in placing a life-size effigy of St Valerie below the altar, with four pillars supporting the table itself. Only when Josefina was able to find another church with a similar altar would permission be granted for the work to begin.

With her mother she travelled again through Europe, visiting churches and cathedrals, and eventually found a *gisant* or recumbent figure of a saint under an altar supported by six pillars in the Church of the Holy Spirit outside Nuremburg. She took photographs and made drawings to prove that a precedent existed, and was allowed to develop her scheme. The authorities were cautious, however, and she was first required to make a life-size model of St Valerie in clay to show what she had in mind. This project was to be Josefina's first major commission. She was only twenty-one years old at the time.

By now Hippolyto was back in England, at the Consulate in Manchester, a city he detested and a posting that he did not enjoy. He was in Manchester during the days of the General Strike in May 1926, and found that there were certain advantages to the lack of public transport: 'I find it more peaceful and quieter, due to the absence of the jarring, nerve-wracking, grinding, scraping noises of tramcars, which are unbearable in Manchester. If in any other respect this town were suitable to me, that would have been sufficient to make it detestable.'

Postcards from Josefina and Freda were held up by the strike, as were his letters to them, and he anxiously traced their progress on a little map, to Prague, Budapest and Vienna, worrying if he did not know where they were: 'During these few days when I could not write to you not knowing your address I have been rather unsettled, I must confess.' He wrote to his fellow consuls in various cities notifying them of the presence of Freda and Josefina, concerned for their welfare.

Josefina sent him a regular supply of poems, plays and essays, often carefully copied out by her mother, which Hippolyto received enthusiastically, but not without criticism. He recognised that the poems lacked the rigour and discipline needed to support their ideas, but he encouraged Josefina to continue, as indeed she has throughout her life. He had given her good advice in an inspiring letter sent to her in June 1925:

> You are like a butterfly, flitting from flower to flower, for the sweet food it loves, in your inconstancy in arriving at a decision as to the real trend of your talent.
>
> All along, you are misguided by your friends and acquaintances, who are not able to help you, for they do not understand the depth of the multiple 'souls' of your artistic temperament.
>
> When you play, your musical friends would you devoted your sole attention to music, only because your music is your own and awakes them to a new sphere of symphony.
>
> Whether you carve on stone or mould, those around you are mystified by your conceptions, and the only way they can find to hide their inability to penetrate the causes of life that is emitted by your work, is to say that they are more philosophical than artistic.
>
> What you write has the gist and candour of the wild flowers, unstudied but itself, modest but coy.
>
> Your prose and your poetical efforts are original in every aspect. They please, they must please, because they breathe the sweetness of your very life, the perfection of your nature and the beauty of your pure sentiments. For this reason you are said to be angelic. Father has said so often, ever since you were a child...
>
> The progress you have made in sculpture is so wonderful

that it would be a great pity to neglect it. The foundations you have built, for this branch of art are so sound that it would be sad to waste them.

Your verses and your prose though still very untrained, are so profound in idealistic philosophy that you should use every means for acquiring the necessary culture to perfect your possibilities in the composition of them.

My advice, therefore, is that you carry on with them all, without any especial sacrifices of time or effort, making of each of your artistic pursuits a pastime and a rest from the labour of the others.

Despite this praise, Hippolyto was always able to provide a serious judgement for Josefina's work, and his early death deprived her of this valuable corrective, especially where her writing was concerned. Interestingly, in his list of his daughter's talents there is no mention of dancing, which Josefina always felt should have been her life's work and her parents were united in opposing.

Hippolyto and Freda were still closely bound by their love for their daughter, and distance was beginning to soften the disappointment and pain on Freda's part. In one letter accompanying a short prose piece by Josefina on the nature of an imperfect world – 'There can be no good without bad, and the bad that we suffer here is in the right quantity necessary for shewing up the good to its best advantage' – Freda regrets having burned Hippolyto's poems: 'I only wish I had kept yours as how interesting now for Fifina to read – to compare your styles. They were good. I remember burning them with tears at Ravenscroft Park because I did not think them true – after all they were true when they were written. I have always expected too much from people.'

As well as providing a commentary on Josefina's poetry, Hippolyto also found himself handling all the mounting correspondence to do with her exhibitions in England, including the acceptance of her *Repentance of St Hubert* for the Royal Academy Summer Exhibition of 1926. Josefina was attracting attention in the art world, and Hippolyto was kept busy providing photographs of her work to journals and newspapers. He had to take photographs out of his own album, which did not make him happy: 'Don't make a mistake about it, I am grumbling,' he wrote to Josefina and he asked her to let him keep the negatives so that he could get prints run off as required.

Hippolyto had dared to criticise some aspect of the gazelle's eyes in the St Hubert piece, but then hastened to reassure Josefina that he must have been mistaken and she was correct all along. He felt, however, that the gazelle was looking at him ironically when he went to see it at the Royal Academy.

The sculpture was much admired, and Hippolyto was very pleased by a review of the work shown in the journal *The Nineteenth Century*. He did not know at the time that the writer of the review, Delmar Banner, was a friend of his daughter, but he assured her that he did not feel that this detracted in any way from the praise delivered by Delmar as critic. Hippolyto, like any proud parent, bought several copies of the journal and sent them to Josefina in Italy.

In his review Delmar criticised almost every exhibit, including a portrait of Miss Gladys Cooper by Sir William Orpen ('the touch is as inartistic as the outlook') and a panel by Jacob Epstein ('the panel is art, even if it is of the devil'). He castigated contemporary portrait painters for not taking time to appreciate and understand their subjects:

> That men of immense intellect and character should waste their time sitting to a painter who cannot understand anything of their lives, their aims or their achievements, is surely simply ridiculous. Admittedly no man can be expected to understand every type of mind; but he should paint none save those he can understand. If a painter is asked to portray a writer, he should read his works; if he cannot understand them, he should refuse the task.

He makes the claim that no one would paint portraits if he could paint landscapes instead, and then takes a savage swipe at one member of the Academy who 'would do well to stick to his fire-screens instead of painting his daughter (if it is she) in a manner that would disgrace a student's first attempt.' Out of this carnage very few emerge unscathed. He praises the architectural entries, and finds the level of the sculpture 'technically higher than that of the painting,' but singles out for unqualified admiration 'an extraordinarily beautiful "Repentance of St Hubert" by Miss de Vasconcellos, which would look lovely in an arched niche among old trees.'

Delmar refers to this review in one of his earliest letters to Josefina, on 18 August 1926, when he confesses that he felt it 'cheek to sit in judgement at the academy – either on my RA judges themselves or on anyone!' His confident and savage critique of the Summer Show does not, however, give the impression that he was doing other than enjoying himself enormously in having a go at prevailing standards. But about Josefina's work he was sincere: 'I am glad you saw my remarks on your work in *The Nineteenth Century*! I meant it.'

Josefina had written to him from Venice, where she was staying on the Lido with her mother and entertaining quite a few suitors at the time. She also sent some poetry which Delmar took quite seriously, steering her away from what he called 'capricious notions about the mysteries of faith.' He added that 'I think poetry is always faith, always *positive* experience, not negative.' He finds the positive in Josefina's sculpture: 'that is why St Hubert especially seems to me so fine. We must have real convictions and living experiences before true art can arise.' He concludes with the question (and the instruction), 'Do you read Ruskin? Do, if not.'

At that time Josefina's most pressing problem was not the absorption of Ruskin's theories, but the practical one of finding somewhere to create the life-size clay model for the figure of St Valerie, as required by the church authorities. Fortunately she had already decided that after working with Bourdelle in Paris the only person she wanted to study with now was Andreotti in Italy, who taught exclusively at a school attached to the University of Florence. It was housed in the Royal Stables of the Pitti Palace, surrounded by beautiful gardens with fountains and pools. Getting accepted as a pupil of Andreotti was likely to prove difficult but fortunately Josefina was able to enlist the help of her father with his government connections. Hippolyto wrote personally to the Minister of Education, who replied with a huge vellum sheet covered in stamps, requesting that the school admit Miss de Vasconcellos.

When Josefina eventually walked up to the imposing entrance hall of the Art School in the autumn of 1926, she was confronted by a huge Fascist soldier.

'No signorinas coming here,' he said.

Well, thought Josefina, this signorina's coming here. She was taken to the headmaster, who said, 'This is terrible, we've never had a woman here before.' He waved the letter despairingly. 'But we must!'

Very reluctantly he agreed and showed her round the college. Her class were told by the Head that they had to behave, because they had a 'Signorina Inglese here'.

'They hated me!' said Josefina. 'I didn't say a word for the first week.' But she worked away on her full-sized clay model of St Valerie and showed them that she was a serious and talented sculptor. Soon she was accepted into the group and was able to hold her own. She remembers that sometimes the students would fight, and if the fight got nasty she would go into the middle and pour a bucket of water over them. 'You had to make your way as best you could. But I learned more there than anywhere. We had to make our own tools. We made a twice life-size figure for the opening of the Pirandello Theatre in Rome. If they needed a dove we would go out into the garden, find a dove, bring it in and put on the easel, copy it, then take it out again into the garden.'

But this was 1926, and Mussolini had gained power in Italy. The young men at the University of Florence were required to do military exercises every morning and Josefina remembers that 'they had a ridiculous bit of drill in the morning. We had to do the fascisti salute. On Mussolini's birthday, Andreotti, who was the most gentle person in the world, had done this lovely sculpture for the Italian mothers who had lost boys in the war. In the marvellous church of Santa Croce. For that occasion every department of the army sent a small number for the occasion and they all marched through the streets. The whole of the Italian army were there. Of course I marched in with my little lot. When we got to the cathedral two soldiers crossed their bayonets to prevent me going in and I dived under them to get in with my lot and got there for the dedication.'

Andreotti was very encouraging about Josefina's work, and once the model was completed, Josefina started on a long round of committees to get permission to carve the new altar. She went up into the mountains in the winter to see her fellow students ski-ing at Cortina, and tried ski-ing herself, although the snow was poor that season. Her friend Giovanni Delago was a champion skier and in 1928 would take part in the Italian airship expedition to the North Pole. After leaving Florence she took the opportunity to visit other Italian cities including Siena and Venice. A flurry of letters followed her about Europe as she captivated young men and left them behind in her travels.

And always she was writing poetry. Sculpture, painting and poetry had become inextricably linked. Freda wrote to Hippolyto from Florence in September 1926 with a poem called 'The Eternal Fountain', and said 'F did a picture and then wrote these lines about it. She is mad to start working and can hardly wait.' The poem begins:

> There is an endless stream of sacrifice
> And pain, whose waters through the ages flow
> A stream of martyrs suffering, human woe
> Oblivious like of shade or Paradise!

The poem ends with a line that is typical of Josefina's beliefs throughout her life: 'Teach to the faithless world, Hope, Love and Peace.'

Shortly afterwards, in 1927, Josefina and her mother took ship for Brazil once more, accompanied by Hippolyto. This time he ensured that his daughter would have no admirers on the long voyage south across the Atlantic by arranging with a young man he knew to be engaged to escort Josefina throughout the trip. Everyone thought that they were engaged, and so no approaches were made to her. At the end of the voyage, leaning over the railing, one handsome young man said to her, 'What a pity you are engaged, Miss de Vasconcellos. I admire you very much.' It was only then that she realised how her father had organised things on the voyage.

The longeurs of the voyage might have been alleviated by a little romance. Deprived of her mallet and chisel during these intermin-able days in the middle of the ocean, Josefina was obviously bored, as this poem reveals:

O Lord… I am bored!
Stiff!… Biff!
Old stupidity – Dullility.
Can't and shan't
Think, in this awful stink
Of Scent, lent
To the air by that old pair
Of 'girls' in curls –
Ancient Pets with Lorgnettes!
Tick,tock… The clock
Repeats untimely deceits.
Ages… pages
Of Life and mental strife
Fly away in a
Second as is reckoned
By the silly
Old Mock-Clock!
Bing, Bong! Goes the gong –
Trumpet peals. Thank God for meals!

Once in Rio, Josefina again succumbed to the magic of Brazil. The soft, warm nights, the street songs, and the beauty of the landscape attracted her deeply. Many years later she wrote:

'Don't you miss Brazil?
The chaotic heights,
pulsating nights,
long for its song?'

'Never fear, my dear –
I hear it still –
all these years apart –
I have it all here –
the beat, in my heart
and my feet.'

She found Brazil as warm and welcoming as before. Staying with friends in a smart apartment on Copacabana Beach in Rio, she was distanced from the awkwardness that had occurred during her previous visit when Hippolyto's illegitimate children had been an embarrassment. When Josefina described the views on a postcard to Delmar she was an artist to her fingertips, finding 'one view which is just like the distance in Leonardo's Madonna of the Caves.' While she was there she carved another version of her work, *The Repentance of Saint Hubert*, which was much admired when exhibited in Rio de Janiero and won the Bronze Medal at the Salon das Bellas Artes in August 1927. She presented the sculpture to the National Gallery in Rio de Janiero and it is still on display there.

Again on the return voyage Josefina wrote several poems and short prose pieces that try to clarify her chaotic thoughts on life. Unlike her later poetry there are no religious references but there is a desire to understand the power behind the universe and man's place in it. In a poem such as 'The Watcher', written in the middle of the Atlantic Ocean, she asks:

> O profound exultation – power
> consuming and constructing!
> Where is the force that can create
> an Evolution, a Chaos, a Unity?

Another poem written at the same time called 'The Old Gods' reveals the same questing spirit:

> The old Gods went roaming, roaming, roaming
> Shadows crossing the sky at dawn
> Black clouds passing the sunset gleam
> Like great birds homing, homing, homing
> Slowly the great spirits are bourne
> On the untroubled waves of a dream.

While in Rio she wrote a kind of meditation on life, in which she asks:

What is the use of living if one cannot find out something new – or is life a continual confirmation of one great Truth? Who shall solve a problem the beginning and end of which is unknown? The problem of Life is ever such; we are always in the middle. What is the use of speaking if one cannot say anything new – or is it the old truths that call out for re-witness, fitting the necessities of all ages?

She goes on to discuss prejudice and toleration: 'What tragedy, what misery can result in the misunderstanding or determination not to see the other side of a question… perhaps it is true that one can only learn, not by being told not to do a thing, but by regretting having done it.'

The conflict between good and evil was always very real to Josefina and these private reflections, written with her poems, show how she was thinking very seriously about the meaning of life. Instinctive artist though she was, there was clearly an intelligence crying out for direction, and this she was to find in her relationship with Delmar.

On her return to Europe, Josefina was given permission to begin work on the stone altar and figure of St Valerie at Varengeville. Her figure of St Valerie is medieval in style to correspond with the twelfth century church, simple and powerful in execution, revealing considerable maturity in its conception. She also designed and made an altar cross in bronze, candlesticks, the tabernacle and flooring.

She made these during the spring of 1928, working largely out of doors near the church. When she was not working she helped her friend Pascaline Mallett teach the village children to swim from the beach below the cliffs. There was an old coastguard station that was used as a changing room, and after the swim and a drink of hot milk for the children, who were not well nourished at the time, Josefina and Pascaline would teach the children songs, dances and games. The Malletts' involvement with the villagers extended to giving regular film shows for them in a barn, using a hand-turned projector operated by their chauffeur.

The Normandy countryside was fresh and green, the orchards were laden with blossom, the meadows were full of flowers, and Josefina was inspired to produce a very fine piece of sculpture. The Archbishop of Rouen, Monseigneur de la Villerabel, dedicated the new altar and cross, and there was much admiration for the style, which although considered modern was also felt to blend well with the architecture of the ancient church. Josefina was present at the dedication and was celebrated at the elaborate dinner afterwards in the historic Manoir d'Ango, where she charmed everyone with her youth and beauty. Her mother was, of course, there too, but so was her father, who was delighted by his daughter's success.

The 1920s were a time of achievement and surprising success for the young artist. She was working in a field where few women were able to obtain commissions and certainly very few were praised as Josefina was. Her work had been on exhibition in London, Rio de Janiero, Florence and Paris, where her *Leda and the Swan* was in the Salon de Tuileries. She had been influenced by the new approaches towards materials – 'truth to materials' – that had encouraged sculptors to carve in native stone and wood rather than Italian marble. Already familiar with the great Chinese carvings in the British Museum, she had used the resources of the Louvre and other European museums to look to the ancient stone and wood carvings from other cultures, which were then influencing Epstein, Brancusi and Moore.

On her return to England in 1928 her future career seemed to be assured, and London was an exciting place to be. Jacob Epstein was valiantly pursuing a strongly independent path with strongly sensual sculptures that caused regular scandals. Epstein was an early encourager of Henry Moore, who was holding his first exhibition in the Warren Gallery and already demonstrating his distinctive style. Barbara Hepworth was exhibiting for the first time at the Beaux Arts Gallery off Bond Street with her first husband, John Skeaping, and William Morgan. With her growing interest in simple shapes, Hepworth's work was already very different from Josefina's, and their show not only focused attention on contemporary sculpture but helped to advance the debate on Constructive Art. Hepworth was to develop the argument further as a contributor to the book *Circle*, published in 1935. Richard Cork, in his essay 'The Visual Arts', expresses the view that 'when Mondrian settled in the same road as Nicholson in 1938, joining earlier artists from abroad like Gabo and Moholy-Nagy, London looked for a while as if it might blossom into a cosmopolitan centre for contemporary art.'[12]

But Josefina did not choose to follow along this radical path. She had a clear idea of where she wanted to go, as she wrote at this time:

> If the world had to choose three of the four arts, I am sure they would prefer to keep Music, Painting and Poetry, for it is they that make the most direct appeal to our artistic sense or imagination – besides, these three Muses form a perfect group, just as the Three Graces in Botticelli's 'Primavera' in which to add or detract one would spoil the beautiful composition. But sculpture, in all her calm, dignified beauty, stands alone, endures the longest; for she is not only an art but a message. It is the voice of man through the ages in which his very thoughts, his noblest beliefs and aspirations are perpetuated in stone. These man-created shapes and faces that look at us so serenely out of the pre-historic past; the archaic Greek, the Etruscan, the Egyptian, the remains on Easter Island, the Incas and the even more remote and mysterious carvings that are continually being dug up; how they help us to realise the triviality of small matters and inspire us to produce work that will do justice to all that is best in our present civilisation.
>
> It is a pretty merciless age, this 'Mechanical Age' of ours, and three-quarters of Modern Art expresses it terribly well – the gross crudity, the unrest, the struggle for domination and the singular disregard of beauty. However its antithesis is a newer and stronger form that expresses itself in a serene purity and an intense striving of mind and soul for a higher and more spiritual beauty. All my hopes are with this last, and it is my belief that it is the forerunner of some future art and a civilisation that it is our privilege to work for and dream of.

With these aspirations in mind she took up a scholarship to the very traditional Royal Academy Schools, where she studied, worked in stone and exhibited in the annual show. One of her tutors was William McMillan, whom Josefina found 'uncommonly easygoing and yet he would not let you off anything. He taught so nicely and he taught with understanding and sympathy, he was a magnificent teacher.' William Reid Dick was also influential. Yet one cannot but feel that a dead hand of conformity to past conventions was very much part of the tuition there, with an emphasis on order, design and accepted standards of beauty. Even at this stage of her development Josefina was beginning to develop the notion that sculpture could provide a focal point for bringing about a personal and spiritual rebirth that would ultimately lead to social and political change.

Always ambitious, and still looking to Europe at this time, Josefina sought the challenge of entering work for the Prix de Rome, and she had completed her exhibits early in 1929. For the Rome Scholarship in Sculpture (a handsome award of £250 annually and the opportunity to work and study in Rome) candidates were required to submit a half life-size nude figure, a head from life, a group of two or more figures in the round, quarter life-size, a model in bas-relief of two figures and five drawings from life: a nude, a head, drapery, hands and feet. Her work was submitted in 1929 and exhibited along with the other short-listed competitors at the Imperial Gallery of Art in South Kensington in January and February 1930. Although she was only the runner-up, *The Times* reviewer singled her out for praise, commenting that she was the only competitor that could be named along with the winner, the Irishman John F Kavanagh. Academic criticism at the time seemed to be opposed to innovation, and it is revealing that Herbert Maryon in *Modern Sculpture* was very critical of Rodin's famous and much-loved work *The Kiss* because of its technical errors: 'the reader might find it a useful exercise to try to find out how the defects might have been made good,' he observed tartly.[13]

But challenges of a different kind were entering her world. As soon as she returned to England in 1928 the determination of Delmar Banner to make her his wife was to have a drastic effect on her confidence and her state of mind. Josefina was so protected by her mother that Delmar had to devise a plan to meet her, so he asked his mother to buy one of her sculptures. She purchased *The Infant Christ* and invited the sculptor to their house at 35 Courtfield Road in South Kensington.

Josefina was shocked by his background – 'the absolutely utter ignorant conventionality. How they treated him. They either spoilt him or bullied him. And he was somehow under their paws. The husband was miserable, his face was miserable, because after she'd had Delmar she decided she didn't want any more children and she turned RC. Knowing his mother was a liar and a cheat, he'd got this tremendous thing against women. She spied on people. He spied on people too. He got that from her. He saw it all. He saw everything. By the time he was seven years old he was cynical.' Josefina herself came upon Emily Banner crouched down outside a keyhole, listening to the conversation within.

That someone so intellectually and artistically gifted as Delmar should also be so unhappy was magnetically attractive to Josefina. As she got to know him better she realised how dominant the power of his mother was, and how Delmar saw her as a means of escape:

> When he proposed to me he put his arms out and said, 'Save me from my parents.' That was his proposal. And so, like a mother, I went to him, he put his arm round me, and I said, 'Yes I will.' I suppose I was so accustomed to everything in my life being different from other children I just took it for one more thing.

They became engaged in September 1929, and seven months later they were married. Two only children, precociously talented, focused on their own careers, with devoted parents dedicated to supporting everything they did – how was this relationship going to develop?

CHAPTER THREE

A Challenging Decade

THE 1930s

among the shades...
Forget your dreams,
creep, like a barefoot child,
No ending's what it seems.
The form that fades
moves to a new design –
Arpeggios of light
fall in bright showers
drenching you awake.

J de V

A romantic spirit denied an outlet – furiously turning the
poetic energy of love into the materials of sculpture.

J de V

Josefina's highly protected upbringing does to some extent account for her innocence with regard to her prospective husband. Even so, in an Art School atmosphere of the 1920s, where homosexuality and bisexuality were surely not unknown, it is hard to believe she was so completely unsophisticated as not to recognise the signs that he was homosexual. Delmar's parents selfishly said nothing to her parents although they knew he was not interested in women except as carers or as people he could instruct. Josefina suited these requirements, as she was intelligent, talented and admired him; she thought he was a genius, and indeed his childhood sketch books show a sophisticated talent. Josefina soon realised that 'in getting me he got everything he needed.' But in fact it is clear that neither partner got what they needed in the marriage, although time would eventually bring them both to a plateau of understanding.

Why Delmar did not discuss his feelings with Josefina before the wedding can only be surmised. He did not leave any diaries or journals which might explain his feelings at the time of his marriage. It is hard to reconcile his deep religious convictions with a marriage entered into in the full knowledge that it was against the basic precepts of the Anglican Church, ignoring the words of a marriage ceremony that began: 'Matrimony was ordained for the hallowing of the union between man and woman; for the procreation of children to be brought up in the fear and nurture of the Lord; and for the mutual society, help and comfort that the one ought to have of the other, in both prosperity and adversity.'

It is certainly true that at the age of thirty-four Delmar could have had little experience of women. Public School and Oxford were very masculine worlds at that time, and after graduating he lived at home in London with an extremely dominant mother. Once when he attempted to leave the house without a hat during a heatwave he heard his mother say to his father, 'Why did we send him to Oxford to go out without a hat!' There was little affection between his parents and his privileged but isolated upbringing did nothing to prepare him for marriage to a warm and passionate woman like Josefina. Perhaps her rather boyish looks at the time with her short bobbed hair and her masculine hands drew him to her. Perhaps his femininity drew her to him. The reasons for attraction can never satisfactorily be analysed but some mutual attraction was present, even though it was intellectual and not sensual. A shared sense of humour helped to bridge over many difficulties.

Delmar's friends were surprised but happy at his decision to marry. At a time when homosexuality was illegal and certainly not considered respectable, a conventional marriage was a wise precaution against social opprobrium. Delmar had described Josefina as 'an angel' in his letter to his friend Henry Bothamley, Vicar of Harlow, and Bernard Groom wrote warmly to him: 'may it turn out to be, as

I believe it will, your greatest work of art and imagination – speaking in more general terms, I am sure that you have taken a wise step, and that your life will be fuller, richer and happier as a result.'

Groom's description of the marriage as a work of art and imagination was to prove entirely correct. Yet many years later, after much suffering on Josefina's part, the friendship and mutual support that this marriage represented proved to be a great inspiration to many people who loved and admired them both.

The wedding on Monday, 28 April 1930 was entirely tailored to suit the social requirements of Delmar's parents. Josefina wanted a small country church with just close family; she got a large High Church wedding at the Old Church, Chelsea, with a reception for hundreds of people at the Rembrandt Hotel. Conducted by Delmar's friend the Reverend Henry Bothamley it was an unremarkable ceremony, with the familiar hymns 'Lead us heavenly Father, lead us' and 'O perfect love' followed by the Wedding March by Mendelssohn. Among the guests was Delmar's friend Mrs Holman Hunt, widow of the painter, resplendent in many layers of ethnic garments and beads. Hippolyto gave his cherished daughter away, and one can only guess his feelings at the time. Freda, of course, was devastated.

The bride had managed, with difficulty, to choose the material for her own wedding dress, a plain white heavy damask made up into a simple gown to her own design. Two years later Delmar did a fine painting of her wearing it. But Delmar's mother exerted so much control that she even vetoed clothes Josefina had selected for her trousseau, and a 'charming little green two-piece' was rejected because green was supposedly unlucky. Two young girls attended Josefina, Delmar's cousin Margaret and Josefina's cousin Sally, wearing pretty flowered dresses with scalloped hems. Delmar looked quite the dandy in morning suit, spats and a gardenia in his button-hole.

On honeymoon they were like two children who had escaped from their parents. And indeed, Josefina's wedding present to Delmar was a set of children's books, the complete works of Beatrix Potter. They spent their first night together at the Mitre Hotel, Oxford, and both found time to write to the Banners to thank them for the day. To please them, Josefina wrote: 'I loved every moment of the day and am oh-so happy. This is only a short note because I'm so sleepy.' For she was also a child released, and the theme of escape from controlling forces is a recurring theme in many of her sculptures, including her last major completed stone carving, *Escape to Light*.

Delmar wrote a longer letter, expressing his love and thanks for 'all the trouble you have taken over my marriage and thro' all the 34 years in which I have been with you. You ought to know that it is at most fully returned.' These duty letters appear to conceal a great deal of hidden feeling: on Delmar's part, a desire to escape, rather late, from stifling parental control, and on Josefina's part, a deep fear of the power of her mother-in-law, Emily Banner, whom she felt to be like the beautiful witch in Coleridge's poem 'Christabel'. The power of Freda's intense love, which had focused on her daughter for so long, would be just as hard to shake off.

It took time to become accustomed to their freedom, and Josefina was happy to travel up to the Cumbrian Fells so that Delmar could paint. But where was the physical love? She was more than ready, but Delmar banished her from the bed – 'it disturbs me having anyone in the same bed,' he told her, and she had to sleep on the child's camp bed that was in the room. Desperately unhappy, Josefina thought that Delmar simply didn't like her. There was no sexual contact: 'his kisses were like pecks of a pigeon picking up grain.'

The true nature of Delmar, multi-faceted and aloof, revealed itself very gradually. Josefina felt that she had married twins: 'one was a frustrated, unsatisfied, unhappy man, enclosed and bitter; the other was the brilliant scholar and artist who had emerged from the child who had been denied love from his mother and turned to his German nanny for affection; who was talented and precocious enough to play Handel's Largo at the age of three on the violin, and could speak English, French and German easily as a child. Unhappy at Cheltenham College where he went to school, and hopeless at sport, he had decided to excel at learning.'

Above all, Josefina eventually discovered that Delmar was going to be, in her own words, 'an inconsolable widow' for the whole of his life. While studying at Oxford, destined for the diplomatic service, he had fallen deeply in love with a fellow student, David, who, like so many of his generation, was killed in the First World War. Delmar never recovered from this loss. He himself had been rejected twice for military service for medical reasons, in particular a lateral spinal curvature that had started from leaning sideways at his desk in school.

Delmar did not confide in his wife for years and Josefina was thrown into a state of despair. His deepest feelings were, she realised later, hidden even from himself. Having married against her mother's desperate pleadings Josefina was unable to talk to her. There was an uncanny repetition of her mother's own unhappy marriage to a man whose nature was not apparent until it was too late. Hippolyto, who might have understood the situation, had been posted back to Montevideo and was out of touch. Most women would have taken the advice of Josefina's doctor and had the marriage annulled, but she felt bound by the promise she had made in church, 'for better, for worse'. And said Josefina wryly, it could hardly have got much worse. Delmar may have seen her as an angel, but the angel wanted more than adoration from afar.

But there were some compensations for a marriage lacking in any physical intimacy. Delmar was fond of her, as a brother loves a sister, and he admired her work. He encouraged her to study theology, and Josefina was grateful that at last Christianity was explained to her in a way that she found satisfying. Her fervent but inchoate ideas about God were given shape and meaning, and it obviously brought some certainties into her life: 'the chief thing which made me become a Christian was the terrific need of it. The need to know that all forms of life and love and growth and personality are precious – however humble – precious enough to be held in a love greater than mine, for ever.'[1]

A year after her wedding, on 30 June 1931, following Delmar's tuition, she was baptised into the Church of England at St Peter's in the East, Oxford. Delmar's friend and mentor, B H Streeter, Canon of Hereford Cathedral, conducted the service. She was confirmed the following day. Yet Josefina's brand of Christianity always seemed to be a very individual and wide-ranging one, very Franciscan, in that her love of nature was much more of a directing force than any amount of religious dogma. When Dewi Morgan, editor of *They Became Christians*, wrote that 'she has meditated with her hands' he was looking at her sculpture, but her poetry also reveals a very sustained relationship with God. She was constantly seeking to explain her experience of life by studying Christianity: 'one felt like a tiny creature that didn't even know what or why I was, passing through a maze of puzzle which had got muddled up – looking for the clue that might clarify the endless paradox of the known and the unknown, the seen and the unseen.' At the same time, she had her own private awareness of the Holy Spirit speaking to her though nature; something that had been with her from childhood: 'although it was so delicate, it remained stronger than any exposition of Christianity I gained from the highly intellectual and spiritual teachings of Delmar. They could not add to what I already had, but they opened the door on the shut side that had held me away from the simple teachings of Christ. The New Testament was my salvation. It answered every question that had ever worried or confused me.'

Delmar's wide circle of friends, academics and teachers such as Bernard Groom, Basil Willey, Edward Downing, Philip Radcliffe and Ronald Balfour would often join the Banners when they visited the Lake District and they brought a great deal of intellectual stimulus to their lives. The Banners would rent a large farmhouse and for one week Delmar's Oxford friends would come to stay, walking all day and taking parts in Shakespeare plays at night. Then the next week his Cambridge friends came for the same activities. There was plenty of laughter and good conversation, and Josefina was able to forget her personal unhappiness for a time. Not many women were invited to these gatherings, although Bernard Groom's sister sometimes attended. The atmosphere was aesthetic and conducive to deep male friendships; very much a continuation of Delmar's public school and Oxbridge background.

There is no doubt that Delmar was clever, witty and amusing, and he played up his eccentricity to great effect, although he used to say, 'I am not eccentric, merely rational.' Josefina remembers that 'he thought nothing of taking scissors and cutting the sleeves off anything he was wearing (up to the elbows) and dropping the bits on the floor. I was told he tore the cuffs off a very old shirt (typical to be wearing it!) in the middle of giving a lecture.'

He was determined to undermine Josefina's natural joy in dancing and music, and if she ever got up to dance to music he would get up too, imitating her and ridiculing her spontaneous response. Soon she stopped playing her guitar and singing Brazilian songs. Delmar did not like that either. In her eighties, after Delmar was dead, Josefina, with the pianist Geoffrey Chacaro, devised a series of dances to poems and music that she performed to friends. She was reaching back to recover the part of her being Delmar had worked hard to destroy. Yet despite these conflicts in the early years of the relationship, the meeting of minds, the academic and the instinctual, was beginning to bring about a highly individual creative force.

Delmar and Josefina lived together first in Wadhurst, near Tunbridge Wells, Kent, in a large detached house called 'West Wind'. Delmar was sufficiently wealthy to support a very comfortable lifestyle within his private means, and he never had to work apart from his chosen vocation. Like all painters he liked to sell his work to discerning admirers and to have it properly appreciated by other people, but he was never subject to any commercial pressures and he could always paint exactly what he wanted.

'West Wind' offered ample space for Delmar to hang his paintings and some of Josefina's reliefs were placed above the fireplaces. Delmar's mural of the fells circled around the drawing room walls; he was to repeat this later on the walls of the farmhouse they eventually purchased in Cumbria. The garden at the back sloped down to open countryside and there was a terrace where Josefina could sculpt. Very little of Josefina's personality reveals itself in photographs of this solidly furnished house, with its two single bedrooms. 'I felt like a ghost in that house,' said Josefina. But as usual she enjoyed working in the garden and the flowerbeds flourished under her care. She planted an avenue of interlocked appletrees and cherished the ducks and ducklings in the pond. On one occasion she rescued two abandoned duck eggs, brought them into the house and helped them to hatch. Seeing the eye of the duckling through the cracking egg was a deeply moving experience for her and she remembered it as an important religious moment in her life.

Not long after the marriage, Delmar's father Wilfrid died on 6 September 1930, aged 58. Delmar dutifully took his mother to Cornwall for a holiday and Josefina accompanied them. Josefina's feelings must have been in turmoil, tormented as she was by her unconsummated marriage, yet still having to keep up appearances.

She had felt sorry for Wilfrid being so much under the control of his wife, and liked him better than Emily. Yet he seems to have made little attempt to understand his son's homosexuality, if he was even aware of it, and certainly did not enlighten Josefina or her parents before the wedding. More sadness came when Josefina's maternal grandmother, Fanny Coleman, died shortly afterwards, in June 1931. They had been very fond of each other, and Fanny's death did nothing to alleviate Josefina's growing sense of despair.

Wadhurst in the 1930s was described by Josefina as 'a very church, bridge and golf community – most of the men going off to London to work.' There they befriended Hugh Walker, a young boy who had been adopted at the age of four by an elderly spinster in the village and who was having an isolated and circumscribed upbringing. The Banners took a deep personal interest in his development, and Josefina in particular found that she could communicate easily with him. They were instrumental in shaping Hugh's future and a life-long friendship was to result.

During the first few difficult months after her marriage Josefina did not complete many sculptures, but she soon found that work was the only way to try to blot out her despair. Sexually frustrated, she threw herself into hard physical labour and went to bed exhausted. The presence of Delmar's mother continued to be oppressive; on one occasion she went through all the drawers and cupboards of 'West Wind' when the newly-weds were out, and gave Josefina a report on their deficiencies when she returned.

There seems little doubt that Josefina's career suffered a severe setback at this time. In 1930 she was runner-up for the Prix de Rome, with sophisticated and much admired sculpture on exhibition in London and elsewhere. She had worked with the best teachers in France and Italy and was well aware of contemporary trends. She was working in new materials like cast stone. She should have been poised for a dramatic leap forward, but the emotional shock of her marriage, and the separation from her mother (she had never needed to write a letter to her before in her life, as they were always together) affected her confidence and artistic vision. Delmar's High Church Anglicanism also engulfed her for a time and caused her sculpture to move from symbolic or mythological subjects to Christian images, and several pieces at that time are stiff and lacking in the wonderful swirling energy of pieces she sculpted in Paris such as *The Repentance of St Hubert* (1926) or *Leda and the Swan* (1927).

This stiffness is apparent in a relief that she carved above the door of the Liverpool Orphanage, an institution that had been founded by Delmar's grandfather. Carving an unknown stone was always a challenge: 'You never know what you will meet when the builders leave a carving stone,' said Josefina. 'Sometimes you can hit a fossil and a great stream of sand flows out. But fortunately this was all right.' Maybe so, but it was not a distinguished piece of work. The figures of a boy and a girl that she carved in cast stone for either side of the entrance were more successful but even they seem lifeless though well-crafted.

She was isolated from her fellow sculptors when her development was at a crucial point of balance: 'I wanted to go my own way, to do what was not in fashion. Any fool can imitate.' But at a time when Henry Moore and Barbara Hepworth were both exhibiting in commercial galleries in London and selling their works, Josefina was on the sidelines. Although she maintained that 'I knew too much about the art world to find it interesting any more,' for a while she seemed to lose her creative drive.

Even her poetry seemed to lose its youthful, if undisciplined, energy. Christian imagery becomes more important than rushing wind and the song of birds. A group of poems was carefully bound into a handmade book called 'Words and Woodcuts', obviously with hopes of publication. Many of these poems seem to represent a battle against despair – 'Sinner's Hope' contains the vivid image:

> Death, like a blind black ferret slips
> To suck the sprite from out my lips;
> My flesh beneath his eager grope
> May chill and fail, but not my hope.

Happier poems are simpler, such as 'Berries in the Hedge', but the tone throughout is serious, particularly in the series of five poems devoted to the heroine Anita Riberas. Josefina sculpted Anita Riberas, showing again how her poetry and her sculpture were closely related.

'Words and Woodcuts' was made remarkable by the prints on every page, some of which have been reproduced in this book as endpieces. The discipline of woodcuts, scraperboard or line drawings suited Josefina's austere style at that time and many are small but perfect images. She put this book together while she was still living at 'West Wind', but she did not get it published. Whether this was because Delmar did not value the poems or did not assist her in publishing is not clear, but Josefina continued to hope that she would have a book of poems published. She could certainly have brought the book out herself and it would have been a very attractive volume, but perhaps she lacked confidence in what she had achieved.

Poetry may have helped fluidity to return to her sculpture, however, and a few years later she carved *Music in the Trees*, a three-quarter figure in Clipsham stone, which was exhibited at the Royal Academy in 1938. 'I always thought it was a bit soppy,' said Josefina, but the delicate sculpture of a naked woman caressed by branches became very popular recently when it was found in the basement of the Southampton Art Gallery and exhibited for the first time since Josefina and Delmar's 1947 Joint Exhibition in London. The ecstasy of *Music in the Trees* relates very directly to much of Josefina's early poetry, with its imagery drawn from the natural world. The 1938 Royal Academy Exhibition also included *Clouds in May*, carved in Hoptonwood stone. In 1939 the Royal Academy accepted her head of the Reverend E W S Packard in stone, and in 1940 a bronze Calvary.

Her most serious project in the 1930s was carving a huge piece of Portland stone left over from Sir Christopher Wren's rebuilding of St Paul's Cathedral in London. The stone was one of the monoliths laid out for Wren to select for the pillars of St Paul's. He rejected it as being not quite perfect, and after waiting for nearly three hundred years the stone was finally given life by Josefina. The work was inspired by Josefina's anxiety at the growing clouds of war, and she envisaged a huge figure of Christ calming the storm.

She began work on the terrace at the back of 'West Wind', often spending long hours up ladders on the same level as birds nesting in the trees. Carving a major stone was just the sort of project she found most satisfying and she loved working outside in her sunny garden. Black with age on the outside, the rejected stone soon revealed its beautiful creamy white colour. The monumental, eight-foot figure was first called *Christ the Judge* but became known as *The Prince of Peace* when it was adopted as the centrepiece for the National War Memorial at Aldershot in 1950. The sculpture was submitted for exhibition to the Royal Academy before the outbreak of war in 1939, but there were very few places for large works and it was not selected. Josefina then had it transported up to their house in the Lake District, where she continued to work on its elaborately carved base.

This base reveals Josefina's fears for humanity: cruelty, killing, the worship of fantasies, the viciousness of the serpent striking fiercely. Christ's blessing and forgiveness stands above this. The statue is enormously powerful and in style seems to relate back to the stone carving of St Valerie she did for the church at Varengeville. Not until after the War had ended would this magnificent sculpture find an appropriate resting place.

Delmar's career as a painter was also developing during the 1930s. He painted a series of oil portraits of what we would now call 'the great and the good': senior clergy, professors, and statesmen, including Viscount Hailsham. They are meticulous and serious likenesses, very suitable for hanging in formal surroundings, but his style in these works seems to be singularly lacking in energy or human warmth. It is interesting to look at the free lines of Delmar's early childhood sketch books, which often seem more eloquent than his later trained style. Drawings and oils of his Oxford friends are more intimate and relaxed. He exhibited three times at the Royal Academy between 1925 and 1928 with paintings on historical and religious themes, and decorated the walls of the Fyvie Hall in the Regent Street Polytechnic with a series of murals, rather wooden in conception, depicting important moments in history. They can still be seen by perspiring students as they write their examinations in the panelled hall. In 1929 Delmar made a visit to the Holy Land and did a series of paintings, mainly ethereal landscapes in watercolour but also some powerful oils. Many of his religious paintings at the time have a clear homoerotic style, with beautiful, muscular young men posing naked or briefly draped in artificial settings.

In 1932 he painted a portrait of Josefina wearing her wedding dress, a painting that depicts a very beautiful young woman with sad and haunted eyes. 'He tried to paint obedience into my eyes,' said Josefina. It was matched by a painting of Josefina and his mother painted as the trunk and the branch of a tree, indicating the central place that his mother still had in his emotions. Emily Banner is at the centre, with a basket of roses; Josefina is perched on a branch, reading to her. The focus of attention is the silver-haired mother, not the new wife. Emily is certainly beautiful, but with a hardness that is very apparent in her face. At the time Josefina did not know what an Oedipus complex was, but all the signs were there for her to read even before she was married, had she been able to recognise them.

Despite the need for ambitious artists to stay close to the centre of things in London, Delmar was always drawn to the mountains of the Lake District and they visited more and more often so that he could paint and draw. Josefina, too, loved the quiet landscapes of the hills, and with her special closeness to nature found some peace there: 'I was very happy as Wordsworth was, living and working very close to nature, finally in the Lake District with Delmar.' They often stayed at Isabella Foster's house 'Beckstones' in Sedbergh, so that Delmar could paint and visit friends who taught at Sedbergh School. Isabella offered Bed and Breakfast in her home near her nephew's hill farm. She became a close friend, and as 'Aunt' Belle provided a warm and comforting presence in Josefina's life. This was especially valued when in 1936 she had to face the sudden death of her father, who had just been appointed Consul General in Liverpool after serving in Genoa.

In June that year Hippolyto and Freda had come to stay with them in Buttermere, and he, too, fell in love with the landscape, saying that he could understand how much they wanted to live there. Ironically this Amazon explorer, the lover of wild and distant places, was knocked down and killed on Catherine Street in the centre of Liverpool only a few months later. He had just got off a bus and was hit by a doctor's car which fractured his skull. Taken to Liverpool Royal Infirmary, he never regained consciousness and died the following morning on 10 September.

Although they had not lived together for some time Josefina loved and admired her father (she was proud that 'the poor people always loved him') and his death, coming so soon after their happy time together, was a tremendous shock. She had always felt closer to her father than her mother in many ways; she shared his love of the natural world and inherited his direct, penetrating stare which often unnerved people. He had unfailingly praised and encouraged her in everything she did but had a steadying influence too. Freda had had a premonition of the accident through a dream, and Josefina, who always believed in the 'Irish intuitive' qualities of her mother, felt that this warning helped her to cope with his violent death. His obituary in the *Liverpool Echo* referred to his 'sterling qualities' and praised his 'firmness of character', combined with a 'genial disposition'.

In a strange way Hippolyto's intense response to the Amazon was not dissimilar to Delmar's close communion with the mountains and high tarns of Cumbria. Delmar was continuing to paint mountains whenever he could escape to the Lake District, and to develop the monumental but romantic style that became characteristic of his mature work. Eskdale was a particular favourite of the Banners, as Delmar liked to paint Scafell from the west, where the red granite rock was exposed. He was one of the first of the Lake District painters to paint from the heights, and his paintings often have a majesty that gives them a powerful religious presence. In those days the Wrynose Pass from Little Langdale over to Eskdale was just a gravel track, and the Banners would go in a pony and trap over the Hardnott Pass to stay at the Woolpack Inn.

Josefina, by now well known locally, was helping out at the Eskdale Show one year when a farmer introduced her to Beatrix Potter, Mrs Heelis, who was judging sheep at the show. Delmar was up in the fells, painting, but Josefina, wearing a dark blue boiler suit and clogs, was busy dishing out huge plates of food for the farmers, some of whom would have left home at three or four in the morning with their flocks to reach the show. There were long trestle tables and benches for the farmers to sit down, each with two sheepdogs at his feet.

Beatrix Potter had become the first woman President of the Herdwick Sheepbreeders' Association in 1930. Canon Hardwicke Rawnsley, one of the founders of the National Trust and a valiant champion of the Lake District, established the Association in 1899 in order to help preserve this rare breed of sheep which are unusual in becoming heafed or hefted to the fells they live on, and do not stray. In that year Mrs Heelis won the silver challenge cup for the best Herdwick ewe in the Lake District. She showed her own sheep widely, and for many years was a respected judge, visiting shows throughout the district. By now a substantial landowner, she had added Penny Hill Farm in Eskdale to her extensive holdings in 1935, and she regularly judged at the Eskdale show.

Mrs Heelis was popular with the shepherds, but even so, Josefina was startled to see an ancient shepherd, rather the worse for wear by the middle of the afternoon, slap the diminutive Mrs Heelis on the back, nearly knocking her flat, and announce, 'My father knew John Peel, and sometimes he was so drunk out of pub he couldn't manage to get on his horse. They had to lift him on.'

'I never thought nowt of John Peel,' was the tart reply. Indeed not. John Peel was the famous Cumbrian who like all Lake District huntsmen, hunted on foot, and was celebrated in the cheerful ballad:

D'ye ken John Peel, wi' his coat so gay,
D'ye ken John Peel at the break of day,
D'ye ken John Peel when he's far far away
With his fox and his hounds in the morning.

When Mrs Heelis left her 4,000 acres and fifteen farms to the National Trust, it was with strict instructions that hunting with otter hounds or harriers would not take place on her Troutbeck Fells.

The Eskdale Show ended with shepherds' calls and waltzing, and Josefina joined in the shepherds' calls because she had learned the skill from her friends in Langdale. Waltzing took place in a muddy field, with everyone wearing Wellington boots, to the strains of the local brass band. The prize for the best dancers, appropriately enough for the area, was an umbrella. By this time vast quantities of beer and food had been consumed, and the shepherds, with their families, trundled unsteadily home.

Here in Eskdale Josefina saw many old traditions that have since disappeared, such as a shepherd's funeral with his coffin surrounded by heather and staghorn moss and laid on a farm cart. And the 'Sin Eater' who called when there was a death, a stranger who emerged from the night and grasped a handful of salt from the chest of the exposed corpse lying in a farmhouse kitchen, swallowed it, and disappeared into the night, taking the sins of the departed with him. Josefina carved headstones for some of her shepherd friends.

When Beatrix Potter was introduced to Josefina at the Eskdale Show, she sized up Josefina in her overalls and clogs, and issued a rare invitation to visit her at home. By this time the creator of Peter Rabbit was being constantly besieged by admirers from all over the world, and she kept herself very much to herself. She received visitors in the cottage at Hill Top Farm, Sawrey, which is now owned by the National Trust and open to the public, but at the end of the day Beatrix and her maid, who always wore a Victorian dress, apron and frilly cap, would put out the fire and walk across the fields to Castle Cottage, where Beatrix and her solicitor husband William Heelis actually lived.

Josefina wrote very hauntingly about their first visit in a letter to Margaret Lane, biographer of Beatrix Potter, and quoted by Delmar in an article published after Mrs Heelis' death:

> When a stranger comes into a Lakeland cottage, Something, diffused through the room as the air itself, recedes into the shadows; watching and hiding there till the new presence has gone. The Stranger knows it will never come out while he is there: – even if the old folk move out, and he takes their place, living there till his footsteps have worn the door-sill lower – it will only emerge when he is in bed. If he comes down in the night there is a cool smell, distinct, but neither sweet nor acid – and he knows that the Past is out and alive in the old house. It is not unfriendly, only still, and 'candlewise'. This same 'withdrawing' is present in a meeting between an 'offcome' and a native of the Dales. A silence, a searching gaze; weighing and sounding. Thus it was at our first meeting with Mrs Heelis.[2]

Josefina and Beatrix were to become intuitive friends: 'She knew a lot without having to be told.'

When the Banners first visited Castle Cottage the door was opened by a tiny figure wearing an old fashioned woollen tea-cosy on her head. Josefina later found out that rheumatic fever as a girl had left Beatrix with a gap in her hair, and she always wore a cap or a velvet head-band of some kind to cover it.

'Coom in,' said Mrs Heelis, in broad Cumbrian. They were led into an old farmhouse kitchen with the dark oak furniture typical of the area, but both of them noticed a Girtin watercolour on the wall, beautiful silver candlesticks, and the fine silver-mounted guns in the hall.

'When she laughed, she would roll and slap her knees,' remembers Josefina. She was delighted to hear that Delmar's private name for his wife was 'Pig-wig' because she sometimes snorted when she laughed. (Pig-wig is the name of one of the characters in Beatrix Potter's story *The Tale of Pigling Bland*.) From that time on, Beatrix always wrote to Josefina as 'Dear Pig-wig'.

On one occasion Delmar asked if he could see the originals of the book illustrations. She paused for a moment. 'Oh aye. I'll get them down from the bathroom. I keep them behind the geyser,' she said. And off she went to get them, from probably the driest place in the house. Delmar described the moment in his memoir:

> We heard the creaking of the stairs as she climbed slowly up, and then, after an interval of little noises, down again, armed with bundles in brown paper, fastened with blue ribbon. We saw how exquisite – beyond our hopes and beyond the means of colour-reproduction – the pictures are. She told us the outlines, which seem to us to strengthen, were not in the first drawings, and remained a distasteful convention to her, but were advised by the printers. She identified all the places; every scene can be found, mostly near Sawrey and Hawkshead; some further off, like those of *Mrs Tiggywinkle* in Newlands; and Pigling and Pig-wig Bland go to live in Little Langdale.[3]

Delmar's professional eye admired 'her realism and her grasp of how things worked' and her 'unpedantic technical finish, her undistorted specific observation.' She bought one of his paintings, a watercolour of Coniston, and took a keen interest in the work of both of them. Beatrix looked carefully at Delmar's paintings and was not slow to criticise but also quick to praise. Clearly she felt that Delmar still had not quite captured the particular essence of the Cumbrian fells, because she wrote to Josefina in 1938 about the need for Delmar to get more light into his studies: 'Your husband has learnt clouds. Light next please. He has the *drawing* that is the foundation.'[4]

She advised him to study trees, when he had the time: 'incredible how many professional landscape painters don't. I mean they have never considered how the branches grow from a tree trunk… if you study an ash you will see every branch from the main trunk or from the stem of the young sapling, has come out in curves, and curved on and on with the weight of foliage. We can tell every tree in winter without reference to foliage, by its mode of growth. So study them some spare moments, Mr Banner, they will repay – they are *in the right place* as beautiful as rocks and they have a nobility of growth which is, usually, entirely overlooked.'[5] This precise observation is apparent not only in her scientific drawings of plants and fungi, but also in the settings to her children's stories.

From the time of the Banners' first visit Beatrix and Josefina became close friends even though there was a wide difference in their ages. Her friendship was a robust one: when she heard of Hippolyto's accident and death she wrote immediately to say 'how grieved we were to hear of the motor tragedy,' but went on in her usual forthright manner to say that 'Life goes on for others in spite of death.'[6] She devotes the rest of her letter to property and house sales.

Her sturdy realism was much appreciated by Cumbrian farmers and she was a respected figure. On one occasion in the autumn of 1937 the Banners were renting Heathwaite Farm above Coniston, and Mrs Heelis was expected for lunch. The whole village knew that she was coming and every cottage window had welcoming faces to greet her. She arrived in an ancient taxi that had barely managed to wheeze across from Sawrey, and was quite incapable of climbing the steep track to the farm. So the village milk float was brought, a pony put in the shafts, and Mrs Heelis was given a plank to climb up, supported on either side. Like a charioteer she was brought up to the farm in triumph, where all the neighbours had sent flowers to decorate the rooms. She did justice to her lunch, but then made a full inspection of the farm before leaving, paying particular attention to the sheepdog pups.

The Banners consulted her extensively about buying or building a property in the Lake District, and her wide experience was invaluable. She cautioned them against buying a farm or cottage that was too far from the road:

> It is wise not to be to remote, for a permanent home. Pig-wig – bless her – is still at the ecstatic stage when she would like to be over the hills and far away – but what about carting coal if there is no road?! What about occasional daily help? Not to mention large canvases and blocks of marble and green slate.[7]

Josefina also benefitted from her advice on two books that she had written and illustrated, one a book of songs for children, the other her book of woodcuts and poems. Beatrix liked the children's rhymes: 'I do love the little rhymes. The Robin, the Daisies, the Brave Dove are perfect for small children,' and advised Josefina to try Warnes, her publisher, 'though the present manager, Mr Stephens has about as much sentiment and artistic taste as one of their own cooking books.' When Josefina wrote to tell of her failure to place the book, Beatrix wrote back saying exactly the right things:

> It was disappointing but not unexpected by me. I am afraid your originals are too delicately beautiful for the modern publishing world which caters for shopkeepers at a competitive price... What is to be done in face of such a world? Children deserve the best.[8]

The Banners' Christmas card that year, with a poem and woodcut by Josefina, pleased her a great deal and she wrote that 'Your sweet Christmas card made me cry!':

> The grass is cut, the flowers fade,
> The Sun dries up the hay;
> Was all this beauty only made
> To perish in a day?

The Infant lies with ne'er a sheet
Nor coverlet of white;
But in the manger, Ah, how sweet
The dried hay smells tonight!

The poem is illustrated with a woodcut of a sickle, wildflowers, a bird and a star.

During the 1930s the Banners had stayed in several farmhouses in different parts of the Lake District, always hoping that the opportunity to buy a place of their own would emerge. Eventually early in 1939, through a stroke of great good luck, they received a telegram from a friend telling them that an old Cumbrian farmhouse, The Bield, in Little Langdale, was for sale. Josefina travelled up to Langdale as fast as she could, hoping that the owner had not already sold it. In those days, word of mouth was the most usual way that these properties changed hands, and they did not change often.

The grandfather of the owner had been the famous grocer smuggler of Langdale, whose cart had a special storage locker for smuggled goods. Most houses in Langdale had secret hiding places for smuggled French brandy, lace and tobacco which came in from the west coast. The Bield was well equipped with two, one in the house and another under the bridge across the stream outside.

The Bield (the name means a safe enclosure in Old English) became more than a home. Backed by steep rock faces and facing out over Little Langdale Tarn and Pike O' Blisco, it is an idyllic spot. But for Josefina it meant continuous labour, even with the help of Dorothy and Molly, two sisters from a local farm who came in to help with the heavy work. The stone flags were cold and the doors were drafty. The drystone walls were packed with moss to keep out wind and weather but the house was seldom cosy. The Banners altered the upstairs level to create a number of bedrooms and a bathroom, because like all very ancient farmhouses this level had originally been one large room for the workers to sleep in, with a small partitioned area at the end for the farmer and his wife. Another typical feature upstairs was a large smoke room built into the chimney, designed to cure quantities of meat for the winter, and this was removed as it took up a large area. Delmar had a studio made at the front of the house in space taken from one of the barns, and from this he had a spectacular view across the valley to the high fells.

At first there was no electricity and water came down in a long pipe from a tank on Lingmoor. The rooms were lit by candles and oil lamps. Although Delmar always ensured that Josefina had help with the housework, she had to cook on an old-fashioned black range and sometimes had to sweep the flues herself. This was replaced by a Rayburn stove after the war. She kept the vegetable garden well stocked and found a refuge within its high drystone walls; often she went out there to weep.

The house was formally blessed on 29 September 1939 by their old friend Canon Aidan Hervey, and many friends and relatives were there for the occasion, including Josefina's mother Freda and Delmar's mother Emily. The Banners liked to keep open house and the visitors' book displays an impressive list of callers: distinguished guests included the artist and head of the Royal Academy, Sir Charles Wheeler, the historian G M Trevelyan, the athlete Christopher Chataway and the artist Owen Jennings. Bishops, professors, painters and musicians all found their way to The Bield.

High Bield Cottage, behind the main house, was part of the property and was rented out as a holiday home to a long succession of families who also came to love the Langdale valley. Over the years not only friends from school and university and their families but parties of scouts and school campers on their land also signed in at The Bield.

Once established in his house in Cumbria Delmar's eccentric habits had full sway. He decided to live by natural hours of daylight, so in winter he rose late and went to bed early. He once lifted a slate in the floor to accommodate a long-case clock that was too tall for the room by sliding it into the hole – not the best treatment for an antique.

For the next six years, while the Second World War engulfed the country, The Bield was a refuge for many visitors who came to experience a short period of peace and tranquillity after the horrific bombing of all the major cities. Freda de Vasconcellos moved up to Ambleside from London for safety during the worst of the blitz but did not stay at The Bield if Delmar was there. Delmar's mother also moved up to the Lakes and was staying in Grasmere when she died on 28 May 1941.

Hugh Walker, their young friend from Wadhurst, together with his guardian stayed with the Banners for some weeks during the wartime period and for a time went to school in Windermere. Delmar subsequently paid for him to repeat his School Certificate Examination year at Tonbridge School from 1947 to 1948 at a time when his guardian thought it best for him to leave school and work in a shop. After gaining his School Certificate Hugh got a commission in the army, went to Africa and finally got admitted to a course at Oxford under the auspices of the Colonial Service. He kept in touch with the Banners throughout his career and afterwards remained grateful to them for an act of generosity that changed his life. Many years later Hugh was reunited with his two lost sisters, Deirdre Curwen and Audrey Steer, who had also been adopted and did not know of his existence, or of each other's. The Banners invited the family to stay together at The Bield, and Delmar said that this was the most exciting thing that had ever happened to them. When Hugh was awarded the MBE towards the end of his career, no one was happier than Josefina.

Many evacuated children came to Cumbria for the duration of the War, and among the rest, in April, 1940, came Brian and Billy, aged only five and four, rescued from the London bombing and from a very disturbed background by Delmar's friend Ronald Balfour. The boys came to stay at The Bield, and for the childless Banners life was to change dramatically from that point on.

CHAPTER FOUR

Safe Haven in the Langdales

THE 1940s

*Which of all these activities I plunge into with such
energy comes FIRST?
My closeness to nature, children and working people.*

J de V

rian and Billy were transported from central London to a
remote rural landscape that must have seemed very strange
indeed. The boys went to the village primary school in Little
Langdale where everyone seemed to speak a foreign language and
they learned that, yes, they could walk on the grass. Soon they were
ranging over the fells, gaining health and strength, and, more
important, security. They spoke broad Cumbrian in a few weeks.
Brian particularly loved helping with the animals at the nearby farm
and Josefina thought he might like to become a farmer when he
grew up. He kept some pet bantam hens, much loved by Josefina,
and Billy kept rabbits.

Before long the boys were formally adopted by the Banners and
remained with them when the War ended. After attending the village
school they went to Huyton Hill Preparatory School in Windermere
and then, because there was often tension between them, Josefina
thought that they would do better at different secondary schools.
Brian was sent to St Bees School on the Cumbrian coast and Billy
went to Rossall, near Morecambe, both fee-paying establishments.

Looking after the two boys had added considerably to Josefina's domestic duties and Delmar did not take kindly to being disturbed by boisterous play. When he took his afternoon nap, Josefina often had to take the boys out in fair weather or foul to avoid causing him annoyance. When difficult problems arose, Delmar would lock himself in the bathroom and run water so that he did not hear what was going on. They were forbidden to listen to football commentaries on the radio because of the vulgar accents of the commentators, and Josefina had to arrange for secret sessions with the boys to follow the scores.

Despite its remoteness, many people came to stay at The Bield. Jennifer Hales, the young daughter of Charles and Madeline Hales, often stayed with the Banners during the war years and Josefina loved having her in the house. Charles and Madeline Hales with their two little girls had come to Little Langdale to escape the bombing of Liverpool, and a long and very enduring friendship was struck up simply by Josefina going to knock on their door after hearing that someone had arrived in the village who might be able to teach piano to the boys. Madeline came to The Bield where she taught the boys to play, and Charles, who was a school teacher, also became a good friend. Charles taught at Huyton Hill School, attended by the Banner boys, and Delmar felt he was such an able teacher that he bought a school for Charles to run, the King's School in Ambleside. Charles was a brilliant headmaster and his school was a happy one. Over the years there would be many such acts of generosity from the Banners.

Jennifer Hales has very happy memories of staying at The Bield at that time, and clearly the youngsters brought life and energy to the house. They bounded about the fells in all weathers, explored the caves in the forbidden quarry and shared a special private language with Delmar and Josefina, who were known to them as 'Poozy' and 'Pig-Wig'. They wrote and performed plays but neither of the boys was bookish, to Delmar's disappointment. Jennifer loved the way that Delmar would always talk to children as though they were adults; he didn't look down to them and his conversations were always interesting. 'They were both very good at making children happy,' remembered Jennifer, and remembers also the glee with which she and Josefina devoured two packets of sweets one day when Delmar was away, breaking the strict rule of having only two sweets per day, after dinner. Josefina made up stories for them and kept the tale of a fat crook called Zambuk running for two years.

At one time there had been a plan to adopt a baby girl, because the boys asked if they could have a baby sister like everyone else, but Delmar stopped the arrangement going through because he disapproved of the child's background; she was the daughter of a Viennese street girl. Josefina had been so much looking forward to the adoption that she started to make clothes for the baby in anticipation of its arrival. She is still haunted by the photograph of the child's face that was sent to her, and confessed that 'I gave away the little garments I had made with more tears for her than for myself.' Looking after the boys saved the situation for Josefina, as she often felt they were closer to her in age than Delmar was, and they had many private jokes that he did not share.

Further pressure on Josefina came from the friction between Freda de Vasconcellos and Delmar. Freda did come to stay in Ambleside for some time during the bombing of London but she still found it difficult to be with Delmar. Josefina had promised to try to see her mother once a month, but Delmar was so jealous of these infrequent visits that he feigned illness, and time after time Josefina had to remain at The Bield to nurse what she soon came to realise were imaginary ailments. Freda became more and more unhappy, while maintaining the lively and positive exterior she presented to the world. Her early stage training in musical comedy stood her in good stead. She continued to hope there was some chance of Josefina leaving Delmar, and that enabled her to keep going.

The Banners knew that the London art world had effectively ceased to exist for the duration of the War, and they could not have expected that the London art world would come to them. At the end of 1940, when London had been severely bombed, the Royal College of Art was relocated to Ambleside. Under the direction of the Principal, P H Jowett, the Schools of Painting, Sculpture, Design and Engraving, with 150 students and their tutors, were moved up to the safety of the Lake District and stayed there until 1945. This influx of rather unconventional young people made a distinct impression on a quiet and very conservative town. Men were billeted at the Queen's Hotel, and the women stayed across the road in the

Salutation Hotel, where they all took meals.

Tutors generally managed to find accommodation elsewhere, and Delmar's friend the Professor of Painting Gilbert Spencer (1892–1979), the younger brother of the more famous painter Stanley, with his wife Ursula and daughter Gillian, stayed for some time with Professor Ernest de Selincourt, the distinguished Wordsworth scholar, at his house, Ladywood, in Grasmere. Spencer did a fine portrait of him there. The Spencers also stayed for extended periods with the Banners at The Bield, as did Professor E W Tristram and his family. Professor Tristram (1882–1952) was Head of the School of Design, and he and his staff faced the huge problem of finding materials for their students to work on, as fabrics in particular were severely rationed. Professor Tristram painted a large number of watercolours during his time in the Lake District.

The Director of the Centre for English Romanticism in Grasmere, Dr Robert Woof, mounted an exhibition of the exiled painters at the Dove Cottage Museum in 1987. In his catalogue to the exhibition, which was called 'The Artist as Evacuee', he discusses Spencer's painting 'Little Langdale from Woodside', probably painted while the Spencers were staying at the Bield. Dr Woof suggests that:

> Spencer usually avoids the drama of the Central Fells of the Lake District, and here the larger hills are hidden behind the carefully painted mist and cloud. Here he prefers to emphasize the pastoral motif, with the interplay of fields, hedges, wall, and wire hoops of the garden wall. and the presentation of the houses and farms lying in a rolling countryside, 'green to the very door'. It is as if Spencer's eye picks out aspects of the northern landscape that more easily harmonize with his southern experience.[1]

Gilbert Spencer described these unsettled years in his auto-biography *Memoirs of a Painter*, referred to by Dr Woof in his exhibition catalogue, where he writes dryly about his service in the Home Guard in Ambleside – 'I stormed the heights of Nabscar, helped to restore the defences of Windermere when knocked down by sheep' – and desperately longs to be back in London. But one happy moment was celebrating the news of the Armistice in 1945 at The Bield:

> We climbed to the top of Whetherlam [sic] and saw the world at our feet whichever way we turned. With Gillian to share our joy, our sense of peace was complete when on reaching home she asked for her skipping rope.[2]

Gilbert Spencer remained impervious to the grandeur of the mountains surrounding him, and in his humorous cartoon sketches of the Home Guard at work he painted the background to resemble the South of England: 'I never came to terms with the mountains, and treated them as sky.'[3]

Gilbert's brother Stanley Spencer (1891–1959) never visited The Bield, but Josefina did meet him in London after the War, where they discussed the qualities of winter, and Spencer interested Josefina when he remarked: 'I like winter. It's so medieval.' Gilbert went to visit his brother in one of the dreary sets of lodgings that he was reduced to living in after losing all his money to his second wife, and Stanley had hidden a life-size nude of himself in the wardrobe so his landlady wouldn't see it. It was painted on wallpaper, and when unrolled, Gilbert said, it bounced towards him in leaps and bounds.

Curiously, none of the Royal College students had made contact with probably the most famous twentieth century artist ever to be associated with Ambleside, the German refugee Kurt Schwitters (1887–1948). He fled to England in 1940, and was interned on the Isle of Man along with many other talented artists, musicians and intellectuals. He came to stay in Ambleside for a holiday in 1943 and returned to live in June 1945. For the three years left before his death, in deteriorating health, he worked furiously on a sculpture project in Harry Pierce's barn in Elterwater in the Langdale Valley. This 'Merz Barn' was to be his masterpiece, replacing an earlier 'Merz Bau' in Hanover that had been destroyed in an air raid and a second construction destroyed by fire in Norway.

Given the nature of the highly conservative Royal College of Art at that time it is not surprising that the students had nothing to do with him. As Robert Woof points out, even the Lake District landscapes that Schwitters painted swiftly to earn money, selling them to passers-by outside the Bridge House in Ambleside, reveal 'a bold expressionistic style... a contrast with the English classical tradition which was maintained by most artists congregating in Ambleside.'[4] Schwitters lodged in Gale Crescent, Ambleside, and Sarah Wilson, in her article 'Kurt Schwitters in England', notes that 'a Professor from the college, a portrait painter, lived in the same house as Schwitters, but was apparently too shy to be introduced; Schwitters had tea with one or two students; yet despite the fascinating potential for an exchange of culture and ideas, no important contacts were established.'[5]

Josefina and Delmar knew nothing about the avant-garde work taking shape in the cold and drafty barn only a few miles from The Bield. Transport was difficult and Josefina usually managed to get into Ambleside once a month for shopping. Besides, Delmar was unlikely to have had much sympathy with an artist who felt that any material, scraps of paper, bus tickets, detritus of every kind, could be made into a work of art. But Robert Woof observes that 'Schwitters' presence in Ambleside was significant, and perhaps prophetic of that international movement which was to sweep away the solid English style which characterises the art of all the evacuees at Ambleside.'[6]

Schwitters died, destitute, on 8 January 1948 and was buried in Ambleside. His remains were later removed to Hanover in Germany. The one completed wall of the 'Merz Barn' was rescued from dereliction in 1965 by the artist Richard Hamilton, then a Lecturer in Fine Art at the University of Newcastle upon Tyne. Hamilton arranged for the entire barn wall to be transported the 160 miles to the Hatton Gallery in the University. It is now a source of pilgrimage for an international audience, and the recognition of Schwitters' contribution to twentieth century art continues to grow.

Although Gilbert Spencer may have tried to ignore the mountains, Delmar was enjoying just the opposite response. Living in the midst of the great crags of Langdale inspired his particular Romantic vision of the mountains and their relationship to man. In the early 1940s he painted a series of large oils of the mountains nearby: Wetherlam, Bowfell, Helvellyn, Glaramara; all painted from a point of view high up the mountainside. Immensely strong but full of mystery, these mountains often dwarf human figures who look across the abyss.

The absence of vegetation and the concentration on the seamed crags give the paintings a mystical quality that is enhanced by swirling clouds and shafts of light. He was meticulous in his observation, using sketches and notes, but he rarely painted out of doors. Mary Burkett, Curator of Abbot Hall Art Gallery and a friend of the Banners for many years, described his approach to landscape in a talk given at the opening of a posthumous exhibition of his work in 1995:

> Unlike many artists, he did not paint from nature. This was not because he did not want to know chosen views intimately – on the contrary, he used to walk every inch of a prospective landscape, analysing the form, studying the colour and taking copious notes on every detail before working on it in his studio. He was looking for fundamental truth and combining this with his rich imagination, producing landscapes of great power and yet with the gentle subtlety of tone which only a few great artists have been able to achieve.[7]

Many of the dramatic paintings of this period are now held by public galleries in the UK. They illustrate perfectly the view expressed in 1941 by the distinguished art historian and critic Sir Kenneth Clark in conversation with Henry Moore, Graham Sutherland and VS Pritchett that 'great landscapes must be painted with a pervading sense of human values; they can't be just records of a tract of country, but of the emotions which that particular scene allows the painter to express. That's why, to my mind, a painter must know his landscape intimately. He must belong to it, and it to him.'[8]

Delmar was closely held within the landscape of the Lake District, but Josefina, although she responded to its beauty, needed more than mountains for inspiration. Yet the confinement of the war years did not prevent her from producing some of her best work, and she, too, found landscape a positive influence in her work.

Although the Royal College of Art was reasonably safe in Ambleside, Cumbria was not entirely free of bombs. In 1941 Beatrix Potter wrote to her friend in America, Anne Carroll Moore, about planes flying overhead on their way to other targets, but occasionally off-loading their bombs on farms and fields:

> We have had noisy nights even in this remote district, as the German planes go over on passage elsewhere, and sometimes unload their bombs when running for home; but there has been very little damage, they usually fall in fields or water. There was one bad tragedy, a lonely farmhouse, where the farmer his mother his wife & 2 children, maid servant and 5 evacuees were all killed.[9]

Josefina's sculpture *Heroic Fragment* had as its inspiration a plane crash on the mountains near them one winter night; they were sitting round the table when they heard the explosion. The crew had parachuted out but had landed on the crags and been killed. Working in very bad conditions the shepherds and their dogs went out and found them hanging upside down in their harnesses, frozen. Josefina's sculpture depicting the hanging airman has now been accepted by the Museum of Army Flying in Stockbridge, Hampshire to be displayed in the Hall which tells the story of the Glider Pilot Regiment. She was writing poetry throughout the war, and one poem, 'Rock-a-bye', which she called a song with music, was in memory of the glider pilots and airmen lost on the Cumbrian Fells:

> The shadow of the cradle
> moved slow on the wall...
> the winter night was sleeping
> with snow soon to fall –
> and I my watch was keeping
> lest baby wake and cry,
> with a Rock-a-rock-a-bye.

On another occasion Josefina remembers finding a perfect hand, and then a man's leg, lying among the rocks on a high fell. The boys were far below and she sent them home while she ran to the nearest telephone at the inn to alert the command at Barrow. The flying boat factory on Windermere was bombed when the Banners were staying in a farmhouse nearby at High Skelghyll, just above the factory, and one bomb landed so close to them that the whole house shook:

Seaplanes were being made hidden in the woods on Windermere Lake. However, it wasn't secret for long because 'Lord Haw-Haw' broadcast the fact and soon after there was a surprise bombing. We were wakened by much noise and then suddenly the whole farmhouse jumped into the air and then landed back with a great thud. Next morning they found that a bomb had been dropped nearby. I think if it had landed on the rock we would have had it, but it went into a bog! How lucky for us all. We were a long time watching the glow of fire around Barrow but there again the bombs landed on waste ground.

During the war years when travel was difficult and even dangerous, Josefina became very close to the farmers of Langdale. She had already come to know many Cumbrians during their stays in Sedbergh, Coniston and Hawkshead before they bought The Bield. She wrote songs and sketches for the Women's Institute in Langdale, and ran a Sunday School for local children at The Bield for several years. It is easy to picture Josefina surrounded by children on the grass outside the house in summer, telling them simple Bible stories, and shelling peas at the same time. Delmar would come down from his studio when it was time for them to go. Josefina always gave the children a spoonful of 'jalop' or tonic before they went, looking after their health as well as their religious education.

She also played the harmonium at the church in Little Langdale, an exhausting procedure involving much peddling with the feet and energetic keyboard attack. Some years later, in 1956, Delmar became a Lay Reader. Although Josefina supported Delmar and went to church with him, she had a lot of reservations about the Church of England. She prefers now to be known as a Christian, not an Anglican, seeking a more wide-ranging view of Christ and his message, and looking always to St Francis for his love of animals and birds.

Josefina visited her dear friend Beatrix Potter for the last time in August 1943. She had a feeling then that they would not meet again, because ill-health was sapping her strength. Beatrix pulled down Josefina's face to kiss her, and then stood at the door, gently waving goodbye with a leaf, like Timmy-Willy in her story *Johnny-Town Mouse*. She died on 23 December.

Delmar had painted his celebrated portrait of Beatrix Potter in 1938 although she did not sit for him, never having the time or patience for it. She stands firmly in her good Herdwick cloth coat with a slightly mischievous smile, clutching an umbrella. Few know that the umbrella belonged to her first love, Norman Warne, who died while they were still engaged. She was deeply upset when she lost the other token he gave her, a ring, while out raking hay, but she found it again among the sheaves. Delmar's portrait hangs in her cottage at Sawrey, with a replica in the National Portrait Gallery in London. He also painted a very pretty portrait of her as a young girl.

Josefina, too, made portraits of her friend, modelling four small busts to represent Beatrix Potter at various stages in her life. First she modelled a rather sad young girl, then a young woman frustrated and confined by her selfish parents: 'no biographers have studied her photographs with enough inward perception to plumb the depth of tragedy in those steady eyes.' Happiness reached her at last with her farm in the Lake District and in the third sculpture she became 'a lass with a friendly shy smile out to explore the freedom of woods and fields.' Then finally she is portrayed as an old woman with chubby hands and cheeks: 'the youngest and bonniest old lady I have ever met – laughing easily, seriously enchanted by beauty – it was plain to see how she was when a teenager and away from the soul-clamp of her parents. No wonder the Warne family loved her – that the child in her understood and loved children.' Josefina gave these models to the Armitt Foundation which has since set up a museum in Ambleside. It now houses some of Beatrix Potter's work, particularly her magnificent botanical drawings of fungi. Josefina was infuriated when, after Beatrix's death, two local people spread the rumour that she did not like children: 'a mischievous misrepresentation if you knew how to read her life – a cowardly form of theft to slander the dead.'

As the War went on, petrol became more and more scarce until the Banners were effectively marooned in Little Langdale, and were lucky if the village taxi driven by Fred Bowness could find enough petrol for them to get to Ambleside once a month: 'Our main supplies came once a week in a cart drawn by a large horse called Duke and driven by a very friendly and rosy-faced man from Great Langdale called Mr Parker who also had a farm there.'

Weather, too, could keep them isolated. In a severe winter The Bield could be snowed in for weeks at a time, and in one long and hard winter Josefina managed to rescue seven snow-blind sheep that had come up to the house for food, by keeping them in the woodshed and feeding them potatoes. That same winter she was being driven in the village taxi with the boys to visit a family in the next valley when they came upon a nearly dead sheep by the roadside.

'It's dead,' said Fred the taxi driver.
'No it's not,' said Josefina.
'It's dead.'
'No it's not, I saw it's eye move. Put it in the boot.'
'I'm not putting that dirty thing in the boot of my car.'
'If you don't I'll sit here in the snow until you do.'

She wrapped it up in her raincoat, put it in the boot of the car and took it with her to their friends, where they warmed it up and gave it a bottle of milk. It survived. Cumbrians might have a reputation for being stubborn, but they had met their match with Mrs Banner.

During another harsh winter a cow was having difficulty calving in the barn attached to The Bield. Josefina could hear it from her bedroom and knew the cow needed help, so she took a lantern and plunged through snowdrifts on a bitterly cold and moonlit night to fetch the farmer. She then helped with the birth of twins, piled up hay around them while they were still damp, and stayed up all night to make sure the calves were snug and warm in the hay.

Despite the unremitting labour involved in running The Bield and caring for Delmar and the boys ('It wasn't easy finding time to carve stone with two extremely active and hungry boys, and Delmar's rather special food') Josefina still managed to complete a number of sculptures during the war years, and the award of membership of the Royal Society of British Sculptors (RBS) in 1941 gave her confidence to keep going. She worked outside in the farmyard while Delmar worked in his studio upstairs. Brian remembers her hammering away at huge pieces of stone yet always being willing to come and help with any crisis: 'I'll do it,' she would say, and come down from her ladder. Josefina admits that often by the time she had prepared her tools ready for use she would have to set them aside again to attend to domestic matters or visitors. At quiet times the bantam hens would come and sit on her knee as she sat working in the farmyard, or would hop over the half door into her studio. Barbara Hepworth wrote positively about a similar time in her life: 'a woman artist is not deprived by cooking and having children... one is in fact nourished by this rich life, provided that one always does some work each day: even a single half hour, so that the images grow in one's mind.'[10] Hepworth, too, had discovered the physical satisfaction of carving:

> Carving became increasingly rhythmical, and I was aware of the special pleasure that sculptors can have through carving, that of a complete unity of physical and mental rhythm. It seemed to be the most natural occupation in the world. It is perhaps strange that I should have become aware of this at the moment when the forms themselves had become the absolute reverse of all that was arbitrary – when there had developed a deliberate conception of form and relationship.[11]

As well as managing to complete the base for *Christ the Judge*, Josefina worked on a dramatic and symbolic piece called *The Last Chimera*, carved from a two tonne block of Hoptonwood stone. Josefina found the stone, by chance, in a stonemason's yard in Ulverston. She had been given a lift into the town by a friend who was lucky enough to have petrol, and while everyone else went shopping for groceries, Josefina set off prospecting for stone. She found two pieces: one was the Hoptonwood stone, and the other was haematite limestone: 'an obvious rarity – a block about five feet tall and one foot six inches square with a hole up the middle. I thought, a fountain! This was the hardest stone of all to carve.'

Josefina bought them both straight away and then had to arrange for transport to The Bield, not at all easy when fuel was almost unobtainable and the stone mason was 'a very sweary sort of man':

> Well, eventually I got transport and both 'stanes' were dumped at home, way up the slope of Lingmoor. The

fountain stone was the right shape to sit on so it was left against the cottage between our front and the stick-house.

But the large one (nearly two tonnes) became rather boring to them and in spite of my anxious arm waving it was just dropped halfway between our front porch and where I wanted it. It was 'Addio! Addio! – and we leave you in the Frio.'

A bit much, considering our man-power was an elderly lady, Aunt Belle, Brian and Bill, myself and Delmar, whose Home Guard duty was to translate German into English if any spies were caught.

What did we do then?

I used my crowbar (a birthday present from Delmar), a long strong wooden spar and blocks from our fire logs. Once I had fixed each move they sat on the spar for weight, I manoeuvred and one of the boys changed the blocks. Once we got it moving it became quite exciting as four inches or six inches a go we got it in the right direction. Once placed it was a matter of better blocks to raise it for carving. Needless to say it took about two days.

The Chimera is a mythical Greek monster breathing fire, with the head of a lion, the body of a goat and the tail of a serpent. Josefina had been thinking about this image ever since she first confronted the Chimera in Florence:

> The idea behind it was based on the Greek idea but enlarged to contain the history of man's 'Chimeras' from plagues, wars, tyrannies and the violence of nature. Where war was concerned – and that is all we could think of then – each Chimera as it came was fought with the matching forces of its own strength – brute force, against force; lies and propaganda against lies. Under the lion's raised paw was the Polish (mother) eagle defending her chicks, and dying for them. I dreamed that the *last* Chimera would be overcome by the strength of innocence and faith depicted by a teenage boy with a scout-knife.

Josefina's sculpture became a powerful plea for humanity to overcome the evil of war. This carving is one of Josefina's finest works and perfectly represents her spiritual and moral dynamism. The outline of the sculpture, which is five feet in length, took its inspiration from the outline of the Langdale Fells which surrounded her as she worked, and the whole piece thrusts forwards in a powerful curve. Brian was the model for the boy in the sculpture. It was accepted for exhibition at the Royal Academy in 1946 ('It nearly broke the lift! – and was well placed').

The sculpture was seen by an Oxford academic and poet, E H W Myerstein, who was interested in the chimera myth, and soon after the exhibition he wrote to the sculptor asking for a meeting. He was invited up to The Bield to stay in late July, but when he arrived things were not quite as he expected, as Josefina remembered very well:

> He was a very large man – 'nicely ugly' and quite striking and wildly eccentric – that didn't matter because we all were – but it was HE who had the shock. Being very short-sighted he had skipped the Josefina in the Catalogue and thought de Vasconcellos was a MAN (anyway as he said later, 'no one could have IMAGINED a woman could carve that!').
>
> As he was a serious gay, and had himself been writing about chimeras, he was dreadfully put out... explaining everything in the most frank and unaffected way. Somehow, perhaps because we had so many other interests in common, and he had been at Magdalen before Delmar, we became friends and I darned his socks.

The death of their friend Major Ronald Balfour in northern France in 1944 inspired Josefina to sculpt another work with its origins in the fearful waste of the Second World War. Ronald had not been engaged in battle but had been writing a report on the damage caused to churches after the D-Day invasion, and was killed by a shell in the town of Cleve on the Canadian Army front. Ronald had brought Brian and Billy to The Bield, and they called him Uncle Ronald. Bill in particular had been fond of him, as was Josefina; indeed, she admitted to having fallen in love with him. Possibly

Delmar had also, as Balfour was homosexual. Several poems written at that time reveal her deep sense of loss, suggesting again how she could be attracted to men who were beyond reach:

> Down by the river
> Where the rocks fall steeply
> There flowing deeply
> The stream sings alone
> With a voice like your own.
> I must forget
> But... not yet.

> Down in the woods where
> Nightingale is nesting
> Shadows are resting
> Below every bough
> Like the shade on your brow.
> I must forget –
> But... not yet.

Thinking of him and the others sacrificed in the war, she lavished time and energy on her sculpture, *The Hand*. She carved it in Honister green slate, the natural stone of the Langdale hills, but brittle and difficult to work. The male figure central to the piece is being supported by a giant hand and looks up to the sky. He is surrounded by birds flying in the rays of the sun, all images of salvation. The Bible text, 'Though I take the wings of the morning or go to the uttermost parts of the sea Thou art there,' lies behind the work. Josefina's sense of personal loss transforms the piece into more than a war memorial and as with *The Last Chimera* the power of the carving is impressive. This sculpture was given to St Bees School where it was dedicated as a War Memorial in 1955.

During this period she also made one of her most attractive family pieces, *Boys Wrestling*. This was based on the figures of Billy and Brian aged eleven and twelve wrestling in Westmorland style. Josefina got them released from school in Windermere by making the excuse of taking them to the dentist, and then sketching them in an adjoining room in the surgery. She felt that she had captured their personalities through the balance of the wrestling. The sculpture was exhibited as part of the Banners' 1947 show in London, and later in Battersea Park in 1960. It has twice been cast in bronze for private collectors.

The creative energy latent in *The Last Chimera* and *Boys Wrestling* may well have been linked to the presence of Brian and Billy at The Bield. Certainly they made for hard work, but they also inspired. It is interesting to compare Josefina's situation with that of Barbara Hepworth, then a mother of four young children, who described her studio in the 1930s as 'a jumble of children, rocks, sculptures, trees, importunate flowers and washing.'[12] But Hepworth also found that for her and her second husband, the painter Ben Nicholson, the birth of triplets had been hugely inspiring: 'The experience of the children seemed to intensify our sense of direction and purpose, and gave us both an even greater unity of idea and aim.'[13]

The 'safe enclosure' that The Bield represented at that time emerges clearly in a simple poem that Josefina wrote one Christmas Eve during the war years:

> The long day nearly past;
> And the family in bed, sleeping.
> I had brought in the kindling to dry,
> And there was no sound, but the peeping
> Of a winter chick under its mother.
>
> Three spirits there are of the kitchen,
> The fire, the clock, and lamp in my hand;
> Each with its own meaning and person,
> Their own beauty and dignity of daily use.
> And in the mixed gold and shadow,
> I stood in the room's warm quiet,
> And blessed the house and the sleepers;
> Also the birds that shelter in the open roof,
> Mice, and other creatures of the field
> That creep for safe sleep into the dry walls
> Of the old watchful Bield...
> The long year nearly over,

> Shall we know where our own work goes?
> Will anyone find it fair?
> Only work as a sower who sows
> And the Lord will care.
> It is 'one of us' now, always there.
> Who made the clock?... Who knows?

Josefina was still hoping to publish a book of poems and had worked out an order from her earlier grouping, 'Words and Woodcuts'. Her new poems were much stronger, less decorative, with a seriousness that came from her distanced but still deeply felt experience of war. Her poem 'Buchenwald', written in May 1945 while on holiday in Seathwaite, was a direct response to the Allied troops entering the concentration camps and death camps of Nazi Germany:

> Do you like crowds? Perhaps for these, too late
> Our love was wakened – lying bone on bone
> In shrunken dissolution, flung by hate
> Upon the scrap-heap of an age of Stone:
> And though their souls are bound no longer there,
> Yet for their sake, whose form the Saviour wore,
> I would my heart could be the soil to bear
> Those worn-out precious bodies. In the core
> Of secret tender darkness, I would fold
> Their deep unseen decay in deeper love.
> Their bones in mine – the rocks where streams run cold –
> Their veins in mine – the roots of trees above –
> Working their composition to rebirth,
> Nursed in the long slow change of healing earth.

This fine poem, passionate yet controlled, offers a very individual approach to the shocking truth about the cruelties that we now call the Holocaust. It emerges very naturally from Josefina's close relationship with the earth; to streams and rocks and trees. The poet seeks to be like the earth, the healing earth, in receiving the bodies so carelessly strewn into pits. Her sculpture *The Last Chimera* certainly seems to share its creative impulses with this poem.

Another well-crafted sequence written at that time was 'Leaves from a Soldier's Notebook Lost in the Libyan Desert'. The five sonnets are love poems and again Josefina has found a mature poetic voice. The fifth sonnet is full of sadness and longing:

> The things I love seem all contained in you.
> A field-path leading home, the blue of hills,
> Stillness of mist-cool harebells hung with dew:
> To be with you alone, to watch you – fills
> My void with peace; for patiently you fashion
> Anew the worn out things of daily life.
> And though you may not know my taintless passion,
> I shall be young for ever; from the strife
> Released, my last long visions will be fair.
> I shall not care how deep the dry sand blows
> Above my bones: O, never move your chair
> From that same corner which in winter shows
> The moving firelight on your hair, your face;
> Lest someone's dreams should miss their resting place.

Yet again one must ask why these poems were never published. They were typed up and a table of contents worked out. She clearly valued her poetry and wanted it to be read. Her poetry would never again achieve this degree of accomplishment. Was she simply too busy, too isolated, or too much under the sway of Delmar? Or did the despair and longing for death apparent in several of them cut across the successful image that she and Delmar were projecting?

With the end of the Second World War there was a slight easing in some of the restrictions that had made normal life difficult for everyone, and people began to circulate again. Petrol was scarce, but the use of private cars was possible once more. The Banners still did not have a car, as Delmar did not travel well in them because of his painful back, so they continued to make use of the village taxi when necessary. Many visitors came to see them, and the visitors' book shows how many friends and acquaintances were now able to travel to that remote spot. Food was scarce, and if the Banners had nothing else to share with cold and hungry walkers coming over the hill, they would make a large pot of porridge on the kitchen range and dish it up at any hour. Once Josefina opened the door to a panting child bearing a large loaf sent from his mother. Strangers had been seen in the village asking for The Bield, and extra supplies were dispatched without needing to be requested.

Delmar had a wide acquaintance among Anglican clergy and was also involved with the early days of the Friends of the Lake District and the National Trust. The formidable Mrs Eleanor Rawnsley, widow of Canon Hardwicke Rawnsley, a founder of the National Trust, lived in Allen Bank in Grasmere, one of the houses occupied by William Wordsworth and his family after they left Dove Cottage. Mrs Rawnsley was particularly fond of Josefina. With what must have been great tolerance she occasionally invited the Banners and the boys to tea, and Brian and Billy sat awkwardly, hair plastered down and on their best behaviour, while a maid in cap and apron carried in plates of tiny sandwiches. The boys demolished everything on offer with speed that amazed even the imperturbable Mrs Rawnsley, not knowing that they had already been well fed with buns at the gates.

On another occasion she telephoned Josefina and ordered her to spend the night. Josefina was used to doing what she was told by Mrs Rawnsley, as indeed most people were, so she went:

> I loved her manner because it was natural to her and it wasn't really dictatorial at all, because she was so versed in religion. And she was one of those women who when you were talking to her you could see her mind working while you talked. She was thinking that every time you said something it reminded her of four other things and she had to chose which one to answer you by. Like doing the rushes for a film and you have five things in front of you and you have to chose one. She was like that all the time.

Josefina felt greatly honoured when, after dinner, some music and a stroll in the garden, she was brought up to the room Wordsworth had slept in. It had been left unchanged for over a century, and was still lit by candles.

'I've put you in Wordsworth's bedroom. Nobody's ever slept here since but I wanted you to have the experience,' said Mrs Rawnsley. She came in and lit the candle, and left me. I was absolutely entranced. It was a beautiful white bedroom, everything white and peaceful. And a candle. I sat in this bed and saw my shadow on the wall, just as he must have done. It was quite wonderful.

The Lake District and The Bield were important for the Banners, but it was again time for them to think about exhibiting their paintings and sculptures in London. Once the boys were sent to boarding school Josefina was able to spend some time away, and she took a studio in Chelsea, at 5 Stanhope Mews, near Gloucester Road Tube Station.

This was the first of three studios she maintained in London. The Stanhope Mews studio was rather dark, and she preferred her next studio at 38 Cresswell Place, a cobbled mews near the Boltons, which had three large windows and an open staircase that allowed good views of the work on the floor below. Josefina filled it full of plants and trailed one right up the banisters. As usual, Josefina had only to touch a plant to make it flourish. With her help, Elsie, a cheerful country girl, she was happy there, although at first her sensitivity to atmosphere made her suspect a distressful death in the house. Indeed this proved to be the case, but the advice of a good friend enabled her to overcome sensations that had affected her work, particularly the Madonna that was destined for St Paul's. Her final studio, just opposite at 8 Cresswell Place, was her favourite, with that essential feature for Josefina's contentment, an old-fashioned courtyard garden.

With a London studio as a base in 1946, she started to make plans with Delmar for a joint exhibition at the Royal Watercolour Society Gallery at 26 Conduit Street, just off New Bond Street. The city had barely begun to face rebuilding after the devastation caused by German bombs and rockets, but the gallery had been undamaged and provided a very beautiful room with marble pillars, elegant stucco and a balustraded upper area. The collection of work was handsomely displayed. The photographer they employed for all their work was Bryan Horner of Kendal, who recorded their paintings and sculptures for thirty-five years.

The exhibition took place between 31 December 1946 and 18 January 1947 and was very extensive, featuring fifty oil paintings and thirty watercolours of the Lake District by Delmar. Josefina exhibited a variety of sculptures in wood, stone, bronze, slate, marble and lead, including some portrait heads and abstract works. Her large sculptures of *Christ the Judge* and *The Last Chimera* were too substantial to go in the gallery, so Josefina, never one to be defeated by any obstacle, got permission to place them outside on a bombsite at 35 Piccadilly. A photograph in *The Times* newspaper shows how crowds gathered round the sculptures. Thousands of people saw them and found the presence of art among the rubble strangely encouraging at a time when Britain was weary and worn after the effects of six years' privation and hardship. Returning soldiers were disillusioned; the writer Rupert Croft-Cooke described it as 'a shabby, disgruntled, impoverished society, alive with deserters, small-time criminals and black marketeers, which moved among the bombed houses and burnt-out buildings of London.'[14]

Prices placed on their work were high and indicated that both Delmar and Josefina had a clear idea of their value. There was a kind of heroism in the way they priced their art, lifting it above the grey world of worn-out clothes, rationed food and ruined buildings that confronted a population in the aftermath of war. Delmar's oil painting *Great Gable from Scafell* was priced at £160, a very substantial sum at that time, and Josefina priced *The Last Chimera* at £500. Their financial investment in the exhibition was considerable, not only to hire the gallery but also to transport the paintings and sculptures from the Langdale Valley to London at a time when Clement Pitman could comment in the exhibition catalogue that Delmar was 'braving the hazards of contemporary transport in order to show his work to a wider circle than that of professional contacts and immediate friends, and proclaim the poetry of the Fells to those who know them but little or not at all.'

Interestingly enough Josefina never crated her sculptures when it was time to transport them from Langdale to London; they went off on the railway cart, later the railway lorry, to Windermere station without any wrappings, a state that somehow imposed a duty of care on all those who handled them on the journey.

Pitman described Josefina as 'a fearless sculptor', and the scale and emotional intensity of her work at that time justify the description. Lady Scott, widow of Scott of the Antarctic and a sculptor herself, purchased one of Josefina's sculptures and wrote to her full of praise:

> Sorry I couldn't get to your private view – I was in the throes of casting, which I do very badly and couldn't leave a hash I was making. However I went today and would like to send showers of congratulations. Prodigious workers you both seem to be! I liked so very much of the work... there were a lot of people there.

Josefina's reputation was assured. She became the first woman Fellow of the Royal British Sculptors in 1948, and became very involved in their work, serving on the council and helping to organise a number of exhibitions. From 1945 onwards Josefina's works were regularly accepted for the Royal Academy Summer Exhibition and she exhibited for sixteen consecutive years until 1962. She had work on display again in 1965 and 1966. Delmar exhibited much less frequently at the Royal Academy and had work placed in only eight shows, the last being in 1964. Some of his swingeing criticisms of other artists had made him unpopular among members of the Academy. But the London studios enabled both artists to promote their work and to carry out commissions. Their independence meant that they never exhibited in a commercial gallery, or used an agent. This may account in some way for the neglect of their work in later years.

Two people working so closely together inevitably created tensions, and although Josefina valued Delmar's judgement, she resented him becoming too involved in her sculpture. In 1949 she deliberately destroyed a very beautiful nine foot figure called *Peace the Phoenix* that she had worked on for many months at The Bield because Delmar kept interfering with the work. 'He kept on saying, do this, do that. Eventually it died on me,' said Josefina, so she arranged for it to be carried to London where she brought it to a friend's studio and hacked it to pieces. The sculpture is listed in the catalogue for their 1955 Joint Exhibition as being 'accidentally destroyed'.

The incident reveals a great deal about the relationship between them. Even then, at a time when Josefina's achievements were widely recognised and her public role increasing, she still struggled with the power that Delmar wielded over her, a power that often meant Delmar deliberately reducing her to tears over trivial matters. He was so jealous of the affection given to Josefina by her cat Sam that he forced her to have him destroyed. Because Delmar went to bed at dusk she had to do the same, and he once crawled out of his window to make sure she was not reading in her room by the light of a torch. For Delmar at that time, control was everything. Not long afterwards, in London, she underwent a face-lift to remove some of the tension that had lined her face. At that time it was a fairly drastic and unusual procedure, and Josefina offered to advise other women who were unsure about the operation. No wonder she was relieved to be living in her London studio, making her own friends and placing at a distance the oppressive presence of her husband, to whom, amazingly, she had remained loyal.

There is considerable irony now in viewing the short film *Out of Nature*, a twenty-minute black-and-white documentary made by Mercury films in 1949. Directed by the Polish film-maker Bernard Kunicki the film depicts an ideal artistic situation, with Delmar striding off to the hills, sketchbook in hand, the two boys wrestling in the garden, and Josefina doing a life-cast and sculpting wonderful works. The scenery is superbly photographed, and there are some dramatic shots of Josefina clambering over rocks in a quarry to find suitable stones to carve. She subsequently sculpted Bernard Kunicki's head, and he became a close friend.

But like so many short films of that period, the commentary adopts an unquestioning tone about the subject, an inheritance from wartime propaganda films, and it was certainly made with great admiration for both artists. *Out of Nature* displays much of the neo-romanticism that emerged from the War and affected many British artists. In film, the work of Humphrey Jennings, in particular, adopted the tone that the historian Angus Calder was to label as 'Deep England'. Robert Hewison, writing in *Culture and Consensus: England, Art and Politics since 1940*, suggests:

The circumstances of war encouraged a neo-romanticism among British artists that was already burgeoning before the war began: Deep England was also John Piper's Derbyshire, Paul Nash's Oxfordshire, Graham Sutherland and John Craxton's Pembrokeshire, Benjamin Britten's East Anglia. The painters' vision derived from William Blake and Samuel Palmer, a mystical sense of the numinous in the landscape that corresponded to a personal, religious inscape. Religion flourished in the emotional intensity of wartime; Anglicanism was an aspect of Deep England that appealed to neo-romantics like the great memorialist of parish churches, John Piper.[15]

It is tempting to add Delmar Banner's Lake District to Hewison's list, as these mountains certainly carried a religious meaning in his paintings. Kunicki's film includes appealing landscape images of shepherds and sheep, country children with flowers, rolling hills and clouds, which formed the background to many films of the period that sought to give a sense of identity to a traumatised land. Or, as Hewison comments, 'This imagined pastoral landscape served as contrast to, and compensation for, all the destruction and stress of war. Somewhere among its bright fields and bosky shades nestled the nation's soul.'[16]

CHAPTER FIVE

New Artistic Horizons

THE 1950s

*It's the task of musicians and artists to lift our beliefs so
that all can see that the ideal is possible.*

J de V

The 1950s saw Josefina taking on a prominent public role in
English cultural life. She organised major exhibitions; she
founded, with others, the Society of Portrait Sculptors; she
executed a number of portraits of distinguished people; and she
endeared herself to thousands with her popular nativity scenes for
cathedrals and churches in London and elsewhere. She had
considerable independence with a London studio, her own bank
account, and good fees from sales of her work. But the 1950s saw
much concern for her mother as well as the two boys, and public
success was often matched by private sadness.

The unveiling of the huge stone carving of *Christ the Judge* as the
centrepiece of the Heroes' Shrine and Memorial at Aldershot on 5 May
1950 was recognition of many years of achievement for Josefina. The
Duchess of Gloucester unveiled the statue and the Bishop of Guildford,
Dr J V Macmillan, performed the dedication. The Borough Surveyor,
Mr Taylor, had placed the statue within a canopy of four pillars, a
baldacchine 18 feet high, designed by Josefina, within a landscaped
garden and in front of a huge cedar tree. The Memorial was dedicated
to the Battle of Britain heroes and to the people of the blitzed cities
and towns. In front of the Christ figure is a rock garden including

stones taken from bombed buildings all over Britain, with the name and heraldic arms of each town.

Josefina attended the ceremony with Delmar, Brian and Billy as well as her mother, who must have regarded the event as a pinnacle towards which many years of careful guidance on her part had led. Josefina, wearing a glamorous wide-brimmed hat and a long checked dress, looked attractive and confident. A civic luncheon followed, and after all the excitement was over Mr Taylor wrote privately to Josefina:

> Last night we went down to the site to inspect the lighting and as the rush and anxiety was over I had time to study your work in the quiet surroundings. It is splendid and I do congratulate you upon it… The countenance you have given the Christ and the work on the folds of the mantle is marvellous. Also the intricate work on the base just staggers me!… I consider that we are most fortunate in having your Christ here at Aldershot and not only will it remind us of its message but also of one of the most charming persons I have ever met.

In 1951 The Festival of Britain encouraged the nation to look to the future, to find a new identity and a new energy, while still looking back to the achievement of the great Victorian Exhibition of 1851. The Festival itself was located on the South Bank of the River Thames, where the Royal Festival Hall was the centrepiece. Along the Thames temporary exhibition halls were devoted to science and serious subjects but there was also plenty of fun, with outdoor dancing and an amusement park at Battersea. The Dome of Discovery and the unusual structure known as the Skylon promised a technological future. People came from all over the United Kingdom; many of them had never visited London before. But there was a genuine attempt to spread the Festival beyond London, and the Edinburgh Festival, which was already established, received substantial funding that helped it to expand into the important international event it has now become.

For the first time since the end of the war, things were looking up, and Robert Hewison, writing in *Culture and Consensus* over forty years later, agreed that 'the Festival was undoubtedly a popular success' and that it was 'one little bit of the welfare state that worked.'[1] Perhaps this aspect was proved when the Festival ended in September 1951 and the new Conservative Government, elected a few months later, promptly razed the site almost completely, with the exception of the Royal Festival Hall and the National Film Theatre.

Josefina's work was exhibited in Lambeth Palace as part of a special exhibition for the Festival. Lambeth Palace had been badly damaged by bombs and this was a chance to open up the Palace to the public, even though the main chapel had been gutted by fire during the blitz. Josefina displayed a large carving of St Michael in yew that exploited the natural grain of the wood and its bark. The ancient yew, six feet long, had been taken from an old cottage in Chapel Stile, Langdale, while it was being renovated. Knowing that they had a sculptor in the vicinity, the owners offered it to her and she accepted it without hesitation. The carving was later bought by Josefina's friend Sydney Walton, who gave it to the ancient church of St Michael in Southampton.

Soon Josefina was being invited to submit work to other exhibitions and to organise prestigious events in London. In 1952, with the sculptor Kate Parbury, she arranged a show of contemporary sculpture in the beautiful house at 45 Park Lane that had belonged to Sir Phillip Sassoon. The show, which was called 'Sculpture for All', was eclectic, involving work by a variety of contemporary sculptors and including artists from overseas. Josefina was already aware of the growing divide between abstract and representational work, and this exhibition was designed to show the richness of different outlooks without the petty divisions typical of much of the artistic world.

Many other sculptors supported this ambitious project, and Jacob Epstein sent along his most recent bust, a bronze head of the actor Sandra Dorne. Lord Kennet declared the exhibition open, and the event was a huge success. Park Lane House became a popular venue for cultural events of all kinds, a focal point for musicians and artists who were looking for new approaches in the post-war years.

Josefina exhibited *Mercury*, a piece that displayed her experimental work with perspex, a material that was interesting a number of sculptors at that time. She had been working with perspex for a few years, having met one of the senior chemists from ICI who dealt with this new plastic during a stay at Wha House Farm in Eskdale. The chemists were keen to see how perspex could be used, and Josefina was sent a number of pieces to try. She also went to visit their experimental laboratories in Welwyn Garden City.

Even using superb Sheffield tools she found it extremely difficult to carve, as the flakes of perspex were razor sharp and flew up into her face. She had to wear goggles and heavy gloves, and despite this her nose was cut by splinters as she worked. The attractions of the new material made her persevere and she made a number of pieces, including an unusual translucent Bishop's crozier for Bristol Cathedral, and, a few years later, a prize-winning head of Everest climber Sherpa Tensing Norkay. Eventually the strain of engraving this very hard material with hand tools gave her neuritis and she had to give it up. She had tried using industrial electric-powered tools when working on stone but at that time the vibration they produced was too strong. Improvements over the years made them easier to use, but Josefina found that power tools were never as sensitive to use as hand tools, which always came first in her estimation.

In May and June 1953, a year after the 'Sculpture for All' Exhibition, Park Lane House was the venue for a Festival of the Arts under the auspices of the International Faculty of Arts. This was Coronation year, and there was a national sense of new social patterns and new ideas emerging with the young queen.

The Park Lane Festival was devoted to the Christian Theme in Contemporary Arts, and Josefina and Delmar were both on the General Advisory Committee. Josefina's work was exhibited, and Delmar gave a Public Lecture on 'Christian Implications of the Arts'. This was part of a very distinguished series of lectures during May and June that included Basil Spence, the architect, and Dorothy L Sayers, the novelist, as speakers, with T S Eliot, Charles Wheeler, Nevill Coghill and Dame Edith Sitwell chairing the events.

Josefina had by now established a reputation for her portrait sculpture as well as her religious work, and Edith Sitwell allowed Josefina to sculpt her. The work was created without a formal sitting, as Edith was always too busy to spend time on it. But she did invite the young sculptor to lunch at her club, placing Josefina on her right and Stephen Spender on her left, with a group of brilliant conversationalists who held Josefina spellbound. Sitwell herself came sailing in 'like a galleon' in flowing black robes, like an Orthodox priest, with an elaborate head-dress to give her even more height, and of course wearing the famous carbuncle rings: 'her big droopy hands were like gloves hung on a washing line.' She told Josefina that 'I dress like this because I was so repressed as a child,' and her feelings were well understood. Fortunately Josefina was often able to capture the features that she wanted to portray in a face by simply watching the subject in a social situation, and she preferred people to be natural and relaxed, reading or listening to music. Josefina's small bronze sculpture of her, *The Green Poetess*, referred to one of Sitwell's poems and found favour with its notoriously difficult subject. She exhibited it at the Royal Academy in 1965.

Sculpture was very much in the public eye in 1953, as the competition for the memorial to the Unknown Political Prisoner attracted attention from sculptors throughout the world. The prize was funded from America, and was undoubtedly related to the hardening political attitudes represented by the Cold War. Reg Butler won the competition with a highly abstract metal construct which was very controversial, but certainly managed to challenge the conventional view of public sculpture as represented by war memorials. Josefina entered the competition and might have considered that with two major war memorials to her credit (*Christ the Judge* and *The Hand*) she should be a serious contender. Her design, which was certainly not one to cause controversy, was not chosen, but she was in very good company with her rejected work. It wasn't all a waste of time; she held a lasting memory of meeting the wartime Resistance heroine Odette Churchill at one of the events connected with the competition.

Despite the attractions of the London artistic world and the convenience of her studio in Chelsea, Josefina was still having to juggle the responsibilities of keeping in contact with her mother, who was then living on the south coast, and looking after Brian and Billy in school holidays and Delmar at The Bield. Electricity was late arriving at Little Langdale because of a dispute over pylons and underground cables in this outstandingly beautiful area, and a supply was not available until 1964. Even the Three Shires Inn in the village was still using a generator, and the schoolroom was lit by oil lamps. As a result there were few labour-saving devices in The Bield.

Life became a little easier when unexpectedly the village taxi-driver, upon whom they depended for transport, decided to give up. Delmar, who disliked cars and felt uncomfortable in them because of back pain, agreed that they had no choice but to have one and that Josefina should learn to drive. She rushed off to buy a car before he could change his mind and quickly arranged for Fred Bowness, the taxi driver, to give her driving lessons. Her first car came to grief on an icy bend and ended halfway up a tree, but the next one lasted longer. Josefina's sense of style led her towards MGB GT sports cars and she owned two of these in succession, which she drove with great enjoyment until well into her eighties.

It was on one of her summers at The Bield while Josefina was carving a huge stone in the garden that she looked up and found a row of boys gazing over the wall, fascinated by her work. She asked them in and showed them what she was doing, gave them lemonade, and brushed aside the apologies of the accompanying master for interrupting her afternoon.

They were boys from an approved school, and the meeting began a relationship between the sculptor and difficult boys that lasted for many years: 'Wherever I have worked,' said Josefina, 'I have visited the approved schools and offered their participation. Young people crave for worthwhile activities; and these boys are happiest when they are doing something for someone else, feeling that what they do is wanted.' Josefina was to work with these boys many times, and eventually founded an outdoor centre for them at Beckstones, a ruined farmhouse in the Duddon Valley which they restored. Her own experience of coping with Brian and Billy, who did not become any easier to handle as they grew up, had given her an insight into the psychology of boys with disturbed backgrounds and she always felt that they deserved a second chance. Again she was motivated by the notion of redemption, but this time it would be dealt with in a very practical way.

There is no doubt that she received much support and encouragement from Delmar in this work, although she was always the one to get involved and get things done. In 1956 Delmar become a Lay Reader in the Church of England and preached from time to time at the local church in Chapel Stile. As well as his interest in church matters he retained a strong interest in all aspects of education. Many of his university friends had become school teachers and when they visited he was keen to hear about their problems and concerns. The Reverend Geoffrey Ellison was Vicar of Holy Trinity Church in Great Langdale and his son, Hugh Ellison, who became a solicitor and assisted the Banners with the establishment of Beckstones, remembers him giving some powerful sermons. Surprisingly he seemed to be able to communicate with the congregation, and one old farmer remarked to Josefina, 'Aye, he rants, but he's nit a humboog.' Hugh remembers his father's initial amusement at Delmar's letters addressed to 'The Vicarcage', but it ceased to be so funny on the tenth occasion.

Becoming a Lay Reader was a threshold of great personal significance to Delmar and he began to achieve a sense of peace that extended to his relationship with Josefina. In time an equilibrium would be created that would bring a measure of happiness to them both.

Despite her own lonely childhood, Josefina had a great natural ability to amuse and entertain children. The person who could carve huge statues of Christ could also write little painting story books for Robertson's Marmalade. In 1951 Robertson's paid her the handsome fee of 50 guineas for a book with what is now the exceedingly politically incorrect title, *A Golly for Samba*. Robertson's liked 'the general appeal to children and the lack of normal advertising jargon' in Josefina's story, which curiously enough tells about a lonely doll who manages to find a partner.

Although many acquaintances called at The Bield, the painter William Heaton Cooper's wife Ophelia (Ophelia Gordon Bell) was her closest friend. As fellow sculptors, they had much in common; Ophelia had also been a student at the Regent Street Polytechnic, although a decade later than Josefina. They shared orders for materials from Tiranti, the supplier in London, and took a great interest in each other's work: 'When I got stuck, I used to phone her up, and when she got stuck, she would phone me.' Much of their work was on similar themes.

The Heaton Coopers lived in a house called Winterseeds in Grasmere with their four young children and used to rent a cottage across the valley from The Bield, High Hall Garth, for holidays. Their son Julian Cooper, now a very successful and highly acclaimed painter, remembers regular visits for tea. He was fascinated by a miniature railway line that transported the salt and pepper around the table – Josefina had made this to entertain the boys. There was also the excitement of the musical glasses, a line of upside-down goblets hanging from the dresser on which Josefina played tunes, and the dressing-up box, always a favourite with visiting children.

There may have been a certain amount of rivalry between the Banners and the Coopers; two painters and two sculptors together. Delmar and Heaton Cooper were using quite similar approaches as they both often took a vantage point from high on the fells, where shapes, colours and the moulding of the rock look very different from a viewpoint on the valley floor. Heaton Cooper exploited the mysterious, faded brown and blue tones of the high fells but Delmar was capable of using a surprisingly bright palette for his large oils. Unlike Heaton Cooper, he frequently included a solitary human figure dwarfed by the mountains, a truly Romantic gesture. Both had a profound belief in God and this was apparent in all their work.

Ophelia, too, was convinced of the presence of God in art, and once wrote: 'Art at its best is a communication from the Creator through man to man. It is also a communication from man to man... Art is a language that is universally understood in time and space. It can by-pass the reason and speak direct to the emotions, so it is very powerful. As it is a language in itself, it is sometimes impossible to translate or explain works of art. We learn the language as we need it.'[2]

They all exhibited regularly at the Lake Artists Society Show in Grasmere, which had not functioned during most of the War, but was re-established in 1947. Josefina and Delmar both became members that year. During the 1950s the Lake Artists Exhibition was quite important, a kind of Royal Academy Summer Show in the Lakes, with smart frocks and hats for the ladies at the opening. Heaton Cooper was President for eleven years. Josefina, now an Honorary Life Member, continues to exhibit there.

In terms of commercial success, there is no question that Heaton Cooper was, and continues to be, a better-known painter than Delmar. The relationship of this distinguished artistic family to the

Lake District, which began with his father Alfred Heaton Cooper in the early years of the twentieth century, continues to be strong. Heaton Cooper's studio in Grasmere was an outlet for prints and books, which allowed his work to be appreciated by many while providing a very necessary income for the family.

Despite all this time-consuming work organising exhibitions and educational projects, and travelling up and down to The Bield, Josefina had managed to complete four portrait heads and to exhibit them at the Royal Academy between 1949 and 1952. But there was a sense among many of her fellow sculptors that the portrait bust was not being given its true place in contemporary art circles.

Three sculptors, Kate Parbury, Eva Castle and Josefina, together with the arts administrator Malcolm Fry, and with the encouragement and support of Franta Belsky, decided to form the Society of Portrait Sculptors. Charles Wheeler, then President of the Royal Academy, agreed to be their first President.

They held their first exhibition at the Imperial Institute in South Kensington from 17 November to 22 December 1953, with 'The Famous in Sculpture' as their theme. Every sculptor they knew was asked to exhibit, and few could resist an appeal from Josefina and Eva. The collection contained 130 works by the most eminent sculptors working at the time in Great Britain. Malcolm Fry wrote in the introduction to the Catalogue that the exhibition 'might well be called a page of history, so varied and interesting are the sitters portrayed, nearly all of whom have made some important contribution to the annals of our time.' He went on to express the hope that 'this newly formed society will bring about a renaissance in the art of portrait sculpture.'

Josefina exhibited her perspex bust of Sherpa Tensing Norkay while her friend Ophelia Gordon Bell exhibited Sir Edmund Hillary; together, the first conquerors of Mount Everest. The collection was wide-ranging and included not only 'great and good' but popular figures such as the actor Peter Ustinov (sculpted by Franta Belsky) and the film star Trevor Howard (sculpted by A J Fleischmann). Jacob Epstein sent his busts of Pandit Nehru and T S Eliot, and Josefina's old tutor, Sir William Reid Dick, provided his bust of Sir Winston Churchill.

Josefina's design skills were used to great effect, as they would be in many future exhibitions. For this prestigious event the organisers went to Sanderson, the fabric manufacturers in London, for some draperies to use in the background display for the sculptures. They were treated generously and allowed to use some of the gold velvet left over from the Coronation in Westminster Abbey. Josefina's gardening friend Joan Thorogood helped with decorative plants for all the exhibitions. Nothing quite like it had been seen before in London, and it was a great success.

Josefina then arranged for the exhibition to travel to Edinburgh for the Festival in the summer of 1954, and the new Society set it up with great artistry in the Arts Centre on the Royal Mile. The Sanderson draperies were again used, but plants were also crucial, and Joan Thorogood contacted a friend in Edinburgh who was a retired horticulturist and who brought them handsome specimens from the Royal Horticultural Society. Josefina was very pleased with the result:

> We had the most marvellous plants to enhance the sculptures. You can't tell what a difference they make. They make an area for the sculpture which is its own and not impinged on by the next very strong one. You get enough space between them. And the plants seem to echo the movement. Nobody does it now. All they do is make it look like a bathroom – scrubbed. Hard polished floor; you hear everybody's heels on it; no seats, you get tired. Like a sanitorium or a bathroom – frightfully clinical. It kills them.

They worked hard, but in the evenings they enjoyed the rich feast of music, ballet and drama that the Edinburgh Festival offered. 'We saw the most marvellous things,' Josefina remembered. 'You never forget those things. We saw a wonderful company doing Shakespeare's *Tempest*. Marvellously done. People who do these think that this sort of thing is ephemeral, but it can affect people for the rest of their lives.' There was a real sense that the post-war world was offering exciting new opportunities for artists of all kinds, and during that summer in Edinburgh the sculptors felt part of the movement.

Josefina also arranged an exhibition of religious sculpture in the

Kirk of the Canongate at the invitation of the Reverend Ronald Selby-Wright, and she found using this space very inspiring: 'I was delighted with its simplicity and room for work and the clear lighting.' In a letter to her friend Justus Akeredolu, the Nigerian sculptor, she wrote: 'I wish you could have seen it because the setting was really perfect and the experience has given me great encouragement and new insight into the possibility of the silent arts as an aid to spiritual atmosphere and worship.' *The Last Chimera* was placed permanently in the grounds of the Kirk of the Canongate and two of her other works, *The Repentance of St Hubert* and *Christus Victor*, are within the church.

She used this experience in preparing her next exhibition, 'Christian Sculpture Today', in St John's Church, St John's Wood in London during May 1955. For the centrepiece she borrowed Jacob Epstein's sketch model of his sculpture of *The Virgin Mary with Jesus at the Age of Twelve* that stands outside the convent in Cavendish Square. Josefina had always admired Epstein for the life and energy of his sculpture, particularly his portraits, which she once described as 'electric'. She was somewhat in awe of him when Malcolm Fry took her to meet him, but she was surprised when he greeted her enthusiastically:

> 'De Vasconcellos. You are the sculptor of the great big pieces!' He knew me. He liked my work. I was so surprised. I was struck dumb. I borrowed the model and put it on a wall and underneath I had an ancient stone trough with a grapevine that went up on each side of it. That's the way to show sculpture. In the arms of nature.

Working with this group of fellow artists gave Josefina a new sense of purpose and she became a particularly close friend of Eva Castle, who was then a very well-known portrait sculptor. Eva had first caught sight of Josefina from the top of a London bus; looking down, she saw a room full of women arranging sculpture, and she leaped off at the next stop to investigate what was going on. Eva was trapped in an unhappy marriage and Josefina helped her to establish herself independently in a new studio not far from her own at Cresswell Place. Their work ran in parallel for a few years: in 1956

Josefina sculpted Roger Bannister, the first athlete to run a mile in under four minutes, and Eva sculpted Chris Chataway, another famous runner of the 1950s.

Elegant and fashionable, Eva was often photographed for the society pages at the time, and seven sculptors, including Josefina, all did versions of her head, which were exhibited together in 'The Famous in Sculpture' Exhibition. Eva feels that her own self-portrait is probably the best, because it goes deeper into the character than an outsider can achieve, no matter how perspicacious. All the portraits captured her beauty, but not many people knew that she had been a courageous member of the Resistance in her native Denmark during the War.

Eva stayed briefly at The Bield towards the end of 1953 and described it as 'hilariously mad', with an austere Delmar reading Jane Austen aloud through every meal. It was a cold and snowy spell, and despite her fondness for Josefina, the spartan nature of the old farmhouse did not encourage her to return. Eva was later married for some time to the actor Tony Britton, and is the mother of the young actor Jasper Britton.

In the summer of 1955, Delmar and Josefina organised another joint exhibition in the Royal Watercolour Society Galleries in Conduit Street. This was even more extensive than their previous show in 1947. The exhibition was in place for a month. Delmar exhibited 31 watercolours and over 40 oils including some paintings loaned from galleries and individuals. During the 1950s he had done pencil portraits of many well-known figures including Christopher Chataway, Roger Bannister and Charles Wheeler. His Beatrix Potter portrait was on loan from the National Portrait Gallery. Sir William Russell Flint, RA, wrote to Delmar congratulating him on his work: 'I was very much impressed by it. The dignity, serenity and deep feeling in landscapes and subjects touched me deeply. How you must love your mountains!'

Josefina showed 54 new works, ranging from portrait heads to door knockers, and had a photographic display of her sculptures in public places, such as *Christ the Judge*. Notably, Josefina's small bronze *Reunion*, modestly priced at £25, was exhibited for the first time. This depiction of two exhausted figures kneeling and embracing was inspired by the story of a woman who had walked across Europe to find her husband after the Second World War. *Reunion* was to be the basis for probably Josefina's most famous works, the *Reconciliation* sculptures that would in years to come be placed in Bradford University, Coventry Cathedral, the Hiroshima Peace Park, Berlin and Stormont. Josefina said:

> The sculpture was originally conceived in the aftermath of the War. Europe was in shock, people were stunned. I read in a newspaper about a woman who crossed Europe on foot to find her husband, and I was so moved that I made the sculpture. Then I thought that it wasn't only about the reunion of two people but hopefully a reunion of nations which had been fighting.

Another sculpture that was especially important for Josefina was her bronze of Anita Riberas, the Brazilian wife of the nineteenth century Italian patriot, Garibaldi. Anita had travelled with Garibaldi's 'Thousand Men' and had given birth to a child in a forest. She was a heroine in her own right, and Josefina's response to her again blended in sculpture and poetry to create a powerful vision. Josefina wrote five poems about Anita and her place in Italian history; the third, entitled 'September 16 1840', describes the birth and gives it a religious context:

> Homeless, with child, on jaded horse;
> As night bears down my time draws near.
> Stand, and reply 'All's well,' to fear
> And heed no pitiful remorse.
> Remember One who in her plight
> Rode bravely under darker skies,
> With all the Future in her eyes;
> And laboured in the straw that night.
> Soon, soon we'll find a kindly bed
> In fallen leaves of forest oak;
> Covered by Garibaldi's cloak,
> And stars for sentries overhead.

The series of poems traces the progress of Garibaldi through Italy with his thousand volunteers and their triumph in liberating Italy. The sculpture is of a strong, handsome woman, at peace with a tiny child in her lap. There is a definite resemblance to the Madonna that Josefina would later sculpt for St Paul's Cathedral.

On 6 September 1955 *The Vision of Bega* was unveiled and dedicated in St Bees Priory in Cumbria. This work consists of two sculptures, the kneeling figure of the seventh century Saint Bega on the right of the altar of a side chapel and the Virgin and Child on the left. The young Irish girl Bega landed on the Cumbrian coast in a small fishing boat sailed by two old monks as she sought to escape from an unwanted alliance with a heathen prince, and as she offered grateful prayers for her safe deliverance, she had a vision of Mary holding out the Christ child to her. She was veiled as a nun by St Aidan of Lindisfarne at Hexham. The sculptures are attractive in their simplicity and do not suffer from the sentimentality that affects some of her later religious works.

An insight into the creative interplay between Josefina and Delmar at that time emerges from a letter of thanks sent to them from the Dean of Durham, John Wild. The Dean had been staying at The Bield for three days while Delmar made a pen and ink portrait of him, and he wrote that 'it was a wonderful experience to sit for the drawing – so peaceful too – and to listen to you both discussing the work from time to time was enthrallingly interesting.' Josefina made a portrait of his head soon afterwards, so this was another example of their shared artistry.

Later that year, at Christmas, twelve British sculptors came together to create a crib for St Paul's Cathedral in London. Josefina was asked to design and coordinate the work. She herself sculpted the centrepiece Virgin and Child; other contributors included Eva Castle, who made the small animals including foxes that stood next to the manger; Marjorie Crossley, who made the Three Shepherds; Adrian Allinson, who made Joseph and the Donkey; Charles Wheeler, who loaned his beautiful Angel Gabriel; and Franta Belsky, who made three cherub musicians. Dean Wild had discussed this project with Josefina when he stayed at The Bield in September, and he wrote to her that 'it may well be one of the most effective means of Evangelism of our age.'

Josefina's sculpture of the Virgin and Child was later cast in terrossa, and in 1957, as the gift of Bernard Sunley, was accepted for permanent placing in St Paul's. It was the only sculpture by a woman to stand there. Josefina felt highly honoured and wrote immediately to her mother thanking her for her support: 'All due to your encouragement and constant help... wished you were here, but felt so near you anyway.'

At Evensong on 21 May 1957, the statue was formally dedicated and accepted 'to stand within your Cathedral church forever.' Over the years it has proved to be very popular with ordinary people, if not with the lovers of more experimental trends in sculpture. James Cameron described it in his regular newspaper column as 'the lovely austere Vasconcellos Madonna in St Paul's,' and a photograph of the statue was used as a Christmas card in 1959 by the Christian Action Race Relations fund to support the thirty defendants at the South African treason trials in Pretoria. Another casting of the work was made for a seminary in Chicago.

The Catholic Herald welcomed the statue as an 'interesting and welcome venture on the part of the authorities at St Paul's in familiarising visitors and their congregations in older Catholic traditions.' Indeed many nuns did come to pray, and Josefina was very moved when at the time of the horrific primary school shootings at Dunblane in Scotland, people came to pray and leave flowers in front of the sculpture. The numinous quality of the Madonna is apparent in the gentle marks left by many people who have touched it as an aid to their prayers. As early as 1965 the surveyor to St Paul's was writing to Josefina to ask for advice on cleaning the sculpture where members of the public had been drawn to touch it. The sculpture has since been moved from the nave to the Chapel of the British Empire.

Shortly after the successful 1955 Christmas crib at St Paul's, Josefina was the subject of a highly complimentary article by C S Sandilands in the fine art magazine, *The Studio*. Sandilands praised the variety of her sculpture and the materials used, but especially commended her mastery of design:

> The ever-present difficulty confronting the creative artist is in every case the general design. This can so easily become an intangible nebulosity. Details, on the other hand, may become

mere matters of craftsmanship that may destroy rather than exalt the whole work. Creative unity is the key to the problem. It is here that the sculptor triumphs.[3]

The article is well illustrated with photographs of a number of works, including her portraits of Norman Nicholson and Roger Bannister. It remains one of the very few serious appreciations of her sculpture.

From this point on, Josefina was much in demand to create large, folk-type nativity scenes for churches and cathedrals. The Reverend Austen Williams, who had come to St Martin in the Fields in 1956 from Bristol, contacted her for what was to be a long association with St Martin's. Austen Williams was soon the centre of a ministry that had many revolutionary aspects. Care for the poor and disadvantaged was very much his aim and his faith involved reaching out to people who would not normally look to the established church. The Social Service Unit (now known as the Social Care Unit, and still very much in business) offered guidance and practical assistance to thousands of people who had fallen outside the bureaucracy of the Welfare State.

Having been a Prisoner of War himself during the Second World War, Austen Williams had particular concern for refugees and for people displaced by war. In 1958 Josefina designed a nativity scene for the crypt of St Martin's with this in mind. The centrepiece was called 'They Fled By Night' and depicted Mary and Joseph resting during their flight from Egypt, with a lively child sitting on Mary's feet. At the same time Josefina was also working on cribs for St James', Piccadilly and for Coventry Cathedral.

Austen Williams was astonished by Josefina's energy: 'She imploded on people,' he remembered, 'but she was never manipulative. She had endless ideas.' He asked her if she would like to design a crib for St Martin in the Fields to stand in Trafalgar Square for Christmas 1959 as part of the World Refugee Year Appeal and she eagerly agreed. It would be sited beside the huge Christmas Tree sent every year from the people of Norway in gratitude for Britain's help in the Second World War.

The Vicar did not anticipate the problems he would face in this seemingly imaginative and unthreatening project. There was a point-blank refusal from the Ministry of Works in May because they felt that the crib would be a threat to public safety. They advised the Reverend Williams that 'the Minister feels sure that you will agree that controversy and disorder should be avoided, especially in this connection, and that it would be wisest not to have a Crib in the Square. He therefore hopes that you will feel that the suggestion should not be taken further.' To their surprise the Vicar did not meekly accept this advice. In fact, he replied immediately: 'I cannot agree with what the Minister feels and I cannot accept that the suggestion should not be taken further.'[4] The campaign for the crib began.

The first salvo to be loosed was impressive: an article in *The Times* headed 'No Room in the Square: Ministry Objects to Crib' brought the project under nationwide public scrutiny. Even more startling for the Ministry of Works, their letter and the Vicar's reply were quoted in full by the newspaper.

It was becoming clear this was no ordinary Vicar. Some months previously Austen Williams had asked George Fearon, a Public Relations specialist, to assist him with matters concerning his church. He wanted to make sure that the work of St Martin's would be always fairly represented by the press, and in this he was well ahead of his time. Fearon handled this challenge with enthusiasm and finesse. He wrote in his book *You Owe Me Five Farthin's*:

> On the evening of the eventful 30 May – only two days after our appeal to *The Times* – almost every evening newspaper in the country made its readers aware in no uncertain terms that officialdom had refused permission for the placing of a crib at the foot of a Christmas tree in a public square. That the square happened to be that of Trafalgar was beside the point. Permission had been refused. We like to think that the champions of liberty would have risen with equal zest had the chosen place been the smallest green in the smallest village. A principle was at stake.[5]

Twelve days after the *Times* article, a question was asked in the House of Commons, and the Minister of Works, Hugh Molson, gave permission in a written reply for the crib. Austen Williams, described by George Fearon as 'a gentle fighter', had won his cause.

Josefina began work on the figures at The Bield and in October Norman Nicholson came to see how she was getting on. Certainly aware of the controversy surrounding the proposed installation in Trafalgar Square, he wrote to his friend Austen Williams warmly praising the work that he had seen:

> Last Saturday I had the pleasure of visiting my friends Mr & Mrs Delmar Banner at Little Langdale and was able to see Mrs Banner's work on the Nativity series intended for Trafalgar Square. I thought you might like to have my assurance that you may await this work with confidence and eagerness. I am not one of those who feel that it is wrong to introduce what is usually called 'modern' works of art into churches. If the congregation is to be puzzled into thinking then this is all to the good. But, inside a church, the setting, the architecture, the whole tradition of liturgy helps to condition the response of the beholder. He senses something at least of the work's religious significance, something of its scriptural reference, almost before he sees it. An abstract or fairly abstract work is therefore easily related to its intention. But in the case of works which are to be exhibited outside, in a busy square, there is no such aid. For that reason I feel that Mrs Banner has chosen absolutely rightly in making the human content of her sculpture quite evident. This work – if it is to have made any impression on the casual passer-by – must belong obviously to the main stem of Christian illustration... the men must be men, the Baby, a baby, and the animals, animals. That Mrs Banner has been able to do this and at the same time produce a work of high craftsmanship and artistic vision is her particular triumph and should be a source of satisfaction to the patrons of this venture. Of this, in any case, I don't pretend to speak with any great knowledge, though the works have a directness and simplicity which I find very appealing. That it may be thought of, casually, as a kind of unusually effective crib will – understandably – annoy Mrs Banner to some extent. But it is precisely because

of this that the message of her work will go over to the thousands in the Square who would not stop to consider the intentions of a more obscure work. Though, if they did stop to consider the intentions of *this* one, they would find them more complex and more perceptive than are immediately apparent.[6]

Josefina returned to London and continued with the work in the cold and unused crypt of St Martin in the Fields, where she often found herself suddenly confronted by vagrants and beggars, some of them violent. One day a verger was attacked and left in a pool of blood; Josefina herself was badly frightened by a deranged man, and after that she locked herself into the crypt. She had only one light bulb on a long flex to work by, and stood in straw to try to keep her feet warm. She enlisted the help of boys from High Beech, a probation home run by the London Police Court Mission, to make the stable and the setting for her figures.

There was considerable publicity when the crib was installed on 16 December 1959, and Josefina was filmed for television as well as being photographed for the *Sunday Times* and the *Evening Standard*. Fearon remembers that Josefina was full of praise for her approved-school boys: 'When I offered her my layman's congratulations for her lifelike group she brushed them aside with a "but look at the remarkable stable." Instead, I looked at the remarkable woman, wondering how she achieved all this whilst running house and home at the same time.'[7] Josefina's crib was seen by thousands of people who came to visit Trafalgar Square as part of their Christmas celebrations.

Josefina again contributed to the work of St Martin's by installing in the crypt an African altar which had at its centrepiece a reproduction of Delmar's early painting of Simon of Cyrene carrying the Cross. Beside it was a life-size figure of an African boy carved by Beth Jukes. Delmar was also interested in the emerging nations of Africa, and he had painted Simon as a muscular African in a setting where the dark tones of Simon's body and the cross contrast dramatically with the pale presence of the Roman soldiers. The original of this large oil was hung in Khartoum Cathedral and a replica is in Johannesburg Cathedral.

St Martin's was much involved in work with African students and politicians who were part of the struggle against Apartheid in South Africa. Bishop Trevor Huddleston and Austen Williams gave a number of memorable sermons, and outside in Trafalgar Square demonstrators protested against atrocities such as the Sharpeville Massacre and the cruelty of the Apartheid regime. The steps of St Martin's often became a sanctuary for demonstrators on the run from the police.

St Martin in the Fields represented exactly the sort of active, responsible Christianity that Josefina could relate to, and she valued the friendship of Austen Williams and his wife enormously. Josefina liked to sculpt the heads of her friends and she made two attempts to make a portrait of Austen's head. The first was in his view too rounded, but the second managed to capture the rugged, angular planes of his face, and he was much happier with it.

Involvement with St Martin's brought Josefina into contact with many religious figures who were also social reformers. She found personal inspiration at this time from meeting Father Mario Borrelli, founder of the Casa dello Scugnizzo, the House of Urchins in Naples. His courage and practical Christian faith interested her a great deal, and she asked if she could sculpt his head. As usual she did not ask her subject to pose, but she was rather taken aback when Borrelli immediately bent over his papers and lit a cigarette. She had to sit on the floor to see his face. Borrelli had lived and worked with the street children of Naples and, like Josefina, he sought to be a redemptive force for those who had been victims of poverty and abuse. A few years later she presented him with a double candlestick and cross in Spanish oak made by boys from an Approved School, but this was no plain cross. Josefina had asked the boys to give her treasures from their pockets, and worked into the cross were a toy cow, three keys, two Irish pennies and a doll's hand. Borrelli came to speak at Sedbergh School, and Josefina donated her sculpture of this inspirational figure to them.

Working in St Martin in the Fields heightened Josefina's concern for the human victims of the unstable political situation in Africa, particularly South Africa. Many people came to visit the African altar that she devised, and with other interested people including several African friends she began to gather support for the creation of an

African chapel in a London church. Contacts were built up with twelve African countries and Josefina planned a chapel which would have contributions from the best artists and craftsmen from all parts of the continent. She felt that 'our relationship with all Africans needs the healing warmth of friendship. Can we over here show them true friendship, by ceasing just for once to regard ourselves as the "Givers" – and humbly hold out our hands for this unique gift – the artistic expression of their faith.'

In England Josefina discussed her plans with Bishop Trevor Huddleston, Dr Norman Goodall, then Secretary to the World Council of Churches, and Canon Raven of St Martin in the Fields. In Nigeria, she was already closely in touch with her friend Justus Akeredolu. So many young men from different countries called to talk to Josefina at her Cresswell Mews studio that a neighbour spread the word that she was running a brothel. Whether the arrival of the bishop's official car fuelled or scotched the rumour is not quite clear.

Her first choice of venue was the Norman crypt of St Mary le Bow, but the architect was uneasy about building work disturbing the old foundations. Then Josefina tried St Martin in the Fields, where she was already well known, and Canterbury Cathedral, but in each case it was turned down by the architect as 'unsuitably out of period'.

Josefina's design was highly imaginative and both symbolic and practical. She imagined the pulpit as made from the prow of a boat, an old slaving ship, with the mast for a cross, presenting the Christian Church as fishers of men. Carvings in African woods by African sculptors of a praying girl and boy would stand on either side of the altar. Wall-lights would be of deer horn or rhino horn, with spears re-shaped to carry the curtains. The font would be a drum and the font cover an old war shield. Children from all over Africa would be asked to contribute a single bead to create a chain, thus symbolically uniting people from different countries. The carpet would be deep blue, and behind would be a warm golden window to cast a glow over even the darkest day. She hoped to form an African choir to sing there.

The whole scheme was wildly ambitious but could have been achieved if the church authorities had been willing to seize the idea. Josefina certainly put immense effort into the project, writing to her contacts all over Africa, using her friends in England and, on the practical side, trying to accumulate supplies of African wood and even tropical plants from Kew Gardens to use in the chapel. The sculptor Everatt Gray was very enthusiastic about the project and wrote to his contacts at Kew who promised him some pieces of African mahogany and offered help to obtain more. But Josefina's notion of having living plants in the chapel was not considered to be practical: 'I do not think any tropical climber would thrive for any length of time in the poor light of the average church,' advised Dr F N Howes, Keeper of the Museums at Kew, not unreasonably.

Many of Josefina's idealistic schemes were successfully carried through. This one, unfortunately, was not. Reluctantly she gave up trying to find a home for the African chapel, and perhaps the Church of England lost an opportunity to foster international relationships that could have served the church well in years to come.

Josefina's public profile was high, and in 1958 she was included on a short-list to enter a competition to design a new fountain in Hyde Park, opposite Grosvenor House. Only sculptors who had already successfully created public sculpture were able to enter, and the scheme required that they collaborate with an architect. Josefina worked with John Stammers and together they planned a sculpture of Hercules defeating the Hydra, with the many heads of the Hydra being the spouts of the fountain. Around the outside of a wide square bowl were reliefs of the labours of Hercules. Delmar's classical knowledge had assisted in the design, and it was a good example of the two creative talents working together. It was a handsome and sophisticated concept, and Josefina won second prize. Her friend Huxley Jones was the winner, and his design, featuring mermaids, was carried out. However there was a cash prize for the runner-up, which Josefina shared with her architect.

Josefina was now spending a great deal of her time in London, and she extended her circle of friends. When she was working on a piece of sculpture she was completely preoccupied, but many friends called in at her studio, day or night. Her house was in the parish of St Mary The Boltons, and she had good friends there connected to the church. Delmar came to stay if he was working on a portrait, and occasionally he would preach at St Mary's, whose vicar then was the Reverend David Ritchie. Their friend the Reverend Roger Carden has a vivid memory of the appearance of Delmar in the pulpit with his thin and wiry frame: 'when he raised his arms in an upward gesture it almost seemed that he was going to ascend heavenwards!'

Even in London Delmar and Josefina seemed to inhabit separate circles but their shared enjoyment of Shakespeare often brought them both to the Old Vic Theatre. Roger Carden saw them as each liking to have their own space. If Delmar's friends came to the studio, Delmar himself would make tea and Josefina would hold court from a perch on the bed, often wrapped in a blanket if it was a chilly day. Delmar was quite likely to serve tea and scones to his friends and eat a bowl of porridge himself.

Delmar's sketch of the Bishop of Bristol was done during one of his visits to London. This sketch was exhibited in the Royal Academy Summer Exhibition in 1958. Other portraits by Delmar exhibited at the Royal Academy during this period were of Charles Wheeler, RA, Paul Packard, the Reverend Father George Potter and Viscount Hailsham. One of his strongest and most sensitive portraits was of his friend John Bellenger, a dedicated youth training officer, happily married with two children, who died suddenly at an early age.

Old Chelsea then was very much like a village, with many artists still able to afford to live there before property became too expensive. Josefina had a number of admirers and some worthwhile relationships, but 'they were never the real thing' and always she returned to Delmar and The Bield.

In Cumbria, too, new friends were emerging who would be a bedrock for her life in difficult years ahead. Mary Burkett came up to live in Ambleside in 1954 and a few years later became Curator of the Abbot Hall Art Gallery in Kendal. Mary was soon part of the Ambleside circle that included Roger Fiske, the musician and composer, his wife Elizabeth, and Norman Nicholson the poet. When Josefina was away in London working in her studio, Mary would sometimes drive out to The Bield to have breakfast with Delmar, which was always the same: Ambrosia rice out of the tin. There is no doubt that Delmar, for all his aloof independence, could also be lonely, and he and Mary got on well. She recognised that 'on the outside Delmar could appear rather ascetic, stern and silent, but beneath the surface there was sensitivity and a very caring person.'

Mary helped him with a series of lectures on Fine Art that he gave in Ambleside, fetching and carrying him from Little Langdale in her car and operating her own projector for his slides. The audience were appreciative but sometimes amazed:

> One night it was terribly hot and stuffy in the blacked-out little room with the audience filling all seats. He was feeling the heat; he had shed his jacket and suddenly looked down at a shirt sleeve; there was a tiny hole in it. Instantly he put his finger into it, all the time continuing to talk, and ripped the sleeve off at the elbow. While the audience gazed in amazement the other sleeve got the same treatment. He made no comment and the talk went on.[8]

Josefina also surprised Mary on their first walk together from The Bield when she strode through bogs and streams without even thinking of removing her shoes. Often she walked barefoot on the Fells.

Another long-lasting friendship was established with Leslie Randall, who worked as a photographer and film-maker to record many of her schemes in Cumbria and elsewhere. He filmed the boys working at Beckstones and some of the activities of disabled children that Josefina was helping with imaginative aids to movement.

She talked about the problems of the blind with Oliver Lodge, a consultant surgeon who with his wife Sheona had retired to Ambleside in 1959 after a distinguished career as an ENT specialist in the West Riding of Yorkshire. Oliver had thought hard about the difficulties experienced by blind children moving, and how they never had the chance to run and play naturally. Josefina agreed, convinced that blind children should somehow be able to dance freely, enjoying the sense of quick motion to warm their blood. She showed him her invention of a carpet with a raised pattern that would give them a new area of freedom and his encouragement helped her at a difficult stage. Many of her sculptures at this time took their inspiration from her thoughts on blindness, such as *Blind Girl with a Dove*, *Prisoner* and *Blind Girl with Lamp*.

Josefina's network of friends spread even wider, and her work for the blind brought her once more into contact with the blind healer

Godfrey Mowatt, whom she sculpted. Mowatt told her: 'I see more often, with more energy of enthusiasm, and with more depth of perception, than most who have the gift of physical sight.' He encouraged Josefina in her view that helping the blind or disabled was mutually beneficial, saying: 'It does not matter whether you are blind or handicapped. We can always be used to help others.' As Josefina would put it, 'cutting out the "good deed" relationship is good for both.'

Another inspirational friend was the blind poet David Scott Blackhall, who was then presenting the BBC programme *In Touch*. Some years later he founded the Milton Mountaineers to enable blind hill-walkers to climb the highest mountains in the UK. David wrote his poem 'Invocation' in 1959 and dedicated it to Josefina. It has been read on every mountain climbed by the Milton Mountaineers in England, Scotland, Wales and Ireland since David died in 1981. The poem begins:

> God grant that I may make a little mark
> Upon my parent's brow, the Mother-earth,
> May set my stone upon the mountain cairn,
> A little stone to mark the turning point.
> Life is the night we wake from, and the dream
> Waits for interpretation. If they ask
> I'll tell them I was harnessed with my neighbour,
> I left a sign, I had a debt to pay.

The friendship with Oliver and Sheona Lodge was to prove very enduring. Oliver was fascinated by Josefina, not only because of her sculpture and her devices for the handicapped but because of her poetry, which he loved. He wrote that 'her lips have been touched with the glowing embers of the prophet Isaiah,' and sent her some of his own poetry. The Lodges went to stay at The Bield, and Sheona wrote about this memorable first visit:

> My memory is of a fourposter bed with a swallow's nest above the pillows. We were not in a bedroom but among mountain tops. Every wall had become a canvas for Delmar, part of the

peaks that stretched into the distance beyond the windows...
In the kitchen an enormous range, a long table and newly-
baked scones and bread we buttered ourselves with real
Langdale butter. Josefina's studio was, or so it seemed to me,
as much a part of the fell as the room upstairs – a mountain
beck, ferns, flowers surrounded by glass that was scarcely
visible but necessary to protect her sculpture, marble, bronze,
stone; an enchanted and almost visionary corner on the way
to Hardknott and the coast.[9]

As a place for artists to work and receive inspiration it may have
appeared to be perfect. But Sheona's perceptiveness took her beyond
the appearance; she saw the relationship as Prospero and Ariel; she
saw Delmar 'as mentor and maybe jailer as well.'

CHAPTER SIX

Sculpture and Vision

THE 1960s

*When you come to a great dark hole in front of you, in
your path of life, fill it with beauty as best you can –
until it is so full, there is no room for sorrow, or anything
else, then you'll find you're free to walk over it.*

J de V

The London County Council 'Sculpture in the Open Air'
Exhibition in Battersea Park in the summer of 1960 saw
Josefina's work placed alongside major pieces by Frink, Picasso,
Caro, Epstein and Moore. The Chairman of the Parks Commission,
A Reginald Stamp said in his Foreword to the Catalogue, 'we have
sought the best we could secure from each school in Britain and
France.' The selectors were not so blind to representational work that
they did not admire the qualities of Josefina's *Boys Wrestling* and this
was a popular piece. Josefina described it in the Catalogue:

> It is a portrait of my boys, aged 11 and 12, practising
> Westmorland wrestling. The pose is technically interesting
> because it is a moment of tension and balance; it also brought
> out their characters. My style varies according to subject,
> material or site; but I try to express as much as possible, as
> simply as possible.

Josefina used a number of foundries in and around London to cast her work in bronze. When *Boys Wrestling* was cast, the directors of the company had a stage built at a safe distance and brought their wives and families to watch the process, particularly the exciting moment when the molten metal was poured into the mould of Brian and Billy wrestling. Even Henry Moore, who was also having work done there at the time, was curious to see what was going on in the pit. Peering down at Josefina, who was making final adjustments to the wax prior to casting, he said, 'You look very nice down there!', and invited Josefina and Delmar to spend a day with him at his studio. As a result of the Battersea Exhibition *Boys Wrestling* was cast in bronze twice for private collectors who wanted a sculpture to place beside a bathing lake in their grounds.

She also worked with the Fiorini family's foundry in Fulham, and most recently she has used the Art Bronze Foundry, also located in Fulham, which was established in 1922 by Charles Gaskin and passed on to his son Michael in the early 1950s. Many major sculptors including Frink and Moore relied on these craftsmen to cast their work. By using the 'lost wax' process the foundries were maintaining an ancient technique: the *Times* reporter Richard Morrison, who visited the Art Bronze Foundry in connection with its exhibition in the Museum of London, suggested: 'If an ancient Roman bronze-maker were mysteriously to appear in Fulham tomorrow, he would find it all very familiar.'

Other interests were crowding in on Josefina, but she managed to complete one of her finest portrait busts, the head of the war correspondent James Cameron, and to exhibit this at the Royal Academy in 1961. She very much admired his robust attitude towards Apartheid in South Africa and against oppressive regimes everywhere. The trouble was that his face revealed so much sadness when he came for the portrait that Josefina was unable to sculpt it and had to give him a copy of Homer's *Iliad* to read to cheer him up. In the same year she exhibited *Prue Fishing*, a charming portrayal of a happy young girl. Despite all her work for Beckstones and her approved-school boys and the disabled, Josefina still managed to exhibit at the Royal Academy. Between 1962 and 1966 she exhibited *Ye Are the Branches* (1962), *Freedom* and *The Green Poetess* (1965), and *Miniature*

Fountain and *Return* (1966). She was also working on one of her most spectacular works, *The Risen Christ*, with the delicate male figure appearing to float upwards without visible means of support. In fact there was a hidden steel armature made by her blacksmith. The figure was installed in St Bartholemew the Great near the old city wall in London and dedicated at a ceremony on Easter Day, 1964: 'The statue looked so magnificent and will be a great inspiration to many, and we are thrilled to have it,' said the Rector of St Bartholemew, the Reverend Newell Wallbank.

Josefina was now a well-known figure in Anglican circles in London. When she was asked to join the Lady Mayoress's committee for the first Festival of the City of London in the summer of 1962, she was keen to show the work of boys from approved schools and was given the Crypt of St Paul's to organise an exhibition. With typical energy and enthusiasm she brought in work of all kinds from twenty-one schools: staircases in wood, kayaks, metalwork, beaten silver, all kinds of crafts and works of art. Josefina called it 'The Carpenter's Shop' to remind people that Joseph had been a carpenter, and Jesus too.

The architect Lord Mottistone, then in charge of the fabric at St Paul's, and an old friend from student days, worked with Josefina to create a short Family Service of dedication on 8 July. Her friends the Cumbrian poet Norman Nicholson and the blind poet David Scott Blackhall both wrote hymns. Norman's hymn, which was sung to the rousing tune for 'Soldiers of Christ Arise', stressed the link between Jesus and the carpenter's trade, ending with the stanza:

> All workers for the Lord
> Come, sing with voice and heart;
> In strength of hands be God adored,
> And praised in power of art.

Boys from Castle Howard Approved School made a special wrought iron processional cross and candlesticks out of garden implements used in work on the school farm: 'carried in procession by two strong lads of 17 years; from there, a group of boys led the singing and many were much moved by it all,' wrote Josefina at the time. The sale of catalogues helped to cover expenses, and the exhibition attracted so much interest that it was kept open for a week beyond the actual dates of the Festival. She enjoyed the fine music and pageantry of the main Dedication Service for the Festival of London in the Cathedral on 9 July, but she was undoubtedly more committed to the work in the crypt below.

As well as organising the exhibition, Josefina displayed three experimental works using perspex: 'Bird Window', made of blue birds on window bars against a morning sky; 'Flying Angels', a mosaic appliqué of coloured transparent perspex; and 'A Vision of the Nativity', an engraving on the curved outer surfaces of two windows from the perspex gun turret of a crashed British night bomber. There was also an experimental window depicting St Paul, designed by Anne Tomlinson using polarised material and viewing screens. This work with polaroid materials, then very new, had been first shown by Stuart Young in the crypt of St Martin in the Fields at Christmas in 1960.

Life was full of interesting possibilities, but in the background, always, was the unhappy figure of Josefina's mother. For a time after the war Freda had lived alone south of London in Bexhill, Lancing and Broadstairs, in a succession of small houses. She still enjoyed listening to music on the radio and went to the cinema frequently, keeping a journal with grades given for each film. She also kept a careful record of the extensive range of books she read: 'books are such a joy to me and I live in them,' she wrote to Josefina. But her daughter's career continued to dominate her life and she signed each letter to Josefina with a sketch of a proud mother hen beside a small chick. She worried about Josefina doing too much, working in the cold, not watching her health, just like any fussy mother, but the closeness of her concern indicated that she had never really moved on from the intimacy of those years when she was so involved with her daughter during their travels together in Europe. On Josefina's forty-second birthday, 26 October 1946, she wrote a loving poem to her mother:

> It is my birthday, and so I write
> To thank you for bringing me to light
> And breathing life in the world that night.

> Thank you for teaching me how to find
> Beauty for ear and eye and mind,
> Memories not to be left behind.
>
> Why should I wish to be young again?
> I am always young in the sun and rain
> Looking at flowers and birds in a lane!
>
> What does it matter when all's said and done.
> Whether we meet in the rain or the sun
> Our thoughts meet beyond them: we two, we one!

Freda pasted the handwritten poem into a notebook and it was obviously much cherished. Feeling at one with her daughter was certainly the case as far as Freda was concerned. She was always overjoyed when there was the chance to meet Josefina in London and often proposed a trip to the theatre on the same day. But she was undoubtedly lonely and usually spent Christmas on her own.

Although Freda had constantly urged Josefina to leave Delmar, she had to accept that this would not now take place. She moved back to London to be nearer Josefina but the rented rooms Josefina had found for her in Kensington did not suit her, as she thought that she was being spied on. Facing a lonely old age and suffering badly from the pain of rheumatism, she wrote out her requirements for cremation in Hampstead Crematorium and decided to put an end to it all. She had often remarked that living beyond the age of seventy was a bad idea, and she was then 79.

Freda's death by suicide on 7 September 1961 imposed a terrible burden on her daughter. Josefina was called to the scene and somehow managed to keep the event out of the newspapers. The body had already been taken away to St Stephen's Hospital, Chelsea, but Josefina was told to go to the wrong hospital and waited hours before being sent to the right place.

On her own, with no relatives or friends to support her, she coped with the inquest four days later and arranged the funeral and cremation. She was determined that no one should know that her mother had killed herself, so only the undertakers and Josefina were present. She sat on her own at the front of the chapel and declined the undertakers' kind offer to sit beside her. Delmar felt removed from it all and did not attend. The Minister was clearly at a loss to know what to say about a complete stranger who had killed herself, but Josefina was comforted when, as though he had been given inspiration, he began to talk of flowers and cats, which her mother had loved.

When it was over, Josefina had a card announcing the death sent round to those who had known her. By keeping the circumstances of her mother's death a secret, she cut off any chance of support from friends or surviving Coleman relatives, and made the emotional hardship even worse for herself. One of the few treasures belonging to her mother that she kept was a book of music teachers' reports showing that she was making good progress with her singing and with playing the violin. Concert programmes from the turn of the century show Miss Freda Coleman singing such favourite songs as 'Still is the Night' and 'A Song of Thanksgiving'. They indicated a talent that wasted away after her marriage, but might have sustained her in old age.

Josefina wrote warmly about both her parents a few year later in her contribution to *They Became Christians*:

> Mother took me to most of the historical and lovely places in Europe and gave all that can be imagined of unselfish and happy companionship. Without knowing it, her delight in, and gratitude for, every good thing however small or humble, and my father's great generosity and real care for people in trouble, were two real Christian foundations for my life.[1]

The idea of suicide continued to haunt Josefina throughout her life. 'It is a hideous curse on a family,' she wrote to her friend Sheona Lodge, one of the few people she confided in, years later, about this personal tragedy: 'Did she not believe we loved her enough to need her presence? In the empty home there was no comfort.' At the time she spoke to no one about her mother's death, not even to close friends in the clergy. Despite her unhappiness and the inevitable sense of guilt that any suicide leaves with the survivors, Josefina continued doing what she was good at: finding ways and means of bringing a complicated project to fruition.

For the next few years Josefina was deeply involved with her work for approved schools. Whenever she was asked to create a Christmas nativity scene she invited boys from these schools to contribute. Each nativity was different and original, and considered by the sculptor to be a kind of folk art. Her tableau for Liverpool Cathedral in 1965 drew on the closeness of the sea and its importance for the city by placing Mary, Joseph and the baby beneath an upturned boat surrounded by ropes, an anchor, a winking harbour buoy, and port and starboard lights on either side. Sails were suspended behind the figures and clever lighting added drama to the scene, making the familiar story new and exciting.

For the 1966 nativity at Liverpool, Josefina designed a lively and slightly surreal scene where an angel propelled a child in a push-chair and another sat on a step playing a recorder and stroking a squirrel. Enclosed by traffic barricades and warning lanterns, it was like a street scene where the birth was clearly unexpected and landed in the middle of things. Boys from Pelham House School at Calderbridge made a carved perspex star, and boys from Redbank School, Newton le Willows made a mobile of seagulls to hang above the crib.

She also involved these young people in making a series of very unusual crosses, rather like the one she made for Father Borrelli two years before. The largest cross, made for St Martin in the Fields, was made up of over 100 pieces: 'small boys and girls in all sorts of places simply turned their pockets out,' said Josefina. 'It was quite a problem to work them into an organic design, and in the end three crosses were made.'

Father Borrelli's street urchins sent white shells; approved-school boys sent cuff links, boxing medals and marbles; one girl sent a comb. Josefina's design set them all together to make a religious item with real significance. The Carpenter's Cross was made for All Hallows-on-the-Wall, the Church for the Worshipful Company of Carpenters, and is made from pincers and calipers, their normal tools. The Farming Cross and candlesticks were made by an approved school specialising in farming, and they used hoes and hayforks wreathed in fronds of morning glory. The crosses and their maker were

42

43

44

42 *The second joint exhibition of painting and sculpture by Josefina and Delmar was held at the Royal Watercolour Society Galleries in London in 1955.*

43 *Josefina at the opening of the exhibition.*

44 *Seven sculptors, including Josefina, made portraits of Eva Castle and exhibited them in 1953.*

45

46

45 Josefina working in perspex in the 1940s, then an experimental material for sculpture.

46 'The Angel of Judgement', carved in oak during Festival of Britain year, 1951.

47, 48, 49 During the 1950s Josefina sculpted several well-known figures, among them Norman Nicholson (left), Owen Jennings (right) and Edith Sitwell.

50

51

50, 51 Josefina was much in demand to design and sculpt figures for nativity scenes in churches and cathedrals. Top is the 1955 nativity scene for St Paul's, which involved the work of twelve British sculptors, and below is the tableau for Liverpool Cathedral, with a Port of Liverpool setting.

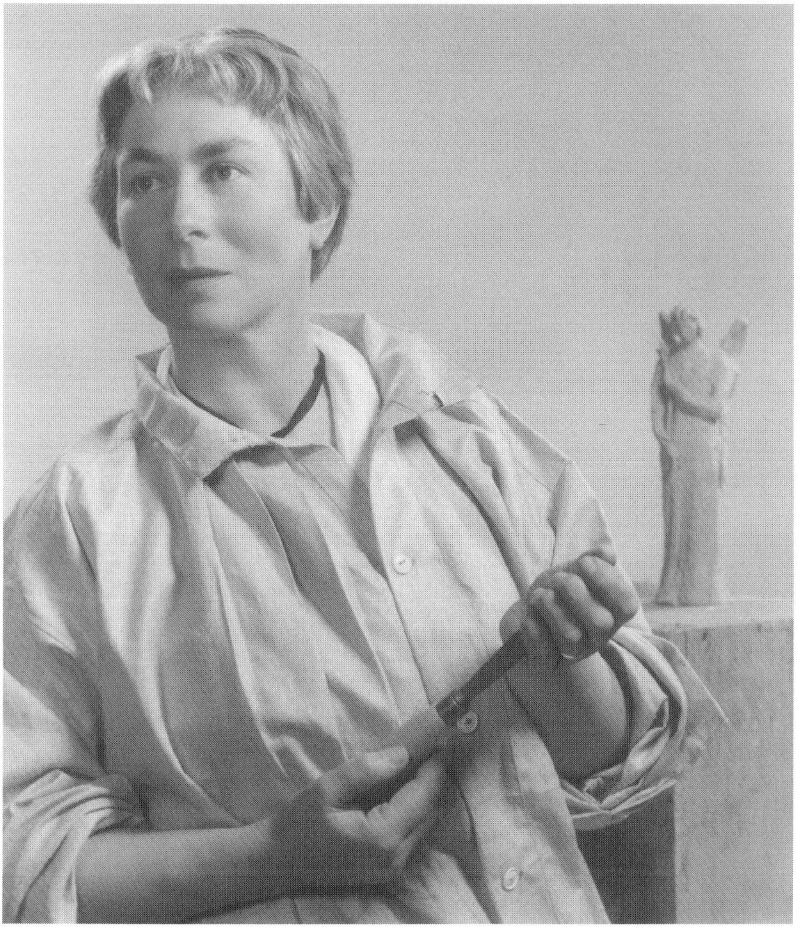

52

53

54

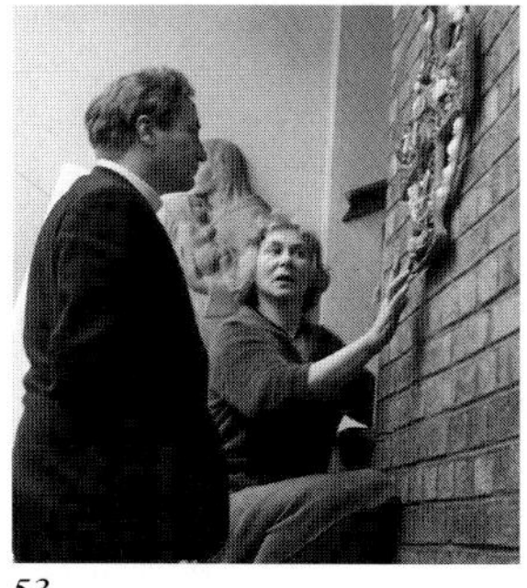

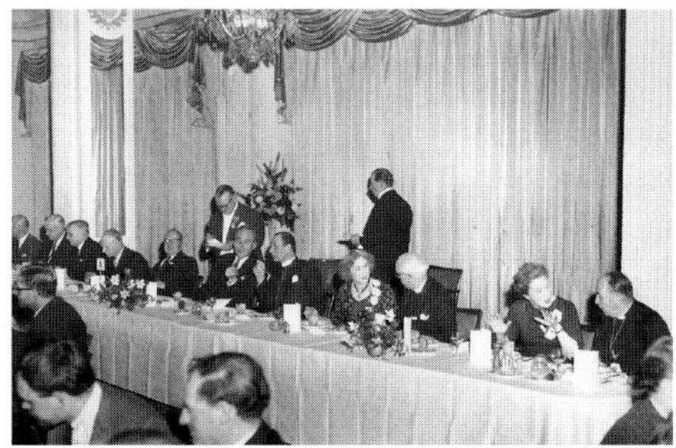

52 Josefina in the 1950s.

53 With Mario Borrelli, founder of the House of Urchins in Naples, and the cross she made for him out of deprived children's treasures.

54 Josefina (centre) was prominent in public life in the 1950s in London.

55

56

55 *Josefina's 'Madonna and Child' was placed permanently in St Paul's Cathedral in 1957. She was the first woman sculptor to have her work accepted by St Paul's.*

56 *The treasured garden of her London studio.*

57

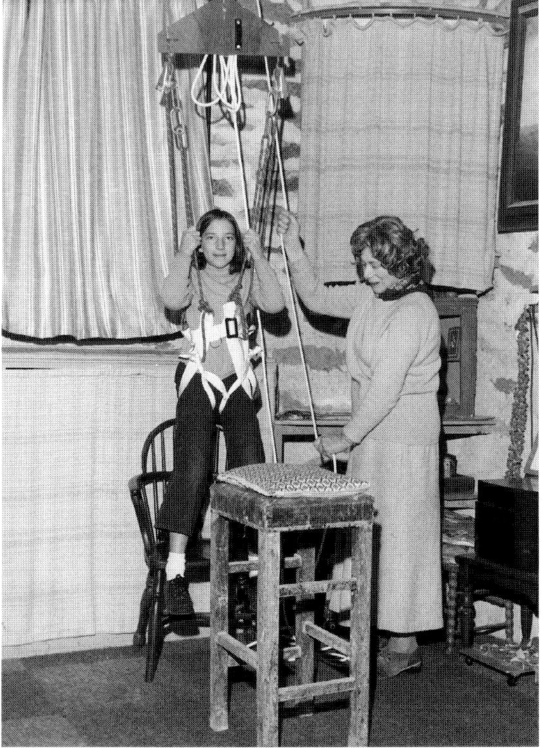

58

57 Josefina demonstrates how to use 'Happy Tapis', a carpet with a raised pattern for blind children that she designed and made. She hoped that it would provide a new area of freedom for blind children.

58 'Track Gliding' was another invention to help disabled people have some mobility.

59

60

61

59 *The Bield with carved standing stones.*
60 *Josefina with her white MGB and the 'Harriet' ship in the background at Millom.*
61 *The 'Harriet' with ramp ready to receive her first disabled visitors.*

62 Josefina and Delmar on their Golden Wedding Anniversary, 1980.

63 'Valiant for Truth', Josefina's monument to Delmar which was completed after his death in 1983.

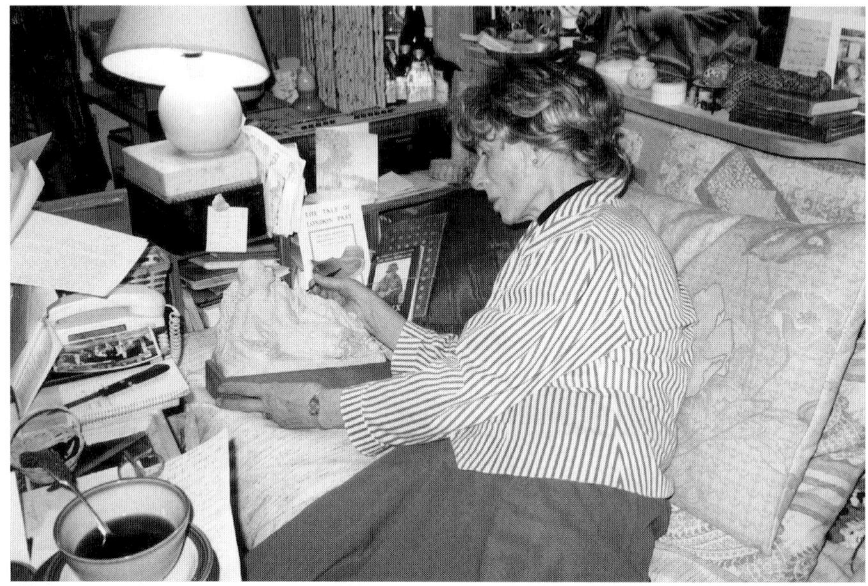

64 *Working in the Old Wash House Studio in Ambleside.*
65 *On the flower-filled terrace of the Wash House Studio.*
66 *Liberation at the age of 85!*

67

67 Receiving her Honorary DLitt from Bradford University in 1977.

68 Josefina was made MBE on 3 March 1985 for services to the community in Cumbria. She was accompanied to Buckingham Palace by her friends Ann Taylforth (right) and Sheila Myers(left).

68

69

70

69 *Blacksmith Stephen Stalker transports 'Father Forgive' to Rydal Hall.*

70 *A version of 'Reconciliation' on the terrace at Wraysholme, being inspected by friends Sheona Lodge (right) and Dr Anne Mathieson.*

71

72

73

*71 Josefina (centre) at her private view, with Tim Collins, MP,
and Mary Burkett, OBE.*

*72 Josefina with Lord Denning and his wife Joan at their home in
Whitchurch.*

*73 Enjoying a concert by Andrew Wilde (centre) and Brian Ainley
at Stone Cross Mansion.*

74

74 'St Michael' is sited in Cartmel Priory in South Lakeland.

75

76

77

'Escape to Light', Josefina's last major work in stone. It weighs 7 tonnes.

75 Marking the stone (the maquette is on the right).

76 Concentrated effort.

77 Nearly complete.

78

79

78 'Reconciliation' was placed in the precinct of Coventry Cathedral in 1995.
79 The latest 'Reconciliation' in position at Stormont Castle, Northern Ireland.

featured in an article in *Church Illustrated* in May 1965, where Josefina was described as 'compelling as the Ancient Mariner and as fresh as youth itself.' Looking at the cross made from children's treasures, it would seem that Josefina was not so far removed from Kurt Schwitters after all when she said, 'I always say to people, if you have any old scrap, give it to me. It might make something useful.'

The crypt of St Paul's was again called into use in 1963 for an exhibition designed by Josefina on the theme of world need. It was called 'Intercession: Photographs and Sculpture of the Theme of World Need'. Josefina used huge blow-up photographs to illustrate the Lord's Prayer, petitions from the Prayer Book and themes from St Paul's Letters. Her sculpture *The Family of Man* (now in Kendal Parish Church) was at the heart of the exhibition. David Scott Blackhall again wrote a special hymn on the theme of world hunger, and this was recorded by the London Welsh Youth choir. The exhibition was opened by the Archdeacon of London and after many people had seen it in London it travelled on to York Minster where it was described by War on Want as 'a really sensational success'. The proceeds from the Exhibition were given to War on Want and other charities.

Josefina's interest in approved schools went back to the 1950s, and now she was led to do even more for these lonely, troubled boys. Again the idea of redemption comes to mind. She felt that with love, a recognition of individual needs and an opportunity to practise the Christian faith, some good could be done. She talked to Norman Nicholson, who lived in Millom, to Lord Denning, and to the Reverend Austen Williams at St Martin in the Fields. Delmar, too, supported the project. With their backing she set about the establishment of 'Outpost Emmaus', a climbing hut and refuge for approved-school boys and boys on remand to give them the Outward Bound type of adventure courses open to more privileged children at high expense. Eventually a committee was formed under the auspices of the Church of England Council for Social Aid and the children's department of the Home Office. An appeal for funds was launched with Lord Denning as Trustee, the Bishop of Norwich as President, and the Bishop of Carlisle as Patron. Austen Williams chaired the committee. In their appeal leaflet Lord Denning wrote optimistically that 'Outpost Emmaus is an inspired conception. It should help many of our young lads – the lonely to find friends, the high spirited to find adventure, the insecure to find security, and all to discover themselves.'

Local committee members managed to find a derelict sixteenth century farmhouse on the west bank of the Logan Beck near Ulpha in the Duddon Valley. It had been left to the National Trust but had stood in ruins for thirty years. Even today this part of the Lake District remains remote and unspoiled, well away from the commercial bustle of Bowness and Ambleside. Beckstones was obtained from the Trust at a peppercorn rent for twenty-one years, and in 1964 restoration by the boys themselves, with the advice of the Honorary Architect, Edgar Glover, got underway. They undertook to restore the farmhouse to its original appearance as far as possible, and an immediate task was to chop down a large sycamore tree that was growing up through the middle of the building.

The first school to send a working party was Castle Howard School in Yorkshire, which had already worked with Josefina on various projects. They managed to roof the dormitory and from then on the building started to become habitable. Pelham House School at Calderbridge sent a party of junior boys to make window frames and a canteen table. The Fylde School, Blackpool, constructed the kitchen block and the common room, and Edmund Castle School, Carlisle, did the electrical wiring. When sceptical Home Office inspectors came to see what was going on in a remote Lakeland valley and saw the boys hard at work in rain and howling gales, one of them remarked, 'It's a bloody miracle.'

The connection with the nearby Eskdale Outward Bound School was crucial. Pilot groups had already been organised under the direction of John Lagoe, who was then Warden. Tom Price took over when John retired and maintained an interest in Beckstones. Local support also came from the Reverend Roy Greenwood, who became Vicar of Seathwaite and Ulpha in 1962 and was Chaplain to Beckstones. It was a very suitable connection as he was a Himalayan climber and had for three years been an instructor for Outward Bound mountaineering parties.

Josefina was committed to the idea of small, family-sized groups, if possible accompanied by an ordinand or theological student as well as leaders from the school, with the aim of providing close, individual help for the boys. She believed that 'boys and birds are much alike – they love freedom, yet have a great homing instinct, are unsentimental and friendly. They enjoy poking about in the country, dislike being watched, and are very resourceful builders.'

There is no doubt that Josefina believed passionately in the aims of Outpost Emmaus: it offered 'an incentive to boys who are struggling to make good – from deprived and dreary beginnings. An incentive to make that extra effort which may earn them – as some lads have said – "The most terrific time of my life".' The Christian message would come through comradeship and example, not through preaching. Adam Ford, an ordinand and leader at one of the early Outpost Emmaus camps run by Outward Bound wrote that he hoped the boys would not think that 'Christianity is another group of people "out to get them". It is not trying to sell them a product against their will, or trying to claim their independence or self-dignity as individuals. Only when they realise that one's interest is in them as individuals for their own sake and that one's hopes and prayers are for them from their own point of view can one hope for a response.'

Josefina felt that there should be a chapel at Beckstones in the calf house, and had very clear ideas about what it should be like. She wanted it to be open to the fells with no door because she wanted the boys to find it 'like a bird's nest', as part of the world of nature so close at hand. But the important tradition of Christianity was there just the same, in the shape of the ancient altar that Josefina found in the crypt of St Martin in the Fields and that was given for Beckstones. On the altar was one of her special crosses made out of pitons and ice axes. The chapel was dedicated to the memory of those who had been killed on the fells in plane crashes through poor visibility or engine failure, and representatives of the Royal Air Force Northern Command attended the opening ceremony.

Although Josefina had been very much the public face of Outpost Emmaus, Delmar had not been indifferent to what was going on. In his unpublished book, 'Jacob's Ladder', he described very movingly his own experience with these disturbed boys, probably during the early stages of the project:

Some years ago, on a Sunday evening in August, dark with distant storm, my wife and I were asked to supper in a camp of eighty 'delinquent' boys from an approved school. After supper we joined in a service in another big tent. It was led by five of the older boys. We all stood, on grass trodden into mud. Because the sun was set, lamps hung by the posts and lit blunted faces that too few had loved, whose searching out of the shadows the remembered touch seemed to lift into a vaster light. Some of them had taken of the stones of that place, and set them up for an altar. Between the stones they had put earth and planted wild flowers; and on the top of it had made a wooden cross, which cast three shadows, as of a Trinity, sharing our darkness and our light. The boys alone chose the prayers, some in the magical words of Cramner; and read them badly. They chose hymns, by Watts and Wesley, and sang them badly. But was it a performance? We joined in. Then they all sang, all eighty as one, 'Nobody knows the trouble I've seen; Nobody knows but Jesus.'

We've met cultivated callousness and wincing sensibility running away from this, the reality of imagination. The negro slave spirituals are the greatest art and the only Christian art, born in Africa or America, and the boys put their soul into what they sang. We saw, as in no college or cathedral office: This is the house of God, this is the gate of heaven...

In this deeply felt description Delmar was using the biblical passage where Jacob in the desert dreams of a ladder stretching up to heaven, and finds that 'this is none other than the house of God, and this is the gate of heaven.' He wrote later: 'I am thankful I was ready to see the offering of those youths in the tent as kin with the living imagination that always forms the ladder between earth and heaven.' Delmar was then engaged with the thinking behind his book about the relationship between nature, art and religion, and his understanding of the need for faith, his concern for individual worth, and the role of faith in society were clearly affected by the very practical successes and failures that he was involved with for several years. The whole Beckstones project was clearly of immeasurable significance for both

Delmar and Josefina, and for many other people as well.

Beckstones became a hive of activity during 1967 and 1968 as volunteers came from Britain and overseas to help complete the building. The *Times Educational Supplement* ran an extensive and very favourable article about Beckstones and its aims. Duke of Edinburgh Award parties, working parties from the International Voluntary Service, and university students all came to help. In a way the work was the project, since every helper could feel a sense of achievement as the building work progressed. Josefina carved a wooden name plate for the gate with an ingenious logo which was used on their appeal leaflet. Beckstones was formally declared open by Bishop Cyril Bulley, Bishop of Carlisle, and was booked to capacity for several years, under the guidance of the resident warden. Even after it opened, Josefina continued to help out with the work there, cleaning and tidying after each group of visitors.

The Reverend Austen Williams came up with his wife Daphne in 1969 to see how Beckstones was functioning, and stayed at The Bield. They spent the night in the huge canopied oak bed with the feather mattress that so amazed all the guests at The Bield, and shivered in the cold, even though it was the month of May. They were instructed to keep the bedroom window open to allow the swallows to fly in and out to their nests above the bed. No wonder Delmar spent most of his time swathed in rugs and blankets, trying to keep warm. Austen remembers being brought into his presence as though he were being introduced to some great sage of the mountains, and was rather overwhelmed by the experience. Yet as he walked out with Delmar the following morning, his response to the beauty of the landscape was intense and made the whole visit extraordinary and memorable.

Leslie Randall maintained a fine photographic record of the rebuilding of Beckstones and also made a 16mm film. Although not part of the organising committee he shared in the idealism behind the venture, and vividly remembers one tough lad placing a few wild flowers in a jam pot, putting it in a gaping window, and saying, 'There, that's more like home.'

Beckstones was a project very dear to Josefina's heart, and she worked tremendously hard to make it a success, as her poem about it makes clear:

I sing the homeliness of things;
Not new and smart,
But nearer to man's heart,
A quality apart.

The hump-backed kettle-holder
Worn to hand;
A lane, unplanned...
Towels – softer when they're older –
The patient land.

The homeliness of God; found in the end –
All else count loss –
The Crib, the Cross.
An evening meal, a Friend;
Bridging all worlds across.

Initially Beckstones ran very successfully, and because the rates charged to stay were modest the accommodation was open to parties from inner cities and disadvantaged backgrounds, just as Josefina had intended. But not everyone in the neighbourhood felt so sympathetically towards approved-school boys. Some local people resented the presence of young criminals in their midst and criticism appeared in the local press. Josefina was steadfast; she had no doubts about the value of what they were doing – 'What does one choose to see? A delinquent or a lonely soul? A derelict ruin or an old home being restored?'

But when does idealism become naivety? Josefina has always seen young people as undervalued and often exploited, and has fiercely defended their rights. Not only was this demonstrated in her practical work with approved schools, but in later, eloquent sculptures such as *Childline to God*, now in Carlisle Cathedral, and *The Weight of Our Sins* (1999), where abused children are specifically identified and linked to a healing vision. Although the establishment of Beckstones had its sceptics, the project did not go unnoticed by Church authorities. Members of the Diocesan Synod in 1973 allowed themselves 30 minutes to discuss 'Social Responsibility Within the Diocese'. Josefina was asked to speak for five minutes on Beckstones. An impossible assignment, and something of an insult considering the years of concerted and dedicated effort that had gone into the project. Not surprisingly, she delegated the task to someone else.

And, indeed, Josefina was not without other projects to pursue. Concern about the future of her adopted son Brian when he had finished his National Service led to the purchase of a farm, Thomas Grove, at Hartsop on the north side of the Kirkstone Pass. Brian had always loved working on the nearby farms at The Bield when he was a boy, and Josefina bought the farm so that he would have a livelihood when he left the army.

Thomas Grove had the highest sheepfold in the Lakes, up near Skirthwaite Beacon, south of Ullswater. Josefina astonished the vendors by walking its boundaries barefoot, through bogs and streams, just as she and Delmar used to do in Langdale. She remained its owner for over ten years, and made considerable improvements to the property. The Milk Marketing Board required modernisation to the shippon or cow-shed and Josefina also converted some of the farm buildings to rent out to local people. The farm itself had a good tenant who eventually purchased it when Josefina decided to sell, because Brian had changed while he was away in uniform and was no longer interested in working on the land. Instead he wanted to write and take photographs, and he moved down to London to work there and also in Africa.

When she was at home at The Bield, Josefina spent a great deal of time considering the problems of the disabled. Her approach was well ahead of its time. While many in the 1960s quite understandably wanted to stress the need for independence for those with physical handicaps, Josefina preferred to emphasise how the helper could also gain from being involved and creating a relationship. In a letter to the physiotherapist Marjorie Bocianowski she wrote:

> There is not yet enough interdependence-relationship in the whole of life... or even the necessary humbling admission of how much there is... If it were for the enjoyment of the handicapped only, there might be some excuse for cutting out their companionship with partners of their own age groups,

and substituting an electrical device instead, but this is not so, because the partners will love it too.

How do I know this? Experience, with rickshaw running with cripples, and with strap running (also with music) with blind, and an unrehearsed mime, with 25 blind children of 'Peter and the Wolf'. Also, by the desire, clearly expressed, by many leaders and members of youth clubs from all over this country, with which I am connected.

In May 1966 Josefina brought her braille carpet or toe map to try out with children at Huyton Hill Preparatory School on Windermere, the school Brian and Billy had attended. She called this *Jeu libre* and the idea was that barefoot blind children would learn to recognise the raised patterns on the carpet and would be able to move freely. They would learn to 'play' the carpet as a blind musician learns to play the piano, and familiarity with the shapes and spaces would enable them to jump and run.

The prototype was made of sailcloth and foam rubber with patterns in coloured cloth. It was in four sections to represent a field, the sun, a rose and the sky, and made in colours to assist the helpers. Josefina had designed three sizes of carpet, so that it could be used in a playpen, an infant school and a gymnasium. Josefina made a braille map for the carpet, and worked out how it could be manufactured by blind workers.

The trial with blindfolded but sighted boys at Huyton Hall was so encouraging that the next step was to try it out with blind people. Her friends David Scott Blackhall and Esther Hodgkinson experimented and made a few suggestions at Woodlarks Camp in Farnham. Josefina went on to choreograph a simple dance for blind children to Vivaldi's 'The Four Seasons'.

The success of the *Jeu libre* gave Josefina encouragement to seek out help from other partners in music and dance who would help to devise ways in which handicapped and blind people could move freely and with confidence. She discussed possibilities with Janet Yardley at the London School of Contemporary Dance and again was ahead of her time in seeking to create opportunities for people who might never have thought that they could dance. Even Josefina did not foresee that a professional troupe of dancers in wheelchairs would be giving performances in the 1990s.

Her second *Jeu libre* was rickshaw racing, where a specially designed chair pulled like a rickshaw gave a sense of movement to the handicapped child. The racing was performed to music and depended on liaison between a fit runner and the driver. Approved-school boys worked with girls who were badly disabled with cerebral palsy, giving them a sense of freedom and movement for the first time.

The braille carpet, despite its innovation and successful use in a prototype state, was never taken up for manufacture, although Josefina tried very hard over a number of years to interest commercial firms. The prototype wore out, and very sadly she threw it away when she moved from The Bield after Delmar's death. But the plans and design remained, and Josefina wisely never lost hope that some day its originality would be recognised and used to help the children it was meant for.

Josefina always stressed the great benefits involved in 'forms of sport and dance where fit and handicapped could meet on equal terms... cutting out the "Good deed relationship" because it would be fun for both.' She said of the partners who came to help that 'it gives them responsibility that young people want. They wish to be useful and their early maturity respected.' Today the notion of interchange is much more accepted as attitudes towards the disabled have become more enlightened.

During the late 1960s Josefina suffered from pernicious anaemia which was undiagnosed for several years. She was permanently tired but drove herself on to make progress with various projects and to continue with her sculpture. She was looking in many different directions and sculpture was only one of her interests. She always made time for friends, young and old, and was very concerned about the future of the young members of the Hervey family, a friendship that went back many years. Ayliffe, aged seventeen, longed to be a dancer, and was being pressed by her parents to enter medicine. Josefina, who had always loved dancing, believed in Ayliffe's talent and encouraged her to follow this ambition. Ayliffe came to stay at The Bield at this crucial time in her life and remembers an inspirational few weeks when she was able to dance in the studio with Josefina while Delmar was having his afternoon rest. Her parents insisted on her studying medicine, however, and her subsequent career had many unhappy phases until eventually she found a niche which allowed her to develop her artistic potential. Years later Ayliffe would dance in the 1995 Granada documentary about Josefina, but by then she did not find herself quite in accord with the highly emotional interpretations which Josefina insisted on, a style that was very much part of her sculpture at that time.

The final years of the 1960s marked an important frontier in Josefina's professional and personal life, as it saw the end of her independent existence in London. Delmar, then over seventy, needed someone to look after him, and Josefina felt it her duty to return permanently to The Bield. He was becoming increasingly frail physically and suffered badly from rheumatism, not helped by the lack of heating in the old farmhouse. Festooned in rugs he sat by the Rayburn in the kitchen and was unable to paint. Even his completed paintings failed to find buyers, and in November 1968 he wrote sadly to Josefina when she was in London that he had sold only two sixteen-guinea watercolours for a year.

His letters to Josefina are affectionate and intimate, full of private jokes, revealing how lonely he was, especially when winter snows made it unwise for him to be out. The farmer fetching hay from the adjoining barn was often the main source of conversation during the day. Letters to Josefina making arrangements to visit friends when she was back at The Bield included anxious details about the times of sunset and sunrise, because he continued to prefer to live his life in natural daylight. During winter in Cumbria, the scope was limited. But he had become reconciled to television, and compared notes on programmes with Josefina when he wrote to her in his own special shorthand style, nearly always on scraps of paper torn from other letters to him: 'Lovely we BOTH see 4syte saga. How one's heart goes out to the young two! & one must not say "they shd hv done otherwise".'

She sold the little house in Cresswell Place to a friend who still owns and cares for it today, tending the flowers and shrubs that Josefina planted. Delmar had always placed himself outside the arts establishment and the arts cliques of London, and although Josefina, too, had very much followed her own path, she had been part of a number of circles in London that had given her stimulus and support. Much as Josefina loved Cumbria, she also thrived in London, where she was several times invited to 'Woman of the Year' Luncheons and other prestigious social events.

Neither she nor Delmar had ever had a high opinion of the arts industry manufactured by the Arts Council, and both were independent of fashion. Influential art critics such as Kenneth Clark and Herbert Read gathered protégés and promoted their work through the Arts Council at home and through the British Council abroad, securing an international reputation for artists such as Hepworth and Moore.

Many artists failed to find a place on these bandwagons, including Elizabeth Frink, who found that the British Council was no longer sending her work abroad and felt an outsider: 'Abstract art was very much the new wave in England, and people suddenly seemed to find figurative art very boring. I felt I'd become unpopular with the arts establishment, though there was still a body of collectors who'd always supported my work.'[2] Yet Frink knew that her work was popular with the public, and felt that this made her suspect with the critics:

> The point is that if a large part of the public know your work – if you become visible to many people – then the critics just don't want to know. For some reason or other the situation irritates them. 'If you're a popular artist,' they say, 'what you make can't be good art.' Is it necessarily bad, or banal, because so many people like it?[3]

Frink continued to do her own work in her own way, ignoring the critics, but it was annoying when the British Council left her out of prestigious exhibitions overseas: 'it became irritating when important collectors used to ask me, "Why weren't you represented in such-and-such an exhibition abroad?"'

At the beginning of the decade, Josefina's work had stood alongside that of the best contemporary sculptors. Now the taste of the arts establishment was firmly against much of the work that she did, and Josefina felt no desire to follow contemporary trends. At the same time she and Delmar, even then, were both convinced that photography and film were the new and important arts of the future, and recent short lists for the Turner Prize have proved this view to be correct.

The evaluation of Josefina's achievement as a sculptor at this stage of her career opens up many interesting questions about the nature of art, religion and moral integrity. It is easy for contemporary critics to judge that Josefina, by remaining true to the human form in most of her work, ignored the inexorable move towards abstraction in twentieth century art. But as Philip Rawson points out in his book *Sculpture*, 'as a language of feeling, sculpture needs a focus if it is to be at all clear.' He adds:

> Even in ordinary life unfocused expression of generalized feeling is not usually interesting. A sculptor who has no other tenor may fall into emotive self-portraiture, which rarely has any continuing interest beyond that of historical document.[4]

There is a considerable conundrum involved in the fact that the further Josefina distanced herself from the British arts establishment, the more her sculpture engaged with serious political and social issues such as the plight of refugees, the search for peace, and child abuse. What set her apart from a younger generation of sculptors was her figurative approach and her religious iconography. Yet the appeal of her work to the ordinary viewer continued to enhance her reputation. She had been sculpting seriously for fifty years, and had seen clearly over the years that what was considered 'new' could very soon be out of date, or even worse, become academically respectable. Elizabeth Frink also felt that fashions in art were fickle: 'The fascinating thing about fashions in art, of course, is that they come round full circle. They reach a certain point, then round they go again.'[5]

So were the critics right to claim that Josefina was avoiding the intellectual challenge of the finest abstract art, which Barbara Hepworth found satisfying?

> Working in the abstract way seems to release one's personality and sharpen the perceptions so that in the observation of humanity or landscape it is the wholeness of inner intention which moves one so profoundly. The components fall into

place and one is no longer aware of the detail except as the
necessary significance of wholeness and unity... a rhythm of
form which has its roots in earth but reaches outwards
towards the unknown experiences of the future.[6]

This may have been the directing force for Hepworth, but
Elizabeth Frink comes much closer to Josefina in her views:

> I think you reach a moment with abstraction when it becomes
> a complete desert. It's very difficult to continue working in a
> totally abstract vein without any root in the visible. For me it
> wasn't available as an option, or I didn't want to avail myself
> of it. Yet of course I was worried, because there was a time
> when abstract work was so popular, and figurative work so
> unpopular.
>
> However, throughout my career I've been on the buying,
> collecting side of the divide in the art world, not the
> intellectually fashionable side, and that's given me a lot of
> stability in many ways.[7]

Henry Moore, too, rejected the purely abstract style, saying in an
interview in 1960:

> Sculpture, for me, must have life in it, vitality. It must have a
> feeling for organic form, a certain pathos and warmth.
> Purely abstract sculpture seems to me to be an activity that
> would be better fulfilled in another art, such as architecture.
> That is why I have never been tempted to remain a purely
> abstract sculptor.[8]

Hepworth, Frink and Moore and many lesser artists all recorded
their views on art and these autobiographical pieces are of great
value today. For such an eloquent speaker as Josefina, it is a matter
of great regret that she did not attempt to put her position as an
artist into words. She clearly felt that the work could and should
speak for itself, but one reason for her relative lack of recognition
today is certainly that she did not, until very recently, start to record

her own personal vision as an artist. Delmar's dominant presence as intellectually superior may have inhibited her from trying to analyse her own work and her response to others, and she always preferred to be active and working rather than sitting back as a critic. Nevertheless such insights and observations from artists are always worthwhile, and this period in her life represented a staging post where her position in the art world could well have been established more firmly by publishing her ideas in written form.

CHAPTER SEVEN

Working for Others

THE 1970S

I and my enemy met,
now free to wander,
but too tired to go.
Suddenly weak, we staggered,
gripping for support,
and fell to our knees...
In the mud, between us,
lay the bones of a child.
We prayed God for forgiveness
and in that moment
were reconciled.

J de V

Although Christian images and themes were the guiding force behind much of Josefina's later sculpture, a strong commitment to international peace has also been apparent in her work. A long and fruitful relationship with the University of Bradford emerged from this concern.

In the late 1960s the Society of Friends (Quakers) were seriously discussing the establishment of academic studies into international conflict and its resolution. A number of universities were approached; none of them considered the idea to be viable. But the newly established University of Bradford had prominent Quakers as its Pro-Vice-Chancellor and its Chair of Finance who were willing to take discussions further.

The first Vice-Chancellor of the University of Bradford, Professor Ted Edwards, was a dynamic and fiery Welshman of strong left-wing views. He and the Pro-Vice-Chancellor, Dr Robert McKinlay, agreed to try to establish a Chair in Peace Studies. Half the estimated cost of £150,000 would be raised by the Society of Friends and half by the University. Robert McKinlay estimated that three years would be needed to raise the necessary £75,000 from Friends and interested people. He was still unsure about the reaction of the University's governing body, the Senate, to such a proposal. Scientists, engineers and technicians are not known to be overly welcoming to high-flown theoretical studies. In the event, Senate not only passed but welcomed the proposal and, more important, approved the funds.

Now it was over to the Society of Friends. Sponsors were readily found, and in March 1972 Robert McKinlay organised a high-level press conference with Cardinal Heenan, James Cameron, the war correspondent, and Arthur Hewlett, Chairman of the Friends Peace and International Relations Committee.

The response, said Robert McKinlay, was amazing. Money poured in. In ten weeks he had secured the necessary £75,000, even without the support of major Quaker Trusts such as Rowntree and Cadbury. Many people had been moved by the appeal and sent small amounts, as much as they could afford. Harry Wheatcroft, the internationally famous rose-grower, sent five dozen Peace roses to plant near the new department. Josefina, who had seen the publicity and been deeply moved by the proposal, sent her sculpture *Reunion* as a gift.

The University suggested that the name of the piece be changed to *Reconciliation*, to link it more closely with the aims of the new department and had it cast in bronze. Josefina, too, began to see more profound connotations for her embracing couple, as her poem, quoted at the beginning of this chapter, suggests. The embrace could be seen as reconciliation between individuals or warring nations, brought together at last, and this meaning has imbued the image with great significance in subsequent years.

The Department of Peace Studies has flourished since its establishment in 1973 with Adam Curle from Harvard University as its first professor. Despite many reservations from critics of the scheme, it has proved to be a worthwhile and influential aspect of the University's work. 'The irony was,' said Robert McKinlay, 'that they were a very aggressive lot. Ideals and opinions were deeply felt and fiercely defended.'

But this was all in the future, and Josefina's return to Cumbria in 1970 as her main base inevitably made her focus more on activities nearby so that she could continue to care for Delmar. He was often highly dictatorial in his treatment of her, to the extent that visitors were shocked. One friend left a note in the Visitors' Book referring to Josefina as 'little Cinders'. Her best source of freedom was her white MGB which allowed her to keep all her different projects going.

Despite Delmar's peremptory attitudes, there was still much to share. For several years Delmar had been working on his book about the inter-relationship between art, nature and religion, and Josefina spent many hours working with him on the manuscript. Provisionally titled 'Jacob's Ladder', the book was written in Delmar's highly intellectual, rather cramped style, and dealt with themes that Delmar had pondered over many years regarding the way that religion and art reflect each other, and how Christian faith is deeply imbedded in the artistic process. He discussed such themes as the place of nature in art, the present predicament of art and religion, and the imaginative crisis facing the young. Delmar regarded the book as a series of questions that needed to be asked and he did not provide answers: 'it is for the vistas of action opened by ultimate questions that we may not least be glad, and bless life.' He painted a series of small but exquisite watercolours of Lake District mountains to illustrate the book. One of Delmar's oldest friends, Bernard Groom, shared his thoughts and was convinced that 'the full significance of your painting will be revealed when and only when the book which you are now writing shall have been duly weighed and absorbed. The two activities will complement and illustrate each other.'

Josefina edited the manuscript painstakingly three times. Delmar had a habit of typing to the very edge of the sheet in order to use every scrap of space; even a word like 'of' would be broken so that 'o' was at the end of the line and 'f' at the beginning of the next; not a state to endear the script to other readers. The process of finding a publisher had gone on for several years. Josefina had been to see a number of editors in London, including T S Eliot at Faber before he died. Delmar was determined to try all possible outlets but was not entirely hopeful about the outcome. He wrote to Josefina in his own distinctive style:

> So few in London or the world see as I see; if they did they wdnt live there. But so far only Faber have had time to READ IT (one month) & only Darton has read it with appreciation (three years!); Collins (Mrs) & Gollancz (Miss Livia) had it two days each; Macmillan, SCM, & Murray, wdnt even look at it tho 'polite'... DDlove, how good of you to help How I wish all yr help so far had borne fruit; but one cannot guess... there are a few (very few) more Publishers who do Art+Religion.

Josefina took the book to every possible publishing house but it was not accepted and still remains in manuscript. Even after Delmar's death she worked again on the script with Dr Theo Harman of the University of Durham and tried in vain to bring the artist's thoughts to a sympathetic readership.

Undoubtedly the rejection of Delmar's book was a great disappointment to them both. A proud and over-sensitive man like Delmar, used to being respected for his artistic judgements, must have felt it very deeply. Like many highly intelligent, impatient people he was unable to explain his thoughts in simple terms, and made no concessions to those who were not as well-read as himself. His paintings remain a clearer statement of his Christian faith. Even so, at the age of seventy-four, he still had work to do, although he was conscious that time was becoming short. He wrote to Josefina in his usual clipped style that 'so fast the years hv flown; so many of our age group have gone now... I wd so like to finish what I can do in the very few years to wch we now hurry... I must not give way but feel better fr saying it...'

Once back permanently at The Bield, and resigned to living and working there, Josefina made efforts to make the house more comfortable. She improved her studio enormously by the serendipitous find of a Gothic shop window which was being loaded onto a skip in Ambleside. It had been the frontage to a hairdresser's, and Josefina commandeered it without hesitation. It made a handsome addition to the house.

Although looking after Delmar took up more and more time, she did manage to make some sculptures. One of her more unusual pieces during this period was the group of Standing Stones she placed in the garden of The Bield. The stones were in fact ancient stone gateposts that Josefina and Mary Burkett found while bird-watching near the tarn at Little Langdale. They had holes carved for poles to run through, a style of gate that can still be seen in parts of Cumbria, dating back to the very first enclosures and farms in the area.

Josefina carved the three stones with biblical emblems and used stained glass in the openings so that light would shine through. She described what she had done:

> Stone One: 'And God said, "Let there be light".'
> On the back are carvings in low relief of early forms of life including a jellyfish, a mammoth and an early bird.
>
> Stone Two: 'And they followed the star.'
> Three lights for the Three Wise Men, but could apply to anyone seeking enlightenment. On the back, the hands of pre-Christian seekers after God are raised, in need, towards the Stars.
>
> Stone Three: 'And the light shineth in the darkness.'
> One light only, in ruby glass – symbolic of the spear hole in Christ's side on the Cross. Through His death letting Light into the world, for all time – Past, Present, and Future. On the other side, the Vine and the chalice.

Josefina's original design for the stones saw them as the centre-piece of concentric circles of paving and flowers representing Time: BC around the stones, and AD on the perimeter. She called it the 'Time Dial' but the setting was never completed. Perhaps this was fortunate, because the stones need no further embellishment. Now weathered and lichen-covered, they make a silent and impressive statement surrounded by the grandeur of the hills. They are held in covenant to the National Trust.

Delmar was right when he wrote of his regret at the loss of friends. In August 1975, Ophelia Heaton Cooper died of a brain tumour at home in Grasmere, and the Banners lost an old and cherished friend. She was only sixty. Josefina could not bring herself to go to the funeral but Ophelia's son Julian remembers seeing her sad face as she stood at the gate of the graveyard of the church in Grasmere, her black clothes blowing in the wind.

Josefina's work for the disabled continued to engage her energies. For several years she had been designing and making prototypes of a system she called 'Track Gliding'. It was all part of her idea to allow physically handicapped children and adults to have some of the joy of movement that others took for granted. The play mat for the blind and the rickshaw racing that she was working on in the 1960s were all part of her vision.

Track gliding was an elaborate scheme using pulleys and a harness in various ways, with the harness being connected to a circular rail that went around the roof of the building. Josefina installed this in her studio at The Bield and worked hard to perfect the device, trying out different materials and fittings. One use that seemed very promising was to hoist disabled children on to the backs of ponies and to hold them securely even if the pony was restless. The harness could also be used to allow badly crippled people to stand upright and to achieve some form of movement. For very difficult cases, the harness could support a light chair to function as a swing, and Josefina gave her people colourful ribbons to draw through the air; an artist's touch to add delight.

She demonstrated her equipment at various centres including Stoke Mandeville Hospital and the Star and Garter Home for Disabled Sailors and Airmen, Richmond. She also demonstrated it at the Robin Hood Riding Centre for the Disabled at Bassenthwaite, where it successfully lifted disabled adults on to horseback and supported them as the horse moved. As a result of working here with the physically handicapped she also designed an adjustable stool to help people sit or stand unaided.

Again Josefina was committed to the ideal of able-bodied and handicapped people working together as partners, so that each could widen the perspective of the other. This continued to be not quite in line with current thinking, which stressed independence as the ultimate goal. The Consultant in Physical Medicine at Queen Mary's

Hospital, Roehampton, Mr I H M Curwen, wrote to Josefina after meeting her in December 1969 and advised her that 'I think these ideas are sound except that the need for assistance makes the child dependent on someone else, whereas independence is usually our chief aim in all activity for handicapped children. This aspect might be overcome mechanically at a later date if you find that "track gliding" is a success.' Despite this fundamental difference, he was supportive of what the track gliding system aimed to do, and added:

> It is certainly an interesting concept for handicapped children of different types. Any child whose disability limits him as regards speed of mobility from place to place misses the excitement of running about in play as other children do. If you can provide these children with a method of locomotion which will satisfy their desire for the sensation of speed alone, I think you will give them great pleasure and introduce them to a number of new sensations.

Josefina patented her track gliding device and had every hope that it would be adopted for use by hospitals and charities. She entered it for the 1975 Inventaway Competition sponsored by the Cognitive Research Trust, founded by Edward de Bono, and won an award of £200. Her hopes of getting her invention manufactured for use must have risen when she received a letter asking her to meet Sven Nordberg of the Perstop Foundation at the Inventaway Luncheon held at the Inn on the Park on 14 August that year: 'Mr Nordberg was particularly interested and I might say impressed, not only with your invention, but with the way it has been put into use,' wrote the Deputy Director, Edna Copley. Years of dedicated effort had gone into this invention, but it was not to be a commercial success. Josefina suffered the fate of many British inventors who worked away with good ideas and few resources: she was ignored.

Josefina is listed as an inventor in *Mothers and Daughters of Invention* (1993), published by the American author Autumn Stanley, where she is credited with the invention of three aids to the handicapped: the dance carpet, the track gliding gear and the adjustable stool. Stanley quotes from Beverley Silvanovis, who wrote in the journal *The Inventor* in 1976, that the carpet and the track gliding gear were 'superb medical inventions'. Autumn Stanley saw that in the dance carpet 'the underlying principle here seems to accord with recent findings in brain physiology, the physical basis of learning, and rehabilitation theory. Josephine Banner's arriving at the idea intuitively, quite without training, is remarkable indeed.'[1] She also noted that women inventors often share many qualities with Josefina: they are only children, their obvious artistic talents are brought on by devoted parents, they attend an all-girls' school, there are other inventors in the family. Dr Alfred Coleman, an inventor himself, would have been proud of his grand-daughter.

Interest in the welfare and development of the disabled was very much at the forefront of Josefina's mind during these years, and she started to think about how they could enjoy the same sort of outdoor activities as the boys who came to Beckstones. Some time ago a party of disabled children had been brought up the Duddon Valley and met a group of senior boys from Beckstones. The boys offered to take them out for a day, and hauled them up and down hills, took them rowing, covered them in mud and generally gave them such a good time that they asked for a place of their own in the mountains. Beckstones was usually fully booked in its early years, and was not designed for wheelchairs. Besides, the legal situation did not allow a change of function to care for the disabled. There was a clear need for purpose-built accommodation for them, and in 1974 the Reverend Austen Williams asked Josefina to see what she could find.

Josefina embarked on this ambitious project with her usual enthusiasm. Because of the difficulties in finding a building in Cumbria, with all the restrictions and problems involved with National Park planning regulations, to say nothing of the cost, she decided to buy a boat. She heard that many trawlers were being decommissioned and her imagination was fired. If a boat could be found and made suitable for children in wheelchairs or on crutches, it would give them a unique experience as a holiday home. In the very early stages of the project Josefina thought that a converted ship might remain in the water, but this was soon rejected on safety grounds. Many friends tried to advise against the project, which they considered to be too chancy and lacking in solid advice from the disabled themselves.

But Josefina was determined, and Delmar was candid in his views expressed to several people that when Josefina's mind was made up, nothing would make her change direction.

The first ship to take her fancy was the Danish *Hans Eggede*, a wooden four-masted schooner moored in Rochester harbour. Although previously damaged by fire, it was still a beautiful ship. But it was too expensive for Josefina and it was sold to a wealthy American, to her great disappointment.

She went on looking at all kinds of vessels: Thames barges, sailing ships and decommissioned trawlers. Often ownership was difficult to trace but she persevered. When she heard of ships for sale at Fleetwood, she contacted the Harbour Master, and although he did his best to discourage her visit she set off in her white MG, scarf flying, and confronted a startled group of seamen and port officials in a smoke-filled pub along the harbour. Eventually she managed to convince them that her intentions were serious, and she was shown around the ships in port.

After looking at several ships she saw the *Harriet*. There was no hesitation: she said to the marine surveyor Tom Cato, 'That's the one for me!' The group of seamen standing around laughed. She had chosen the pride of Fleetwood, affectionately known by the sailors there as 'the grand old lady of the seas.' After some delays she eventually purchased the *Harriet*, using £3,000 of her own money, and the ship was then given to the Harriet Trust, established in 1978.

The *Harriet* was a rigged ketch with two masts built in Fleetwood in 1893. Made of pitch pine on oak, she was 62 feet long and 21 feet wide, and had been used as a fishing boat. The last master of the *Harriet*, Captain George Fletcher, had served heroically in the Second World War, when he sailed as bosun of the *Edwina*, one of the little ships that rescued men from the beaches of Dunkirk. He joined the crew of the *Harriet* in 1942 after being injured in that rescue, and skippered her for 32 years. When the time came to sail the *Harriet* to Millom, he was on board, along with his friend Captain Alex Mellon from Millom.

As with Beckstones, a local committee under the auspices of CAN (Combined Action Now) was set up to run the project on behalf of the Trust, with Mr Anthony Mason-Hornby, followed by Mr Roland

Woodward of Millom, as the first Chairmen. Lord Denning was President of the Council, and the Archbishop of York, the Bishop of Carlisle, the Earl of Carlisle, Baroness Masham and Lord Wells were Patrons. Later the Reverend Austen Williams and Norman Nicholson were added to the list of Patrons. There was a vast amount to do. Money had to be raised and permission granted to beach the boat on the south Cumbrian coast. It soon became clear that an additional building would be needed to provide more conventional accommodation, with the boat being used as a recreation area. At this point Josefina's University of Bradford connections became useful, because the Vice-Chancellor's son Christopher Edwards was an architect and his then wife Ayliffe was a doctor with a special interest in helping the disabled. They both became advisors to the project.

Josefina pushed on, brushing aside difficulties and solving problems. She was a dynamic force, and for some people, probably too dynamic in getting her own way. A friend remarked at the time that there was one word in our vocabulary that she did not recognise and that was 'impossible'. Every imaginative project needs someone to persuade everyone else to aim beyond their reach, no matter how much irritation they cause. Yet again, Josefina was the one to do it.

On Wednesday, 9 February 1977 the *Harriet* sailed into Millom harbour escorted by a smaller trawler in case of unexpected events. They had waited three weeks for a clear moonlit sky and a high tide to see them in. It was a hazardous journey for the old ship because the coast was known to be full of rocks and shifting sands and during the night the depth detector failed. To make matters worse, the weather deteriorated rapidly after high tide. But Captain Mellon had set the harbour buoys himself and knew every inch of the approach. He brought the grand old lady safely in, using an original plumb line, despite early morning mist. A few days later the BBC 'Look North' programme filmed the ship at its mooring and interviewed Josefina and some of the crew; very useful publicity for the project.

Eventually after many meetings and a great deal of effort, agreement was reached to beach the boat at Borwick Rails on the old ironworks site at Hodbarrow in Millom. The largest land crane in Britain and a low-loader were hired and the 64-ton *Harriet* was lifted safely on shore in November 1977, in howling wind and lashing rain. The work went on all day and into the night, finishing by the light of torches and flares. Josefina, who had been wet through since eleven in the morning, did not leave the harbour until ten at night, when the ship was safely held in wooden supports on land. That night the country was lashed by one of the greatest storms for many years, smashing many boats tied up in harbour and destroying part of Morecambe Pier. The *Harriet* had been lifted on to land just in time.

In June 1980 it was moved again to a permanent site on the edge of the Duddon Estuary where there were fine views out to sea and to the surrounding Cumbrian fells. Oystercatchers waded nearby, and flights of seabirds soared overhead. Herons stalked in the shallows of the river and on one occasion a rare egret was seen on the estuary. Bee orchids were found in the corners of the old iron works. Children confined to wheelchairs on the deck could feel surrounded by birds and the ever-changing light from huge western skies.

The local community took the project very much to its heart and fund-raising began immediately. Copeland Council and the Cumbria Tourist Board gave major grants, and arrangements were made for some of the building work to be done by the Youth Opportunities Programme and the Manpower Services Commission.

Josefina herself wrote scores of letters to trusts and charities. Very few of Josefina's extensive group of friends, all written to personally, failed to contribute. Many individuals and organisations gave useful items as well as money, and devoted their time as volunteers. Local pubs had collection boxes, scouts and guides held bazaars. Hundreds of letters bear witness to the effort that went into the project on Josefina's part.

The complexities of setting up a building suitable for children in wheelchairs were immense, with fire precautions for the old wooden boat a priority. Unexpected help came from the boat builder Tommy Myers, who was given the title Honorary Shipwright. He and a carpenter directed the work of the young helpers. He also designed and made a special motorboat, the *Tracy*, with access for disabled children to enable them to go out on fishing trips when they were staying at the Harriet.

As the Harriet scheme came successfully to fruition, the Beckstones project was coming to an end. It was hard to find appropriate and reliable people to serve as warden, since no salary was paid and the only incentive was free accommodation and the chance to walk the fells. Funding difficulties were beginning to affect the number of schools that used the facilities. The local voluntary committee considered all these problems, and with the lease on the old farmhouse about to expire after many years of successful use, no warden and few bookings, the decision was taken to allow the property to pass back to the National Trust. It was disappointing for Josefina but she felt that by that time much good had been done and that Outpost Emmaus had served as a prototype for other, similar initiatives in different parts of the country. The building itself is still used by a climbing club, so young people continue to benefit from it, and the energy expended in its renovation was not wasted.

Throughout the 1970s Josefina's work for charity and the disabled meant that often her sculpture took second place. She served as President of the Guild of Lakeland Craftsmen from 1971 to 1973, which required her to take up the cause of potters, weavers and other craft workers who were normally excluded from the exclusive circles of pure fine art. Members of the Guild at that time remember her as having lots of good ideas herself and being a dynamic figurehead, but being rather less successful in listening to the ideas of others. In particular, Josefina, who had never been without money herself, found it hard to understand that other artists and craftsmen had to earn a living from their work. Apart from actual commissions, she could afford to sculpt and cast works to be donated to appropriate locations, but not everyone was cushioned by a private income as she had been all her life.

During the first few years after her final return to Cumbria only a Virgin and Child for Blackburn Cathedral in 1974 was completed. But the placing of *Reconciliation* at the University of Bradford in 1977 was to open up a whole new phase in her career.

Reconciliation was unveiled by Nobel Peace Prize Laureate and Deputy Secretary General of the United Nations, Sean MacBride, on 4 May 1977. One of Ireland's most distinguished twentieth century figures, he flew over from New York for the occasion. On the same day Josefina was given an Honorary DLitt at a special degree ceremony which also awarded a DLitt to Sean MacBride. It was a tremendous honour and deeply valued. Recognition by an academic institution whose ideals were not only to advance learning and knowledge but 'the application of knowledge to human welfare' meant a great deal to her. There was also a certain satisfaction in knowing that after many years her unique intelligence and sensitivity had been recognised by such an august group.

The University's Public Orator, whose duties require him or her to make a witty and erudite speech in praise of the recipients of honorary degrees, noted that this was 'the first occasion... that we have paid our highest tribute to a practitioner in the visual arts.' He referred to Josefina as 'giving visual expression to some of the profoundest episodes in the Christian tradition, notably the Nativity and the Resurrection. Working in materials as ancient as marble and as modern as perspex she has, as was said once of another, touched nothing that she has not adorned.' He also spoke of 'the sense of compassion which informs her professional creativity' in her work for offenders and the disabled, and he concluded, 'She has brought the full force of her talents and concerns to bear on the making of *Reunion*, which will grace our campus in perpetuity.'

Curiously enough, the sculpture, although placed in a square adjacent to the Student's Union and very much in the centre of student life, has never been vandalised; no red noses, no funny hats, no graffiti.

Josefina's connection with the University of Bradford continued and strengthened. She donated several of Delmar's paintings to the University. When Professor Edwards died, she made a sculpture of white peace doves against a rose marble background called *After the Storm* and gave it to the University as a memorial to him, in recognition of his contribution to Peace Studies. Josefina had liked his trenchant style and admired his ability to get things done; he admired her ability to get other people to do things for her! *After the Storm* was placed in the new extension to the Library on 15 May 1998 and the University sent a chauffeur-driven car to collect Josefina and Robert McKinlay for the celebratory event.

The Department of Peace Studies now has more than 250 students from all over the world, and with the publicity surrounding *Reconciliation*, and her own personal qualities, Josefina undoubtedly made her contribution to its success.

CHAPTER EIGHT

A New Beginning

THE 1980s

To me the mysteries of life are important – they are
God's Poetry... we hear the sound and like it, but don't
know what it means.

J de V

Josefina and Delmar had been married for fifty years on 28 April 1980. There was no special celebration, but friends sent cards, flowers and gifts. A sense of quiet fulfilment was felt by them both. They had endured – 'we felt that we had made it – a great satisfaction,' said Josefina.

The day after their anniversary their old friends Norman and Yvonne Nicholson called to see them. It was to be one of Yvonne's last visits as she was terminally ill, and Norman, who had suffered from tuberculosis as a child and had always been delicate, confounded all expectations by outliving her, and caring for her to the end. Delmar and Josefina too were feeling old. They made their wills just before their anniversary, and neither was in good health. The next two years saw Delmar becoming even more demanding as he sat in a chair wrapped in crochet rugs, suffering badly from arthritis and rheumatism, needing constant attendance from Josefina. His sight was failing and his last paintings are blurred and indistinct, very different from the exact portrayals of rock and sky that characterised his best work.

Other people still found help and inspiration from Josefina's presence, even in unexpected ways. In the spring of 1980 Sheona

Lodge's daughter Fiona was very ill in Wraysholme after receiving chemotherapy for cancer. Josefina, who although much older was one of Fiona's few close friends, came to dance for her, and Fiona's sister Anne Mathieson remembers that 'it was a lovely way to beguile a young woman at death's door. It was Josefina's own idea and she was certain, she said, that Fiona would be pleased to have her dance and indeed she was. It helped us all to have the creative spirit of Josefina's dancing as a beacon in that dark night.' And then, said Anne, 'she breezed away – more action than words.'

At this time, Josefina came to depend on the practical assistance of Mrs Ann Taylforth. Ann and her family needed somewhere to live and they moved into High Bield Cottage behind the main house in July 1981. Ann was able to help at The Bield and to carry on with other work as well. She continued to look after Josefina for the next twenty years. Her friendship and help were indispensable and greatly valued. Even in her responses to Josefina's sculpture, Ann's spoken approval, or her eloquent silences, were well understood.

As well as caring for Delmar, Josefina was also occupied with final details for the opening of the Harriet Trust Outdoor Centre. She wanted her great supporter, Lord Denning, to be present, but he was not well enough to travel, and although the date was put forward by several months he was still unable to attend. Finally, on 4 May 1983, the opening ceremony was performed by the Chairman of Millom Council, Councillor Bessie Schiff. Josefina's old friend Austen Williams travelled up from St Martin in the Fields to Millom with his wife Daphne to see the project come to fruition. With the Reverend Joe Isaac of Millom he blessed the tiny chapel, curtained off with a fishing net, that had been made in the prow of the boat. After touring the team house, the warden's quarters and the boat, the visitors had a fine northern tea in the Palladium in Millom. 'It was a totally happy moment,' remembered Austen Williams, 'with a great sense of achievement.' He was then Chaplain to the Queen, and cut a fine figure standing on the deck in his special scarlet cassock.

Now equipped with two dormitories, a warden's house, ramps and every facility for simple holiday accommodation for the disabled, the *Harriet* took in its first children in 1983, offering 'Maximum Opportunities for Independence With Safety' according to the publicity leaflet. Christopher and Barbara Powell were the first wardens, and in the next few years they welcomed children and their helpers from all over Britain and abroad. 'It seems like a dream,' said Josefina at the opening ceremony, but it was no dream. It was the product of a huge effort and great inspiration to see it through. Not surprisingly, after the opening Josefina's health began to decline; she had pushed herself to the limit in order to see the Harriet Trust successfully launched.

Delmar, too, had been gradually growing weaker for several months. Hugh Ellison saw him for the last time as he lay in bed upstairs at The Bield and Delmar remarked to him, 'the veil is very thin.' And so it was, but he had failed to notice that Josefina was also ill. She had been unconscious for two days when she was found by a neighbour, but refused to leave The Bield until arrangements had been made for Delmar to be cared for at Balla Wray, a nursing home near Hawkshead, and all her own appointments had been cancelled. Only then would she agree to go to Lancaster Royal Infirmary where she was immediately rushed into surgery and intensive care with a perforated ulcer.

Once removed from his familiar surroundings Delmar quickly and quietly faded away. Leslie Randell was one of the last to visit him, and as Delmar listened to Leslie reading him his favourite Wordsworth poems, he was peaceful. Mary Burkett came too and was deeply moved when Delmar said to her about his wife, 'She's a saint. She's an angel. She's the most wonderful woman in the world.' Ann Taylforth was with him when he died in his sleep on 8 November 1983 at the age of 87, without seeing Josefina again. After two operations she was fighting for her life in hospital and did not recover for many months.

Ann Taylforth arranged for Delmar's funeral at Holy Trinity Church, Chapel Stile, Great Langdale, on 12 November. Canon Eric Rothwell conducted the service and the Reverend Raymond Heawood, Vicar of Langdale, led the committal in the cemetery. The church was full. Three weeks later, when Josefina emerged from intensive care, she was told of Delmar's death by a Methodist chaplain in the hospital, but it did not come as a surprise. In due course she carved a tombstone for him with the epitaph:

> Delmar Banner – (1896–1983)
> Painter, writer, lay Preacher,
> Loved many friends and the Fells –
> He'd a sweet smile.

To the outsider this epitaph may seem strangely distant for someone who had been part of her life for over fifty-three years, but perhaps it focuses on what was shared in this unusual marriage and the qualities Josefina admired to the end. Josefina knew that conventional platitudes would in no way sum up this creative and unusual man.

After Delmar's death, Josefina received scores of letters from people whose lives had been enriched by their visits to The Bield. There is no doubt that the atmosphere of artistic endeavour, majestic surroundings and the closeness of God in the lives of Josefina and Delmar had a profound effect on everyone who had been there. Many wrote about the special sense of peace they experienced during their visits. Some had stayed at High Bield Cottage for holidays with their families and remembered vividly the impression that Delmar had made on them, and how they admired his paintings. As they wrote, many were looking at his visionary mountain views hung on their own walls. Prayers were said in many churches in the UK and abroad; Holy Trinity Church in Tulsa, Oklahoma, which held one of Josefina's sculptures, said prayers for them both on the Sunday after his death.

There were letters from those who had received practical help from the Banners, including the local farmer whose severe fine for allowing sheep to stray on the road was paid for him. Messages came also from the young men and women who had been encouraged to find their true paths in life, sometimes against the wishes of their parents. Despite Delmar's personal austerity he had been generous to many, and this was not forgotten.

Josefina made a slow recovery from her operations (peritonitis followed the perforated ulcer), with extended stays in convalescent homes, and was not ready to return to Little Langdale until February 1984. She stayed with Ann in Bield Cottage and never lived in The Bield again. As she gradually regained her strength, supported by Ann, Josefina was facing the problem of what to do with her own future. Living at The Bield was no longer practical; the house was too large and she did not want to live there on her own. That aspect of her life was over. But would her health allow a new phase to open up?

Before she sold The Bield and Bield Cottage, arrangements had to be made to house Delmar's collection of paintings and her own large sculptures. Their two studios were full of work. Not only that, if she were to move to a smaller house, much of the heavy antique furniture that had suited the old farmhouse would have to be disposed of, along with a great deal of china and linen. Most of the valuable antiques were simply given away to friends. Delmar's paintings were donated to provincial galleries, the Victoria and Albert Museum, and the University of Bradford. The Abbot Hall Museum in Kendal, then under the Curatorship of Mary Burkett, accepted work by them both.

Delmar and Josefina had held firm views about the sale of Lake District properties to outsiders and Josefina decided to sell The Bield to local people whose family had been there for generations. High Bield Cottage was sold to Ann Taylforth's sister and brother-in-law to ensure that Ann could continue to live there at a low rent. Disappointingly, her hope that The Bield would be a family house once more did not come to pass and it is now used for very expensive holiday lets.

Josefina had always liked Ambleside and had many friends there. Then, as now, the town contained an interesting group of artists, musicians and retired professional people who made up a stimulating social circle. Much of this revolved around Wraysholme, the large house in Millans Park owned by Oliver and Sheona Lodge, Frank and Edwina Saunders' house Ashley Green, and Muriel Cuppage's fine old farmhouse at Skelwith Bridge. When Josefina bought a small terraced cottage, 4 Fair View Terrace on Peggy Hill above the town, in the late spring of 1984, she fitted snugly into the house, but also into a group of supportive and sympathetic friends.

Two or three years passed before she felt quite liberated, but eventually the weight of caring for Delmar fell away and she embarked on a happy time when friends, shops and the Health Centre were all within easy reach and the inspiration to sculpt returned. Just down the steep hill from her cottage was an old stone wash house, probably originally a shepherd's lodge, and in 1985 she bought this to use as a studio. As with The Bield, there was a formal blessing for the Old Wash House: on 28 October 1986 the Reverend Michael Irving came to bless the house and the work within.

Now Josefina felt that she was free. She could do just as she liked. And what she liked were often the things that Delmar had hated: dancing, evenings out, dinner parties with friends, going to concerts, writing poetry, spending money. She had time to enjoy clothes and to make elaborate hats for friends, something she used to do for her mother many years before. Professor Margaret Macpherson ran a writing circle for a group that met mainly at Wraysholme, and Josefina occasionally joined in. She started to write a series of poems that would later be set to music for her to dance to. Margaret Macpherson observed perceptively about Josefina's love poetry that rather unusually the focus was on the feelings of the loved one, rather than the person who loved.

She had lost contact with her Brazilian relatives and now she wrote to them again. When Josefina had money, she spent it, and one of the first things she did was to send an air ticket to her cousin Lucilia Vasconcellos d'Alincourt Fonseca in Brazil to enable her to visit England. Lucilia's is the first signature in Josefina's new Visitors' Book for Fair View Terrace, dated July 1984.

Gradually Josefina's physical strength and her artistic inspiration as a sculptor returned. Her assistant Shaun Williamson completed Delmar's memorial, the limestone carving of *Valiant for Truth*, based on John Bunyan's *Pilgrim's Progress*, and it was placed at the YMCA Outdoor Centre on Windermere. Delmar had always said that he wanted this as his memorial, but Josefina had left it incomplete, not wanting to finish it before he died. It is a classical male torso, arms upraised, strong but simple. The plaque on the base explains how Valiant for Truth crosses the river to heaven at the end of life's journey, and raises his arms to shield his eyes from the glory ahead. It also expresses Josefina's hope that the sculpture would be 'in a place where young people meet, as an encouragement and inspiration for them to seek for truth in their lives.'

Recognition for all her years of work for approved-school boys and the disabled came at the end of 1984 when she received word that she was to be made an MBE 'for services to the community in Cumbria', and this was announced in the New Year's Honours list. Accompanied by Ann Taylforth and Ann's sister-in-law Sheila Myers,

Josefina went to receive her award at Buckingham Palace on a cold crisp March day, when a sprinkling of snow had dusted the Palace courtyard white. She wore a full-length fitted black suit and a wide-brimmed black hat with a pale mauve ostrich feather and looked every bit the successful woman of her time.

There were still some clouds on the horizon, however, and the two adopted sons continued to be a concern. Brian had been seriously injured in a car accident while filming in Africa, and on returning to England he was unable to deal with the pressures of conventional life. For thirteen years he lived rough on the streets of London and for most of that time Josefina did not know where he was. Then one day her old friend Eva Castle saw Brian sitting on a bench outside a pub in Chelsea and brought him to her flat. Over a period of months she and Josefina kept in touch and Brian decided to return to Cumbria where Josefina shouldered the considerable burden of looking after him.

Josefina felt that Brian had been 'punished by life' and she never forgot the distressing circumstances of his early years in London before he and Billy came to live at The Bield. She wrote this poem about their relationship at that time:

> Certainly it seemed that I had known you ages,
> read and re-read you like a well known book –
> but yesterday, I found some uncut pages,
> that all my care had chanced to overlook.
> I found a way that led me to a tree,
> shading an altar dedicated to God,
> a broken toy, a small Gethsemene –
> and lonely paths, that no man ever trod.

For Josefina, this was a heart-breaking time. She felt that she couldn't abandon him; he had been abandoned by other women in his life and she must stay with him now. Ambleside was a very conservative community and Josefina was well known. She showed not only loyalty but great courage and generosity in supporting Brian through many difficult years. Bill, too, had not had an easy life, lurching from one trouble to another. He died of cancer in the spring of 1986 and was buried beside Delmar in the churchyard at Chapel

Stile. He left three children from his first marriage and two from his second, and these grandchildren and in turn their children have brought great joy to Josefina.

Unexpectedly, the end of 1986 saw Josefina unable to do much work at all, because rushing up the stairs in her cottage she fell and broke her right wrist. This was badly set by a student nurse in the local hospital and caused her weeks of pain until finally she managed to see a surgeon at Lancaster Royal Infirmary who urgently reset the bone. Being Josefina, she taught herself to write with her left hand and wrote several poems while she was recovering.

In many of her projects Josefina was strong and confident, ready to push ahead when others found excuses not to bother. Yet there was still an unanswered longing to be loved, not as an inspiration or as an emblem but as a woman. She sought spiritual help from Dr Martin Israel in London, a source of enlightenment to many people, and found that he understood her implicitly. He accepted her need to care for others and advised her to 'use every moment helping other people to see God working his way in your life. This is also the only way to personal fulfilment.' Josefina sculpted his head bent over in prayer and began a long-lasting friendship with him.

His book *Precarious Living: The Path to Life* was a revelation to her, dealing as it did with childhood perceptions that she too had experienced and not quite understood: a profound consciousness of evil, a mystic understanding, and a deep love of nature. Martin Israel wrote:

> I knew, early in my life, the joy of identification with nature in her many forms: the countryside with its changing pattern of beauty, from spring blossoms to the yellow summer grassland, the flowers of the field, the autumn tints of brown and red, and the sharp cleansing winter barrenness when all was desolate and yet full of that true beauty that comes of a shriven landscape. In nature there is not merely the outer form, but also an inner realm that palpitates with psychic and spiritual life. To him who can observe there is nothing empty save the emptiness of a vapid, selfish human being intent only on himself and his needs.[1]

No wonder that Josefina felt they were in perfect accord. Martin Israel also had experienced a highly sensitive childhood: 'I was in perpetual communion with my surroundings and with a world far greater than my physical surroundings. Each object, each flower, the sky and the atmosphere were bathed in a supersensual radiance.'[2] His moment of vision at the age of sixteen, when he experienced 'the silent music of eternity,'[3] was immediately recognised by Josefina as a moment she, too, had felt as a child.

He came to visit her in Ambleside and advised her never to leave there: 'it is your milieu and the inspiration comes flowing from the Lake District.' Josefina became a huge admirer of the man and his work. Her sculpture of him is full of passionate regard. It was said about Stanley Spencer that painting people was his way of loving them. For Josefina, moulding the heads of those she loved was an emotional as well as an artistic experience; distanced to some extent, but intense. She sent him poems and sculptures but as a very busy man, much in demand for his special skills as healer of damaged minds and bodies, he found it difficult to respond to her depth of feeling. Nevertheless he constantly encouraged her in her work: 'creativity is the essence of life, and its service to others the greatest gift,' he wrote to her in 1988.

Twenty years earlier, Josefina had written in her contribution to *They Became Christians*:

> I believe now that one has to go through all this… The growing point of the spirit, all through life… sensitive enough to feel sorrow or anxiety, need, anguish, hope, exploration, fear and faith – the growing point that, unless it has the courage and compassion to remain sensitive, will cease to be a living tendril and harden to dead wood.[4]

It was prophetic in the sense that Josefina must have known that she would always be a seeker, yet in the same essay she wrote that she was certain 'that the love of God is a bridge upon which to traverse the unknown.' So she embarked on a new life, independent, but not invulnerable.

She found a new friend in Jonathan Wordsworth, an Oxford academic and a Trustee of the Wordsworth Trust at Dove Cottage. In clearing The Bield Josefina had given some of Delmar's paintings to the Trust, along with a beautiful Ruskin drawing of Rome and some books, and Jonathan had handled the negotiations. Their friendship strengthened, although Jonathan, who was much younger than Josefina, had a busy life and a family elsewhere. They admired each other; she admired his intellect and sensitivity to poetry, and he admired her artistic understanding. He was a welcome guest at Fair View Terrace and Josefina enjoyed going to lectures at the Wordsworth Trust in Grasmere. He and Sheona Lodge replaced Delmar as trusted critics of her work.

Jonathan was not alone in his attraction to Josefina. Many younger men were drawn to her and she to them, but all remained in awe of someone who had come so far and done so much. Perhaps Josefina seemed to demand an intensity of response that few people could answer. Perhaps the love that she and Delmar had achieved, so painfully, was, in fact, never going to be superceded. Much of her sculpture at this time reveals the kind of sensual longing of a younger woman. Lovers embrace, hold each other gently, touch their cheeks. The maquette *Beyond Time* is almost erotic in the closeness of the embrace. Her poetry is full of desire suffused with religious imagery, but it is resigned to failure. This short poem written at the time has some of the pent-up emotion of Emily Dickinson in the feelings it expresses:

> I buried Love, beneath the stone
> that lies across my hearth –
> but in the morning, all alone,
> I heard a passing laugh.
>
> I buried Love, below the gate,
> that leads to Carefree Lane,
> a waste of time – it was my fate
> to hear him laugh again.
>
> I buried Love, below a bed
> of Herbs, when night was black.
> The plants all flowered, and I fled –
> for Love was laughing back.

She still felt herself to be a passionate and unsatisfied woman, yet men saw her as a kind of icon. Few who met her were untouched by her transcendent qualities. As she always had done, Josefina was imbuing her work, both poetry and sculpture, with a heartfelt emotion that reached out vividly to those who encountered it. As a seventeen year old she had discovered a hero to worship in Pliny the Younger, and in a strange way she never met anyone who eclipsed his image. Several of her young friends were homosexual, a continuation of a pattern of attraction that endured throughout her life.

Josefina managed to retain a youthful appearance and was as slim and delicate as a young girl. She dressed in full-length, feminine skirts and was always distinctive. Few of her friends had ever seen her dancing and they were amazed that a woman in her eighties could still be so creative and so physically agile. On one occasion fellow sculptor Meryll Evans arrived at Josefina's cottage to continue working on a portrait head she was making of her friend and was taken aback to find herself settled in a corner of the ground-floor living room while Josefina danced for her. She made costumes and devised whole programmes of dance, often weaving her own poetry into the music. These became more and more elaborate until in 1990 Border Television filmed her dancing at Wraysholme, accompanied by the young pianist and composer Geoffrey Brown (later known as Geoffrey Chacaro).

Geoffrey had been awarded a scholarship to study music in Brazil and he and Josefina found a great deal in common. The fact that there was nearly fifty years difference in age between them was of no importance. She made a cast of his hands and did a fine sketch of him in 1988, rediscovering yet another skill that had lain fallow for many years. While Delmar was alive she did very little painting or sketching, but now she was able to enjoy this, as she had while sketching fellow students in the 1920s. She started to paint in oils, which was easy to do in a small space and gave relief from strenuous physical work on large sculptures. In contrast to the fluidity of her sculpture, the paintings are often stiff and diagrammatic, and cannot be considered to be entirely successful. She also planned and gave a whole evening programme of dance, poetry and music at Rydal Hall for her friends and guests. Josefina did not look her age and she was blooming in the new creative world that had opened for her. Some friends felt embarrassed by an elderly woman dancing with such obvious emotional commitment, and thought privately that she was making an exhibition of herself. Others admired her courage to do just what she wanted in old age.

But there was still a sense of responsibility towards Delmar and their shared artistic life. Josefina was able to arrange for a third joint exhibition of her and Delmar's work; a commemoration of their achievement together. This was managed by Bradford Art Galleries and Museums in collaboration with the University of Bradford, with the exhibition held in Cartwright Hall, Bradford and in the University from October to December 1987, and subsequently at Cliffe Castle in Keighley, Yorkshire. The exhibition ended at Abbot Hall in Kendal, from March to April 1988, when over 200 people attended the launch by the popular BBC broadcaster Brian Redhead.

Delmar's exhibition of paintings was entitled 'Call to the Fells' and consisted of a variety of his life's work, including major oil paintings, watercolours, portraits and drawings. His painting desk and palette were also displayed. The catalogue quoted Delmar's words, 'the longer we live in the effort to paint, or to understand whatever life offers to our imagination, the more deeply do we see that true art is a confession, a belief, a praise.' As a retrospective exhibition it revealed clearly what a serious painter Delmar had been, never deviating from his own high principles regarding his art.

Josefina's part of the exhibition, with the title 'Perchance to Dream', displayed only 19 works, but they covered a long career, from *Well of Peace* made in 1920 to *Priere* in 1987. The six works completed in 1987 indicate that her inspiration was returning after some difficult and painful years. She also displayed some of her poems that related to the sculptures, creating an undeniably moving atmosphere. Freed of Delmar's more academic criticism, Josefina's work was becoming much more emotional in tenor; too sentimental in the view of many observers. The practical difficulties of stone carving meant that increasingly she was modelling instead of carving, and this led to a softening of her style. The sculptor Fenwick Lawson, who works in wood, feels that 'it is too easy to be seduced by what you look at in modelling – a gesture of occupying the same space. Your knowledge is expressed in that moment. But carving doesn't allow that to happen. Months and even years can pass, and the process is informed by a stream of impressions.'

There is no doubt that Delmar's rigorous self-criticism had also influenced Josefina, and much of her work was now beginning to look over-decorative and weak; too much dominated by the concept of an idealised human figure from which she was unable to break free. That said, her ultimate rejection of anything that displeased her was 'Delmar would have hated it,' so his judgemental presence was never far away.

Having made all the complicated arrangements for these exhibitions, Josefina then had an unexpected invitation to visit Brazil once more. She was asked to join the celebrations for the Centenary of the founding of the Republic of Brazil in Rio de Janiero in November 1987. It was a chance to see her much-loved cousin Lucilia again and all the other Brazilian relatives after a separation of many years, and she did not hesitate to go. Lucilia accompanied her to the ceremony in front of the equestrian statue to Marechal Deodoro da Fonseca, their great uncle. Josefina joined the dignitaries for the event and was celebrated herself as a distinguished guest.

But back in England various pressures were beginning to appear, anxieties about finances and her own health. In the summer of 1988 she decided to sell her much-loved cottage and move to a flat and studio in Isel Hall near Cockermouth, where she had previously stayed as a guest. Isel was now owned by her friend Mary Burkett who was anxious for the large and ancient house to be shared by creative people. Much of Josefina's capital from selling the cottage was given away; the cautious voice of the bank manager ignored. Delmar had always carefully managed their finances, and at no time in her life had Josefina had to worry about day to day expenditure. She had never worked, not even as a tutor to art students. It made her happy to help others, and she was generous without stopping to count the cost. Loyalty to Brian and to Bill's family was always important. She wanted Brian to be independent so she bought him a caravan. But she was herself becoming very vulnerable in not having a home of her own, and not protecting the funds that she had.

Leaving her cottage was a serious wrench and the move did not go smoothly. In order to save money, friends brought her belongings to Isel on an open truck. One of the bags blew away and Josefina's manuscript music, of her own compositions, was scattered to the four winds. Fortunately a party of walkers came across most of the papers and, realising that they were of value, gathered them up and managed to return them to her.

At Isel Josefina installed a garden table and bright yellow parasol in the flat to off-set the grey stone walls. Although she lived at Isel free of charge she invested a considerable sum of money in modernising the rooms, turning the game larder into a bathroom and the coal bunker into a kitchen. The work was done by trusted builders from Langdale, but bringing workmen from so far away added to the costs. Like many old buildings Isel was difficult to heat and Josefina was not now quite so impervious to cold conditions as she used to be when she sculpted outside at The Bield. She stayed at Isel off and on for the next year and a half, but was never entirely settled there.

While at Isel Josefina was commissioned by Carlisle Cathedral to sculpt figures for the alcoves high in the end wall of the Fratery and she embarked on a passionate scheme called *Childline to God*, which featured a life-sized Christ, supported by two angels, gathering to him abused and injured children. These figures were first sketched on the walls of the large Elizabethan kitchen at Isel so that a group from Carlisle Cathedral could see them. They approved, but preferred to call the sculptures *The Good Shepherd* instead of *Childline to God*. Josefina was angry and disappointed about this as she wanted to make a hard-hitting moral statement with the sculptures. They were completed and installed in 1990, and shortly afterwards on 3 May 1991 Josefina had the honour of showing them to the Queen and Prince Philip when they visited Carlisle Cathedral on the occasion of the 450th anniversary of the foundation of the Dean and Chapter of Carlisle. Some years later, when a head and shoulders of the Jesus figure from *Childline to God* was exhibited in Manchester Cathedral, together with photographs of the children, Carlisle Cathedral agreed to revert to the original title.

The distance between Ambleside and Cockermouth had not seemed very great to Josefina when she was still driving, but her last car, the white MGB, had been sold. Without a car at Isel she began to feel rather isolated, despite the attractions of living in such an historic house with a beautiful, tranquil garden which she loved. She started to paint once more, enjoying the freedom to use colour – 'a special treat'. Two of these oil paintings, 'Petals Falling, Isel' and

'June Evening, Ill Bell', were exhibited in the 'Art in the Garden' Exhibition in Kendal a few years later.

Still, she had many visitors and arranged for sessions of poetry and music to which she invited her friends. Geoffrey Brown gave a recital at Isel in October. For Christmas, she devised a *son et lumière* called 'The Seeds of Time', a retelling of the birth of Christ, with references to the history of Isel Hall, although this was never performed. She found the ancient house and garden endlessly fascinating, and wrote that 'living at Isel Hall gave me some insight into the inherent power of its strength and age. Nature's moods were intensified by the supremacy of the site and the double curve of the Derwent. Swallows and many birds come to nest, and the gardens breathe sweet contentment.'

But she had enjoyed living in Ambleside, and she particularly missed her close friend Sheona Lodge, who was now a widow after the death of her husband Oliver in December 1987. After the winter of 1988–89 Josefina decided to turn her Ambleside studio, the Old Wash House, into a tiny living space and to return to Peggy Hill, just across the road from the cottage she had previously owned.

The Old Wash House (also known by Josefina as *La Vielle Blanchisserie* or Ye Olde Wasshe House) consisted of only one room, and Josefina built on a small bathroom. Her bed was a kind of bunk used as a settee by day, and the kitchen was in the corner where the copper and chimney used to be. Outside the studio a terrace hung high above Stock Ghyll, the rushing stream that flows through Ambleside, under the quaint Bridge House where Schwitters used to sell his paintings, and on to join the River Rothay and Lake Windermere. Josefina again had to restrict her possessions but she found great joy in her cosy house and the sunny terrace which she filled full of plants. Later her blacksmith Stephen Stalker made metal trellises to support wisteria and clematis and to give more privacy. It was tiny, but by the late summer of 1989 she was happy there, perched above the stream, surrounded by flowers, with birds flying in and out of the open door. Jonathan Wordsworth had called it 'a reassuring place to work' when he first saw it in 1985, and so it proved to be.

Inside, the studio was packed with neatly stored possessions, usually folded away into wicker baskets or carefully placed on shelves along the walls. There was even space for a grand piano. Here Josefina sculpted, played the piano, composed, entertained with flair, and wrote plays and poetry. She was busy with her work, her causes and her good friends. Even her grocer came under her the spell, as her poem about cheese, 'Second Thoughts (Josefina to her Grocer)', reveals:

> 'Derek! – Will you tell me please,
> What's the name of that Grotty Old Cheese?'
> Falling back, as though he'd been shot, he
> Wildly exclaimed, 'You must be dotty! –
> It's the greatest Treasure of all my Collection,
> Mature, Majestic, beyond perfection.'
> 'I see,' said I, 'I'll hide my fears,
> And have some. On a fork I'll spike it,
> And if it comes running home in tears,
> You'll know I didn't really like it.'

> *Envoi*

> From age to age – it suits me fine –
> Fromage Romantique, food divine!
> O, praise it best on bended knees.
> Derek responded kindly, 'Quite –
> It's always nice to know I'm right.'

What grocer could resist a customer like that? Even her bank manager wrote thanking her for a 'poetic letter'.

But unforeseen events could still disturb her equilibrium. The rushing stream beneath the studio that gave her so much pleasure could also be a threat. Torrential rain and an overflowing beck washed away part of the retaining wall that supported the Wash House, and repairs were very costly. Josefina had to find over £5,000 for the work, as her insurance company was not willing to cover the damage.

Meanwhile, she had started working on a major creation, a statue of *St Michael*. Standing proud and heraldic in the centre of the studio, it took up most of the space, and Josefina wrote on her 1990 Christmas card: 'I'm starting on a new St Michael (7ft tall with its base) and enjoying the effort... but I don't seem to concentrate on anything else – burning saucepans and trying to swallow pills with their plastic covers on. Ah well – en avant – and Ann helps to keep me civilised.'

The message was energetic but the short poem on the card, 'A Sculptor Remembers', indicated some regrets about the way her work was being received:

> Jesus-dear Infant-mine I suppose, by now?
> Your form I've fashioned, nine times...
> Last year, under a bough of
> Christmas Tree's dark shade, they placed you;
> none could see the sleeping face I'd made
> with so much love and courtesy...
> Jesus – dear Infant – mine-or I Yours?
> I'm shadowed too-forgetting everything
> O Child divine, excepting You.

St Michael would not be destined to languish in the shade. Worked first in plaster and then cast in bronze, with dramatic metal jaws framing the saint as he struggles with the dragon of evil, the sculpture has been one of Josefina's most admired works. Stephen Stalker made the jaws from welded steel. First exhibited in Manchester Cathedral in 1991, it now has a permanent position in Cartmel Priory where it is seen by thousands of visitors every year.

While she was working on *St Michael* at the Wash House, Josefina was visited by Sir Harry Secombe on 31 October 1990 and filmed for the ITV programme 'Highway', which was broadcast from Kendal and South Lakeland shortly afterwards. It included a shot of Josefina's major work *The Family of Man* in Kendal Parish Church. This sculpture shows children from different races gathered round Mary and the Christ Child: African, Chinese and European. Josefina presented the group huddled under a blanket as in a contemporary refugee camp in the Middle East. The programme generated a great deal of correspondence as viewers wanted to know more about this inspirational woman, who was also briefly shown dancing with a parasol in Wraysholme. Josefina was on the way to becoming a national figure once more, the first time since the 1960s she had been recognised in this way.

CHAPTER NINE

International Acclaim

THE 1990S

From the first I have been a simple communicator using plain form as Wordsworth used plain words... but over the years, mystery has increased, like changes of weather over the Fells.

J de V

At a time when most people would be content to rest after a lifetime's achievements, Josefina was rising to new challenges and welcoming new adventures. She spurred on her friends and supporters, often exhausting them and aggravating them but always proving fun to be with. As well as continuing to support her many charities she was still hard at work as a sculptor.

Inevitably the decade would see the deaths of many close friends: Norman Nicholson had already died in 1987; Sheona Lodge died in 1997 and Lord Denning in 1999. But Josefina's ability to inspire and comfort young people as well as her own generation meant that many new friendships emerged, at home and abroad.

Even in great old age Josefina continued to inspire and encourage. She recognised the qualities that made every individual special and drew them into focus. When she found out that sculptor Meryll Evans had been a champion fencer, she wrote urging her to bring that energy into her sculpture. She encouraged Shaun Williamson to pursue his individual style of sculpture and to persevere in his work, not always easy, in training young unemployed boys in Whitehaven to carve wood and stone. Her inspiration encouraged musician Leslie Meurant to compose a number of works for piano and choir, in particular his 'Creation' Concerto no.2. Together they devised a musical play called 'Les Livres Vivants' based on the treasures of the Armitt Trust in Ambleside, a private library which has now been housed in a fine new building in the town. It is a charming, old-fashioned fantasy, with dancing bookworms, historical figures and the Warne children (Beatrix Potter's audience) all depicted. Unfortunately the support required to stage the piece could not be found. Leslie also set poems and writings for a work to commemorate the Holocaust called 'Shoah', but although Josefina hoped for a performance at a church in Windermere 'with important people in the audience' this did not come about. Instead, a private concert for twenty-five invited guests was hosted by Anne Mathieson at Wraysholme. Leslie had a CD made with the mezzo-soprano Katherine Johnson singing to his own accompaniment.

Ideas continued to tumble from Josefina's imagination, often combining the arts in ways that took more conventional thinkers by surprise. She devised a series of television programmes that combined seven arts: music, poetry, painting, architecture, films, sculpture and living. Few people would have accepted the challenge of making such relationships between the arts or understood the concepts involved, but she was determined to carry on where Sir Kenneth Clark's influential television series on the History of Art had ended. Too daring and complex for contemporary television, the series did not progress beyond the planning stage.

But if one project failed to succeed, others came in to take its place. A commission in 1990 to produce another sculpture for the Reverend Curtis Junker at the Holy Trinity Episcopal Church in Tulsa, Oklahoma, led to the *Joyous Mary and Babe*, which delighted the congregation. The church already owned a crucifixion in oak and bronze by Josefina which stood on the altar of a side chapel. Josefina decided to deliver the new work personally in April 1991 and invited Ann Taylforth to come with her to help with arrangements.

With the sculpture encased in a sleeping bag labelled 'Dallas or Bust' they set off for Gatwick, driven by Stephen Stalker. After an encounter with suspicious customs officials who inspected the sculpture for hidden packages, and further fisticuffs with the airline who wanted *Mary* to have a seat to herself at extra cost, the sculpture was finally loaded into the hold as excess baggage. Josefina had not wrapped the work, as she thought, quite correctly as it transpired, that it might be inspected during the journey. Besides, she had always found that when transporting fragile sculpture it was best for those responsible to see what they were doing. Even so, slight damage was done in transit and Josefina had to make swift repairs on arrival in Texas.

Curt Junker and his wife met them at the airport and were helpful in every way, even solving practical problems like drying out Josefina's clothes which had got wet while the luggage stood on the tarmac at Gatwick. When they finally arrived at Holy Trinity Church, people were waiting to greet her and she still had enough energy to talk to them all and explain her work.

The Archbishop of Canterbury, Robert Runcie, was visiting the University of Oklahoma at Tulsa in order to inaugurate a Chair of Ecumenical Studies, and he and Josefina took part in a special service. He wore full regalia, and she wore her Royal British Sculptors' robes in the procession. They passed beneath the stained-glass window executed by Frederick Cole of Canterbury which depicts the sculptor Josefina de Vasconcellos, the poet T S Eliot and other figures taken from American history.

Hospitality was lavish, and Ann, who had never been to America before, was amazed by the luxurious houses with their guest suites and swimming pools. She was a great success with everyone she met, her dry Cumbrian humour going down well. Their twelve-day trip was packed with events and interviews and Josefina thrived on it all. Her 86 years were lightly worn.

She arrived back in fighting form, ready to make progress in a long-running campaign in support of the Lake District hill farmers against the National Trust. It was a minor conflict for a seasoned warrior like Josefina; the Trust clearly didn't have a chance. One of her previous neighbours in Langdale was in dispute with the National Trust over his lease. Feelings were running high, and the officials of the Trust seemed to be very distanced from their tenants. Josefina went straight to her old friend Lord Denning in London and he sent her to see the Minister of Agriculture. She also contacted Dame Jennifer Jenkins, who was then Director of the National Trust, asking for her support in the formation of a Tenant Farmers' Association 'as the only way in which reliable information and specialised advice can be fed in to the local NT committee – thus bypassing the reports of ignorant or biased Land Agents.' No room for misunderstanding there.

On Friday, 21 June 1991, a very long stream of traffic wound its way down the narrow road to Stool End Farm at the very top of the Langdale Valley for the Shepherds' Meet Lunch. The guest of honour was the Minister of Agriculture, Baroness Trumpington. This event had been organised by Josefina as a chance for the Minister to meet the shepherds and to launch the Association. The shepherds came with their wives and their dogs and some of Josefina's aristocratic friends came too. The Bishop of Carlisle sent a message of support. The farmers' wives laid on a handsome lunch in the barn, which had been well decorated with garden flowers, some of them arranged in shepherds' boots.

Baroness Trumpington was welcomed to Langdale by local solicitor Len Hayton, a descendent of many generations of hill farmers, who reminded her that 'without the National Trust the countryside would be the poorer, but above all, without the hill farmers who do the work on the land, the valleys and hills would be lost.' He commended the formation of the National Trust Tenant Farmers' Association to 'represent the interests of the farmers' and paid tribute to Mrs Josefina Banner, 'who has been the inspiration for this meeting today.'

After lunch there were demonstrations of country crafts such as horse-shoeing and sheep-shearing. Border TV and newspapers were given very full briefings of what lay behind the event. Beatrix Potter would have been proud, and Josefina was certainly thinking of her dear friend who had also had many differences of opinion with National Trust officials over the years. Canon Rawnsley, who never shirked a good battle with officialdom over land issues, was no doubt enjoying it all from afar.

Setting up a local organisation to advise the National Trust was a clever way of handling the dispute, and succeeded where a more confrontational approach would have failed. Josefina's determination and her contacts in high places were put unstintingly at the service of her old friends and the people she probably valued more than anyone else in the world, the shepherds of Cumbria.

Once the position in Langdale had been satisfactorily resolved, Josefina, at the suggestion of her friend Sheila Lemoine, began to make preparations for a one-man show in Manchester Cathedral during December 1991. She had a number of new works which had not been exhibited before; works that were dramatic and vigorous and displayed aspects of her thinking that had become more prominent during the eight years since Delmar's death. Less classical in form, her new sculpture was charged with emotion. St Michael was on public display for the first time and was much admired. Josefina wrote in the exhibition catalogue:

> He's a sort of 'God's Ariel', and I hope you'll find the laughter hidden in him? I often see courage and laughter marching together – and the beauty in it – reminiscent of some words in a prayer, 'high hearted happiness.'

Blind Girl With a Lamp and a copy of the *Joyous Mary and Babe*, her sculpture for Tulsa, revealed a fluidity and femininity that was immediately attractive to many, although too sweet for some. Josefina intended the blind girl to be symbolic of those who, despite their difficulties, find a guide to support them through life.

In contrast to the positive figures, the strength of *Father-Forgive*, an agonised Christ upon the Cross, probed deep into Josefina's relationship with God, as did the longing expressed in the uplifted face of *Priere*. The exhibition also included *Infant Jesus with Sparrow*, a rather sentimental representation of a sleeping child. Dedicated to Greenpeace, this presented a curious contrast between the robust confrontational style of the environmental pressure group and Josefina's sculpture.

In scope, the exhibition was truly varied and a very substantial effort for an elderly sculptor working without any assistance except for the armatures and casting. Sheila Lemoine's organisational skills and general support had made it all possible. Perhaps the effort was beginning to show, however, and during 1992 Josefina's health deteriorated. After suffering a great deal of pain, she entered the Lancaster Royal Infirmary in August for a major operation for gallstones. Although feeling cheerful and positive, and having equipped herself with a selection of glamorous negligées and nightdresses in order to receive visitors, Josefina was apprehensive. She suffered greatly after the operation and confessed in a letter to Sheona Lodge written on 12 August that 'it has been such an awful time, I never knew pain so bad... I prayed to die (loudly) and longed for it.' Again Ann Taylforth was warned by the hospital that she might not last the night.

Next day she described her state as being 'a big cave in a mountain-side full of pain – I prayed but its seemed dry and empty – at dawn I heard some wonderful music of Chopin in my head returning like gentle sea waves – suddenly I realised this was (God-Jesus) speaking to me – flowing in like spirit-blood. I owe this to reading Francis of Assisi... Francis experienced the creative love of God in all Nature, (good and bad weather!) experienced the love flowing through it all – so of course through music and other human creations of beauty – however humble – or by children – through God. Words about this experience are not enough, it is the actual reality and openness to receive, knowing it is real that makes it work – turn thought into fact!'

The other side of Josefina showed itself in a jokey postcard sent to Sheona not long after this ordeal:

> My presence in heaven caused doubt,
> When my tiny horns started to sprout.
> 'What sins brought you so low?'
> I replied, 'I don't know –
> I'd better go back and find out.'

Josefina somehow found the strength to recover and to get back to her own cosy quarters in the Wash House, picking up the threads of her many concerns once more. Music had helped to pull her through her illness and music was always part of Josefina's life in Ambleside. She had managed to squeeze a concert grand piano into the Wash House and she continued to play herself as well as compose, often working with her friend Leslie Meurant, the pianist, composer and photographer who lived nearby. She also continued to be a friend and supporter of the young pianist Geoffrey Chacaro, who had worked with her on the dance poems.

Now she met another talented young performer at the outset of his career, the pianist Andrew Wilde. Andrew had studied at Chetham's School of Music and the Royal Northern College of Music in Manchester and was soon giving recitals in London and in Cumbria. He and Josefina struck up a warm friendship and again all barriers of age seemed to disappear. Josefina attended several of his concerts and promoted him among her friends. She gave him a copy of her sculpture of Chopin and Delphine, which he valued highly. He wrote to thank her for the gift:

> It is next to me on the piano, as I write now. It will always be a reminder of how one should approach life, and one's art, because a certain message radiates from it telling us that there is nothing so precious as those first moments of discovery – two people very much in love like the first blossom of the gentlest Spring morning; the soft sighs of nature herself embalming human existence... Josefina, thank you for believing in me and for demonstrating this by your kindness and for personally sharing with me such a magnificent creation.

As she had with so many friends, Josefina embarked on a portrait bust of Andrew, working from photographs and memory. They were both pleased with the result, which captures his ardent energy, and it was cast in resin bronze. The relationship was creative for both of them. Josefina had a new source of inspiration and Andrew drew encouragement from the messages he received from Josefina before performances.

Despite her other interests, Josefina continued to take a close interest in the Harriet Trust, although not officially a member of the committee. Initially the enterprise functioned well; bookings were brisk and the unusual site, right on the edge of the Duddon estuary, was exciting for children. But the exposed position was starting to create problems for the old ship, and managing the project started to create more and more difficulties for the voluntary committee. Donated equipment wore out and had to be replaced. Standards had to be kept up and strict new regulations for residential accommodation adhered to.

The *Harriet* herself began to deteriorate. The mast became

dangerous and had to be taken down. The deck started to rot and the handrails were unsafe. Dry rot was found in parts of the boat that had not been ventilated properly. Increasingly committee meetings were focused on how to maintain the *Harriet* instead of providing for the disabled.

Lady Mary Jardine, who had taken over as Chair, took the decision to abandon ship. Josefina, who was no longer on the committee, received word that her beloved *Harriet* was to be burned without delay because of dry rot. Distraught, she was determined that at least something should be salvaged and she asked the National Trust to lend her two carpenters for a day. In great haste they stripped out the fine wooden panelling and brass fittings from the cabin and carried them off to store at Rydal Hall, where Josefina was working on a sculpture.

In fact the boat was not burned, and the panelling could have safely stayed where it was. Josefina was now determined to rally the Harriet Trust into embarking on another fund-raising campaign for the project. In August 1992 she again asked Lord Denning to lead an appeal. He did so, but pointed out in his letter that he was unable to give much help to the campaign because of his age. He was then 93. His wife Joan wrote to Josefina in her usual friendly way but was clearly indicating that her husband was not able to cope with another onslaught from Josefina. Meanwhile Josefina was still writing persuasive letters to funding bodies and individuals, although even she was beginning to admit to her age: 'It's very odd being OLD. One makes an effort and then, suddenly, one's strength is gone!'

But she was resolutely opposed to seeing the *Harriet* go up in flames and the Committee was faced with a difficult situation. Repairs to the rapidly deteriorating boat were likely to be very expensive. Lady Mary Jardine observed: 'It is true that the *Harriet* became a challenge for the Trust, just one of those things a committee is faced with rather than a tremendous burden. We were in the business of providing holidays for disadvantaged youngsters, not preserving old boats, so it was very fitting that we were able to keep her long enough for Friends of Fleetwood Museum to raise the money to tow her back to Fleetwood in 1998.'

In the meantime Lady Jardine arranged for the TV personality Anneka Rice to visit the *Harriet* in July 1994 as one of her Challenges and renovate the vessel so that it could again be used by children in wheelchairs and on crutches. Anneka brought another fishing vessel to lie beside the *Harriet* but this caught fire during the filming, adding more drama to the extensive saga of the Harriet Trust in Millom. At the time Josefina was not very happy about the Anneka Rice Challenge, seeing the project that was so very dear to her personally being energetically taken over by someone else. It was not the first or the last time that she would clash with other powerful women. But on reflection in October 1994, after the TV film had been shown, Josefina wrote to Lady Mary congratulating her on her 'imaginative realism' and her 'inspired idea' which had generated a great deal of positive response towards the Trust and its work. Josefina wrote that 'seeing all that has been done (and so excellently) has made me contented and at peace about the Harriet Trust.'

As long ago as 1983, after Delmar's death, the old skipper of the *Harriet*, Captain George Fletcher, had written to Josefina advising her that 'I hope you are going to retire from the active part you have been playing for the Harriet Trust. Its time to "lay to" now, and let somebody else take the helm.' Wisely, she decided to do so at last.

Increasingly Josefina was realising that her energy needed to be conserved for her sculpture, and she decided to make another major work in stone. On 24 March 1994 a huge eleven-foot block of magnesium limestone weighing eight tonnes was lifted by crane into the grounds of Rydal Hall. Josefina, dressed in her warm dungarees, spent the whole day supervising the operation, assisted by Shaun Williamson and other helpers. She was delighted with the stone which already had the rough shape she desired when it emerged from the blast at the quarry near Doncaster in Yorkshire: 'it is superb – Shaun and I each gave it a few chisel cuts to test – and it rang like a bell!'

At one point she had proposed working on her new stone in Sheona Lodge's garden at Wraysholme, seeing no problems with a crane swinging the massive stone over the house from the road. Sheona, while always happy to support her friend, was less than enthusiastic about this, and was relieved when Josefina found a space to work at Rydal Hall. Josefina began straight away even though the trees were still bare and cold winds swept down the valley. Work went slowly but the stone gained character in the roughing out and Josefina was happy with its place in the peaceful garden, closely enfolded by the hills.

This stone was to become *Escape to Light*, a work Josefina designed but had some assistance with the actual physical labour of carving. For the first time, she enlisted the help of pupils and other experienced sculptors such as Shaun Williamson and Dr David Pearson. Colin Hayes, a monumental mason from Kendal, came to remove some larger depths of stone with a pneumatic chisel. *Escape to Light* is another in a series of works that symbolises the fight of man against evil. Its surging shape is not dissimilar to *The Last Chimera*. Once more the human figure struggles against the jaws of evil, helped by curving flights of birds, the wind and waves. Josefina described her vision as:

> A symbol of the spirit of man escaping from the evils of this world and from his own part in the destruction. Without seeing, or being attracted to the light, there is no escape from the power and darkness of evil – but the soul of mankind is gifted with an inner light that can respond to Everlasting Light.

The original maquette had been of a female figure but Josefina felt that the thick solidity of her stone required the strength of a male figure. She saw it as a kind of 'Folk-Everyman' in sculpture, with the symbolism appealing to people who were neither Christians nor artists familiar with sculpture. At one end of the piece she carved a bell to acknowledge the ringing tone the stone made when it was first struck. She hoped that the sculpture might go to the former Nazi concentration camp at Auschwitz as a memorial to the millions who died there but this did not take place.

Josefina celebrated her ninetieth birthday on 26 October 1994 with a party at the University of Bradford, but the following year she planned more events to return hospitality to her many friends. In May 1995 she held two Brazilian Evenings in 'The Golden Rule', a friendly pub on the very steep hill that leads out of Ambleside towards the Kirkstone Pass, and known locally, fairly obviously, as 'The Struggle'. To these parties Josefina invited everyone who had played a part in her life: shepherds and aristocrats; artists and plumbers. She lifted the slate for drinks, provided food on both evenings and arranged for Brazilian music to entertain her guests. These parties broke down the old class barriers of Cumbria and were remembered long after.

Soon there was further excitement of a different kind with an opportunity offered by Coventry Cathedral for Josefina's *Reconciliation* to become a sculpture known throughout the world.

Many people in Britain and Germany had been distressed in 1992 when the Bomber Command Association commissioned a sculpture of the wartime Commander in Chief of Bomber Command, Sir Arthur 'Bomber' Harris, to stand outside St Clement Dane Church in the Strand. Questions were asked about the moral standing of a man whose judgement had been seriously questioned by historians. It was his decision to fire-bomb the non-strategic city of Dresden in 1945, killing over 80,000 people in a blaze that burned for seven days. When the statue was in place, but before it was unveiled by the Queen Mother, Canon Paul Oestreicher of Coventry Cathedral attempted to place a peace symbol beside it, and newspaper photographs show him, white-robed, hands outstretched, confronted by a line of helmeted policemen.

A number of influential people not normally associated with the Peace Movement were unhappy with the sentiments surrounding the 'Bomber' Harris statue, and among them was Richard (now Sir Richard) Branson, Director of the Virgin Group of companies. Working with Coventry Cathedral and the Department of Peace Studies at Bradford University, Richard Branson agreed to finance the casting of two bronzes of Josefina's *Reconciliation*, which over the years had become an unofficial logo for efforts towards international peace. One sculpture would be placed in the ruins of the old Coventry Cathedral, destroyed by bombing in the Second World War, and the other in the Peace Park at Hiroshima. Both works would be unveiled in the summer of 1995, fifty years after the dropping of the two atomic bombs on Japan.

The idealistic International Ministry at Coventry could not have anticipated the storm of criticism that this project unleashed. A gesture of international friendship was turned into an opportunity for the media to attack the all-too-successful Richard Branson for insensitivity and for meddling in affairs that he did not understand. The National Federation of Far East Prisoners of War Associations protested loudly against any hint of reconciliation with a Japanese government that had not apologised or offered reparations to those who had suffered starvation and cruelty in Prisoner of War Camps. The familiar British habit of knocking the successful brought about accusations that Branson was simply trying to further his commercial interests in Japan.

In many ways a generation gap had opened up between the views of those who had fought in the Second World War and the new outlook represented by young people such as Richard Branson. He, like many of his contemporaries, felt that while not forgetting the past, it was time to set aside the great burden of blame and retribution imposed on Germany and Japan. He was quoted as saying, 'It may well be that those seeking reparations are absolutely justified but that is only one aspect of how British people feel. Two generations have grown up since the war. I just want to say it is time to move on.' In the *Daily Mail* on 1 July he said that 'it was time to show a symbol of the end of conflict. Since the end of the war we have had 50 years of friendship and over the years many of the Japanese have apologised.'

That he did genuinely feel this is clear in a letter he wrote to Josefina in June before the sculptures were in place: 'I'm so glad you feel the same about Hiroshima. Let us hope that in a thousand years your beautiful statue is still in Hiroshima Peace Park as a celebration of mankind never being so cruel again.'

The Ministry at Coventry rallied in defence of their scheme and the Provost, the Very Reverend John Petty, expressed the hope that 'our gesture may ultimately improve the relationship of all.' Even Josefina, who could never have expected attention of this kind, was sought out by the press, and Christian Thurston, whose Oddfellow's Gallery in Kendal had begun to show her work, defended her desire to seek peace. Eventually Josefina produced her own Press Release, explaining the genesis of the sculpture – 'It is about people' – and her own vision that the man and woman embracing over barbed wire were praying 'that this would not happen again – to their children, or any body else's children.' She added, 'I have had the honour of meeting some of the survivors of Hiroshima and am deeply grateful to have had my work chosen as a symbol of sorrow and friendship.'

Richard Branson and an official party from Coventry, including the Lord Mayor, the Lady Mayoress and the Provost of Coventry

Cathedral, were flown to Japan on Virgin Airlines and the sculpture was unveiled in Hiroshima on 12 July 1995. Canon Oestreicher wrote a profound and moving prayer to be used at this ceremony and the one to follow in Coventry:

> Holy Spirit of life and beauty, inspirer of Josefina, sculptress and lover of humanity, we rejoice that when justice and peace embrace, a new world is being born.
>
> May we, from twin cities dedicated to healing the wounds of history, rededicate ourselves to building that liberated world in which men and women war no more and live together in peace and joy.
>
> Amen.

The white veil covering the sculpture in Hiroshima was brought back to Coventry and used again to unveil the second *Reconciliation* on 6 August, the fiftieth anniversary of the dropping of the atomic bomb on Hiroshima, when an estimated 140,000 people died. This time Josefina was able to be present, as was Richard Branson. The same plaque was placed beside both sculptures:

> In 1995, 50 years after the end of the Second World War, this sculpture by Josephina De Vasconcellos has been placed by Richard Branson on behalf of the people of Coventry as a token of reconciliation.
>
> An identical sculpture has been placed on behalf of the people of Hiroshima in the bombed ruins of Coventry Cathedral, Coventry, England.
>
> Both sculptures remind us that, in the face of destructive forces, human dignity and love will triumph over disaster and bring nations together in respect and peace.

Significantly, on the same day the Mayor of Hiroshima, Takashi Hiraoka, delivered a Peace Declaration in which he said that 'we want to apologise for the unbearable suffering that Japanese colonial domination and war inflicted on so many people.' Perhaps in response to those words, which so many had waited to hear, the

Provost of Coventry Cathedral wrote to Josefina at the end of August expressing the view that 'there does seem to have been a shift in the consciousness of relationship between our nations this month. If we have made a contribution to that, then we are grateful to you for being so instrumental in it all.'

Following the unveiling of both sculptures, Josefina and Richard Branson received many letters from England and Japan expressing a deep response to the image. Lord Denning wrote to Josefina that *Reconciliation* 'is a masterpiece which will remain for centuries in the two settings to tell future generations of the trials we have been through and have overcome'. A wheelchair-bound eighty-year-old woman wrote to Richard Branson to say that 'I can't wait for someone to wheel me round to see it again... it is so beautiful, so much so that it made me cry; so symbolic of the end of war, the end of hatred... let's hope it proves to be so.'

For Dr Robert McKinlay, who had retired as Vice Chancellor of Bradford University and was living in Ambleside, the stated aspirations towards peace on the part of leaders from many nations represented a very hopeful moment. The role played by the sculpture he initially placed at the Department of Peace Studies had become even more important than he could have envisaged. Miniatures of the sculpture are now presented to world figures by Coventry Cathedral as their annual Peace Prize because it is truly universal in its significance and cannot be seen to belong to any particular faith or community. As Josefina herself said, the image represents regret for the past, friendship for the present, and faith for the future.

She wrote regularly to Richard Branson from then on and they seemed to develop a close bond. She sent him poems and he wrote to say: 'It's a humbling experience meeting you, listening to you, reading your words, seeing your art. It's also humbling realising the joy you get from believing – if someone as special as you can have such a strong belief, it should be easier for the rest of us.'

Josefina always created a specially close relationship with her friends when she sculpted their heads and she now proposed making a bust of Richard. With someone as busy as Richard Branson a sitting was highly unlikely so she began working from photographs. Capturing the introspective side of her subject, which she wanted to do, instead of the positive, cheerful dynamism he normally projected to the public proved to be extremely difficult. She worked on the bust for years, trying out different approaches, seeing him as explorer and navigator; as 'Coeur de Leon'. People who saw the earlier versions of the bust, including fellow sculptor Meryll Evans, encouraged her to keep going but she was dissatisfied and eventually destroyed the model: 'I could *never* perfect it to my level of acceptance,' she concluded.

She had been trying to imbue the face with so much that it proved to be almost impossible to achieve; perhaps her own words were in the end more apt to describe him: 'A man I have tried to portray... is the one who sails the seas in his own ship, who loves the silence of starlight, the companionship of seabirds – and who sets his course for home.' It was a disappointment, but in many ways it was a relief to be free of her struggles with the Branson bust and to be able to work on other projects. Josefina may have had a rather romantic view of this highly motivated entrepreneur, but she knew when her work was not up to her own high standards. In fact she did return to the project a year later, having thought again about what she hoped to achieve.

The extensive publicity surrounding the *Reconciliation* sculptures brought Granada Television to her in July 1995 and she took part in a programme directed by Josephine Millington that included some of her close friends, including Sheona Lodge and Leslie Meurant. The sculptor was filmed hard at work on *Escape to Light*, playing her grand piano in the Wash House, and explaining the meaning of her carved gateposts at The Bield. The programme also showed the ceremony at Coventry Cathedral and the dedication of St Michael at Cartmel Priory. Josefina looked well, and certainly much younger than her ninety years, although her back was giving her quite a lot of pain and curvature of the spine was becoming apparent. But her energy seemed to be unfailing, and soon she was preparing for a new exhibition.

On 17 September 1995 her old friend Mary Burkett opened a retrospective exhibition of sculpture and paintings by Josefina and Delmar at the Oddfellows Gallery on Highgate, Kendal. As usual with these events, a large gathering of friends and supporters attended, and shared in Mary's praise:

> Nothing is ever too much trouble for her to do for her friends; her generosity and warmth of spirit fill any place where she is

> – tolerance, magnanimity – you all know what I mean. Her
> sculpture and painting are in fact the result of all this, coupled
> with her total, shining faith. The compassion which you see
> in her work, the strength, the love, the sincerity, all come from
> her own experiences.[1]

Mary accepted that some of those present might find Josefina's work sentimental and the religious connection 'too much'. But, she added, 'I would suggest that they are not seeing clearly her deep spiritual message.'

Even after such an exhausting event, Josefina had not forgotten that it was the birthday of her adopted son Brian, and typical of her she was determined to celebrate this. Bundling him into the back seat of Sheona Lodge's car, she took him out to dinner and the cinema in Windermere.

Despite Josefina's apparent unfailing energy, she was realistic enough to accept that occasionally the help of a younger sculptor might be needed to carry out her wishes. In the forty years since the huge carving of *Christ the Judge* had been installed at Aldershot as part of the Heroes' Shrine, the sculpture and its surroundings had experienced much wear and tear. The huge deodar cypress tree that provided the backing for the sculpture had come down in a storm. The garden had become neglected, and the statue of Christ had been vandalised. Rushmoor Borough Council decided to renovate the garden and were amazed to find that the original sculptor was not only still alive but keen to get to work.

Despite her initial determination to do the repairs herself, she had to accept that her best contribution to the work would be to design the features for a new head, and to allow the young craftsman Simon Smith to do the carving. Simon came up to see Josefina in Ambleside and Josefina gave him a choice of models. To her great joy the committee agreed completely to a new and softer expression for Christ. She did make a personal contribution by recarving a damaged hand, but the actual work of the head itself was carried out by Simon with a concept that Josefina considered to be far better than the original. Additional work on the stonework in the garden and on the plaques was carried out by Simon Essex.

The memorial was rededicated on 3 November 1998, but Josefina did not feel strong enough to attend. It was unveiled by the Mayor of Aldershot, Councillor Peter Moyle, who expressed the view that the shrine had become a memorial to peace during the past half century. But he added that 'the message of the statue and the memorial, although written over fifty years ago, is as true today.' Josefina sent a message of good wishes to be read out by Jim Davidson of the Friends of War Memorials who had been active in supporting the renovation of the Shrine. Jim Davidson also planted the idea for a new memorial called Peace Launch, which excited Josefina tremendously and she designed a sculpture consisting of a gun barrel crowned by a dove of peace, surrounded by four children in distress, with a great deal of inspirational poetry. This idea did not get beyond the planning stage, but it was the sort of scheme that inspired Josefina and kept her forging ahead.

Living in the centre of Ambleside meant that Josefina could get to concerts and social events fairly easily, either by taxi or with her many friends. But although she was still happy in the Wash House, certain problems were beginning to emerge. The steep hill became very slippery when icy and the loyal band of helpers, many elderly themselves, were unable to visit. Josefina herself held on to the handrail and made light of the problem. For many years in all weathers she hurried down to Wraysholme every evening to have cocoa and a chat with Sheona Lodge beside the Aga, sharing her zest for life with Sheona and bringing her much happiness during her last years.

She also worked on various pieces in Sheona's garden at Wraysholme or under the balcony at the back of the house. Sheona remembered 'seeing her under our balcony, snow on the ground, working on a piece for St Martin in the Fields that needed repair, coming in to the kitchen blue with cold. Curling up on the sofa like a dormouse. After tea she sprang up and said to the two exhausted men who had been helping her, "Come on, we've another twenty minutes before it's dark." She was only eighty something then.' Even so, she contracted pleurisy twice and was advised to avoid working in cold places for long periods of time: 'third time would not be lucky,' advised her doctor.

Problems less easy for Josefina to deal with included casual harassment from local youths who banged on the door of the Wash House at night and even climbed on to the roof and started to remove the heavy slate tiles. Seeing the bent figure of a very old woman, neighbourhood children shouted out that she was a witch. Josefina was never lacking in courage, but she began to feel nervous at night, even though friends reassured her.

Crime also entered her world when a thief smashed the window of the Oddfellow's Gallery in Kendal and stole one of her sculptures valued at £1,800. Appropriately enough, the sculpture was called *Escape*, one of five cast from the original. Josefina was reported as saying that she took it as a compliment that someone was prepared to go to prison to acquire one of her works.

She was also worried by problems with her hands and had constant pins and needles. An operation was arranged, put off and eventually undertaken, but was unsuccessful; there was no improvement. Even so, her hands remain remarkable for an elderly woman: strong, smooth and unmarked.

During much of 1996 Josefina worked regularly on *Escape to Light* at Rydal, helped usually by Dr David Pearson, a retired anaesthetist and a sculptor himself, who would collect her from the Wash House in his car and bring her to the site. She would mark out what she wanted on the stone and her helpers would chip away with mallet and chisel. Rachel Polkinghorne, Ann Taylforth and Brenda Bevit worked occasionally, as did Shaun Williamson. Dr Pearson was entrusted with safeguarding the future of the project, because in March that year Josefina was ill and feeling very vulnerable. She sent a Special Delivery letter to Dr Pearson, charging him with the responsibility of finishing the work if she were to die before it was completed: 'I think that if I died tomorrow you would know how to finish it.'

But she recovered, kept going, and was so clear in her own mind about what she wanted that the contributions of her helpers were not always retained. Having worked all through 1996 on the sculpture with Josefina, Dr Pearson was disappointed to be told that she intended to recarve his scallop shell and fish because they did not fit into the overall scheme. The carving was too scientifically correct and too crisply finished to blend with the flowing lines of the sculpture as a whole. His dragonfly remains on another part of the stone. Dr Pearson was philosophical; he had found the whole experience of working on the stone an interesting challenge that he would not have done without. His friendship with Josefina survived, but he did no more on the stone.

Work continued intermittently, but although Josefina had hoped to finish *Escape to Light* in 1997, over four years passed before the sculpture was complete. No permanent site has yet been found for the work, although Josefina hopes to see it on a plinth in water, with the inscription: 'We are all pursued by evil, both from within ourselves and without, and as nations we sin. "Let he who is without sin cast the first stone." '

The winter of 1996–97 was distressing for Josefina when on 27 January 1997 Sheona Lodge died, peacefully, at Wraysholme, aged 96. Many friends and relatives mourned her passing, but Josefina felt quite bereft. Their friendship had been deep and Sheona, while being much more down to earth than Josefina and feeling herself sometimes cast in the role of grandmother rather than equal, had rejoiced in her friend's creativity and 'her greatest gift, the transcendence of happiness over tragedy.' Josefina had felt the security of Sheona's love and understanding for many years and the loss of her friend was very painful. Shaun Williamson had previously carved the headstone for Oliver Lodge and Sheona's daughter Fiona, and now he added Sheona's name to the simple natural slate incised with kingfishers. Yet Josefina's faith allowed her to feel that Sheona was still very much present and still an influence for good.

Almost immediately, Josefina decided to sell the Wash House and to move from Ambleside. Always impetuous, she sold her studio for a very small sum to a friend, who swiftly resold it for a much larger amount. Josefina's grasp on finances somehow always got involved with friendship and once more she failed to gain financial security from the loss of her much-loved home. Her friends were shocked at the suddenness of her decision and wanted her to stay as part of the circle where she was known and where supporters could lend a hand when needed. But her mind was made up and she went.

Josefina moved to Kendal, to become Sculptor in Residence at the Oddfellow's Gallery, which was then run by Christian Thurston. He offered her a small but sunny attic at the top of Prince Charlie's House on Stricklandgate, with an area in the gallery to display her work and to meet people. This was the second Oddfellow's Gallery in Kendal, as Thurston had previously run a smaller gallery in the Oddfellow's Hall on Highgate, Kendal. He had organised a retrospective exhibition for the work of Josefina and Delmar in 1995, and supported her work for the next few years.

Josefina's room was again a small space filled with huge endeavours. She created a kitchen and shower-room under the eaves and in the other room she sculpted, wrote and slept in a huge armchair. By this time pain in her back had made sleeping in a bed uncomfortable for her so this arrangement was quite satisfactory. Living right in the centre of Kendal with traffic passing day and night was quite a change from the quiet lanes above Ambleside, but the bustle suited her and she had many visitors. The gallery had a small café where she could have lunch and other shops and restaurants were nearby. She repeatedly told her friends that it was the happiest time of her life, and in many ways it was, because she was almost completely free of responsibilities. Being Sculptor in Residence meant that she could be in the public view when she felt like it, or could retreat to her own apartment when she wanted privacy. The Gallery gained by having her there, as visitors found her presence fascinating.

But she was often very, very weary. In a letter to her old friend and fellow sculptor Eva Castle she admitted that she was 'almost always tired. Make breakfast (cornflakes) then REST. Tidy room – do flowers then REST etc. But quite happy just to sit and look at flowers or read a book. Still manage some work at odd times. Ah well – still have a sense of humour and hang on to it. Not the sort of thing to ask St Anthony to find if I lost it!!'

However, the arrangement at the Gallery was highly irregular, as the burglar alarm meant that she had to be locked in her room at night, marooned up several flights of steep stairs. Had there been an emergency it would have been very difficult to cope, and Ann Taylforth might have had to come from Little Langdale, an hour's drive, to let her out. Fortunately nothing untoward happened while she was there but her friends were, not surprisingly, anxious about the situation.

Throughout her life Josefina had written poetry (her poems were first published in the *Bournemouth Graphic* in 1920 when she was 16) and now she found time to prepare a small pamphlet for publication.

She worked hard on the poems, and accepted some critical advice from close friends who read her work. In 1997, with the help of her friend Lilian Cooksey who set the booklet for private circulation, Josefina published *Perchance to Dream*. The thirty-six poems are delicate, romantic and seem almost like the work of a young girl who still believes unreservedly in the transforming power of love. When she was interviewed on BBC Woman's Hour in November that year about what it was like to be very old, she had a great deal to report.

One of her new interests was the Mildmay Hospital, which worked with Aids sufferers in London and overseas. Helen Taylor Thompson, chairman of the Board of Governors of this Trust, happened to see Josefina on television and wrote to ask if she would kindly donate a small sculpture for a fund-raising auction that they were holding. Josefina replied immediately to say that she would not send a small sculpture; she would send three medium-sized ones instead. The event was held at Blenheim Palace on 18 July 1997 and Josefina attended. Mildmay was taking a particular interest in children with Aids and Josefina was very concerned about these innocent victims. This was the partial inspiration for her next major work, *The Weight of Our Sins*, which she completed two years later.

In February 1998 Christian Thurston organised another major exhibition of her work at the Gallery, called 'Moments of Truth', and a very large and enthusiastic crowd attended the Private View. Sculpture, paintings and poetry were displayed, and Josefina incorporated music as well by arranging for Geoffrey Chacaro to give a short piano recital as part of the event. Christian was now showing work by Josefina and Delmar as well a number of local artists. Although Christian was notoriously slow to pay his artists what he owed them, Josefina was grateful to him for his interest in her work.

That year also saw the end of the long and convoluted story of the trawler *Harriet* in Millom, largely through the efforts of Mary Neesom, the last Warden of the Harriet Trust. The Fleetwood Maritime Museum wanted the ship back, as an essential part of their history, and this seemed an ideal solution to the problem of what to do with a decaying vessel that was still fiercely loved and protected by its owner. Elaborate preparations were made to lift the old ship into a cradle, then on to a barge to be floated across Morecambe Bay. As with its arrival in Millom, the weather did not cooperate, and gale force winds delayed the departure. Eventually, on 18 August, the *Harriet* set off on what was definitely its last voyage and arrived safely in Fleetwood Harbour after dark. It was a very satisfactory end to the story, and the fate of this historic vessel would probably not have been such a happy one had the Banner stubbornness not taken hold and refused to let go. The Youth Hostels Association has taken over the running of the Centre, which still gives priority to young disabled visitors.

Josefina found that living in Kendal was convenient in many ways but it did mean that she was now further away from *Escape to Light* at Rydal, and progress was slow. She was very dependent on friends to take her there and help with carving the stone itself. But the vision had emerged from the stone and she was pleased with results.

The Weight of Our Sins, completed in October 1999, deflected Josefina from the Rydal stone for some time. Her concern for abused children over many years prompted this sculpture, a group of six life-sized children struggling with an eleven-foot cross. Each child represents neglect and mistreatment by adults: Aids, landmines, serial abuse. The weight of the suffering is borne by the children; they bear the cross as Christ bore the cross to his crucifixion. The eye carved on the cross is the eye of Christ seeing the children in distress. Stephen Stalker made the metal cross. Josefina described her response to the work:

> I am so close to the children, they are real children to me. I know all their sufferings. It is a personal experience: they remain in my heart. These children are related to all the children suffering in the world. If you don't feel the reality, it becomes an idea instead of an experience – just a thing of one's brain. Ordinary simple people have a gut feeling; they know whether it's just a good idea or a felt experience.

Many found this work disturbing and were puzzled by the symbolism. To those who did not believe so firmly in the tenets of Christianity, the sculpture could appear to be a condemnation of religion (the Cross) crushing children, and indeed the present concern for young people abused by religious figures might support this view, although that is certainly not what the sculptor intended. On an artistic level, the piece falls into the category of propaganda rather than a transformation of the sculptor's indignation through myth and imagery, which would have been her usual approach. Josefina seems to have become so enraged by the whole question of child abuse that she lost sight of her artistic instincts, although she defends it by comparing it to Rodin's *Burghers of Calais*. It is worthwhile remembering that in the catalogue to their 1955 Joint Exhibition Delmar expressed the view that 'art is not craft, nor escape into "beauty" nor "self expression" nor "representation" – nor propaganda. It may involve them; but it must not be confused with them.' The 'serious impulse and end' that Delmar saw behind all their works was perhaps being pressed too far.

Josefina decided that the piece should be transported on a pilgrimage from Kendal to London during the autumn to raise money for charities concerned with children and to heighten awareness of the Tenth Anniversary of the UN Convention on the Rights of the Child. Her original plan was for the sculpture to be wheeled on a trolley by teams of young people, collecting money on the way for various charities, but this proved impossible to organise.

Eventually, after a Dedication of the sculpture in Kendal Parish Church at the end of October, she brought it to Shrewsbury Abbey in Stephen Stalker's pick-up truck. There, a programme of events had been arranged involving local schools and charities, and featuring a piano recital by Josefina's friend Andrew Wilde on 6 November. After Shrewsbury the sculpture was placed at St Martin in the Fields in London for temporary display over the Christmas period. The Mildmay Trust for Aids victims was particularly interested and supportive, and other charities involved were Amnesty International, the Children's Society, NSPCC, Road Peace, Save the Children, Sight Savers and UNICEF. To this extent Josefina's aim of using sculpture as a means of focusing the attention of people on social issues was successful.

Making this eloquent sculpture and accompanying it on the pilgrimage was a tremendous effort, both physical and mental. It was a passionate statement of protest and a clear rebuttal to those who found her conventional religious sculptures too sentimental. While she was modelling the abused children Josefina also worked on the figure of a happy child, *Childrise*, in order to keep herself from descending into despair. She was now 95 years old and the labour involved in modelling all these figures had been immense. She remembered watching Henry Moore in his studio working on a sculpture half the size but with two strong young men to help him with the work. She had made *The Weight of Our Sins* almost single-handed.

Her emotional commitment to causes dealing with abused and suffering children was extreme and she had little patience with people who were not prepared to throw themselves wholeheartedly into the campaign. Josefina was very happy to accept the credibility and esteem of certain institutions when they were behind her, but she was impatient with their slow-moving procedures, which to a strong-willed person like herself looked like inadequate effort on behalf of worthy causes.

It was an exceptionally busy time for Josefina, because during the period the sculptures were at Shrewsbury Abbey she was called on to function once more on an international stage, as a new *Reconciliation* was unveiled in Berlin on 9 November 1999, the tenth anniversary of the fall of the Berlin Wall. It was temporarily placed outside the new Reichstag building near the site of the Church of the Reconciliation, which had been blown up by the East German secret police, the Stasi, in 1985. When the ruins of the church were cleared, the ancient Bible used for services was found beneath the rubble, its tooled leather cover undamaged, and Josefina made a cast of this to place between the two kneeling figures. The Bible is bound with barbed wire to be a reminder of the wall that divided the city for so many years. The plinth was made of ground-up seashells from Ireland and set into it, behind the Bible, were pieces of concrete from the Berlin Wall along with small pieces of rubble from Hiroshima, Nagasaki and Dresden. The base was coloured a rather bright shade of pinkish purple, brighter than Josefina would have liked, but there was nothing she could do about it at that stage.

Preparations for the event had been delayed by the discovery of an unexploded bomb very near the site; a booby trap left by the Stasi when they blew up the church. This meant that the sculpture was unveiled in a building site full of machinery and piles of sand, and Josefina did not see the sculpture on its base until the actual unveiling. Helen Taylor Thompson accompanied her to Berlin, where they stayed with an Order of Deaconesses who had been associated with the Mildmay Mission Hospital in its formative years in the nineteenth century. Helen offered to wheel Josefina to the ceremony in a wheelchair, as it was a little far to walk, and she reluctantly accepted. But when she saw the huge crowd of television crews and guests waiting at the site she abandoned the chair and made the effort to walk the rest of the distance, leaving Helen to park the chair hastily behind a pile of building materials.

Surrounded by a swirling crowd of robed churchmen, television crews and politicians, Josefina sat down quietly beside the sculpture on her little folding stool, wearing her Royal British Sculptors robe. A tiny hunched figure sitting in the rain, she was hardly noticed until the ceremony started, then everyone wanted to know who she was and how the sculpture came to be made. Rachel Polkinghorne from Border Television was there and filmed the event as part of an on-going pictorial biography of one of Cumbria's most famous twentieth century artists.

This *Reconciliation* will be part of the Berlin Wall Memorial Site, and an important symbol for the re-unified German nation. In *Berlin Wall*, a book of essays that describe the historical events surrounding the building of the Wall and the destruction of the church, Pastor Manfred Fischer expressed his conviction that the new Chapel of Reconciliation 'will have effects far beyond the Reconciliation Parish itself,' and Theology Professor Peter Bloth of Humboldt University wrote in the same book:

> What does 'reconciliation' mean here? Christian belief attests to the fact that reconciliation is more than, and different from, tolerance. With reconciliation, one doesn't simply 'let things slide', and particularly not when confronted with brutality and contempt for human life. Reconciliation, rather, strives to make valid and visible how God's actions in his sacrificed and living son Jesus Christ have definitively worked to benefit humanity everywhere in the world – that is what ecumenical means! Every wall of unfreedom, every form of contempt for human dignity falls short of that which, according to God's will, should determine human life. Thus, the word reconciliation, encompassing both the actions of God and those of humans, is not only appropriate

in describing the engagement of this church parish on the Berlin Wall, but it can also demonstrate what the church has to offer all individuals, the directions and forms in which it can accompany them in the world today.[2]

As with all the unveiling ceremonies of her *Reconciliation* sculptures it was a profoundly moving experience for everyone involved, and especially for Josefina, who shared the view expressed by Manfred Fischer: 'if we have faith in symbolic actions, then we know that symbols have a silent power which can make the "impossible" possible.'[3]

Josefina had not forgotten the suffering of Dresden, and earlier in 1999 she had asked Canon White to bring a small replica of *Reconciliation* to the city. This was presented to the Head of State of Saxony who wrote to the sculptor praising the efforts that had been made towards peace and reconciliation between the twin cities of Coventry and Dresden, both victims of the ferocious bombing of the Second World War.

On her return to England Josefina was totally exhausted. She had been travelling, meeting people and speaking in public for several weeks and she had not spared herself in promoting the causes she believed in. Unfortunately on her return to Kendal she was faced with yet another crisis involving somewhere to live. Financial difficulties beset Christian Thurston and he was unable to keep up his lease on Prince Charlie's House. Josefina had to move out. In early December she came to stay at Wraysholme in Ambleside where she had always felt so much at home, and remained for nearly two months with Sheona's daughter Dr Anne Mathieson and her family until new arrangements could be made. She was tired and anxious and fatigue made her deafness worse. Over Christmas she gradually regained her strength and her spirits, and began to plan her future. After all these years she was still giving financial support to her adopted son Brian, and this responsibility was a serious concern to her.

At the end of January 2000, Josefina rallied her helpers and moved her possessions from the Oddfellow's Gallery to Holehird Cheshire Home above Lake Windermere. She had seen the century out, and she still felt ready not for retirement, but for new opportunities. There would be plenty in the year to come.

CHAPTER TEN

The New Century

My willow cabin
has reached its 'grott-age'
a second best
to 'Life's Dark Cottage'.

One of those things
by luck or fate,
I went and built it
at the wrong gate.

No 'Romantic ears'
for to hear my calling...
ineffectual tears
to waste, were falling.

But some of the withies
'Took' – to flower
like a bright Bay Tree –
made a Willow Bower!

It creaks, it leaks,
but squirrels run in it,
a chantry at dawn
for Robin and linnet.

Beauty, urgent as Life, insisted,
– pushed and shoved –
to be held and loved...
I never resisted.

J de V

Thrusting a wild bird into a tiny cage is the only possible way to describe Josefina's situation at the Cheshire Home at Holehird. Like many people who survive to a great age, she felt like a young person trapped in an old body, unable to do what she wanted when she wanted, with the precious relics of an active life packed away in black plastic bags. Her room at Holehird looked out over Lake Windermere and to the mountains beyond, and the gardens surrounding the house were superb. But the room was small and even modelling miniature figures was difficult. Dust and clay went everywhere when Josefina was at work.

Independence had been hard-won for Josefina, and she feared that living in a residential institution might deprive her of the opportunity to do as she liked. Yet the staff were kind and the management of the Home enlightened, catering as they did for many different people, young and old. She had put her name down for Holehird two years before, but she still did not feel that the time was quite right. When she went there after living in the Oddfellow's Gallery, friends were relieved to know that she was well looked after in such an attractive and safe environment, but wondered if she would be able to reconcile herself to the loss of complete freedom. Their fears were justified.

She was writing a great deal of poetry. 'I write poems as easily as a cow drops dung,' she advised her friends with great candour. As she looked back on her life, her poetry allowed her to gain perspective and understanding of experiences that had shaped her, often with great pain and suffering: 'dark and light/have veered/in the thread/ of my Life line.' Her wry poem, 'Willow Cabin', written in August 2000, reveals some acceptance of the state of her life at that time; not ideal, but still functioning for the things that mattered.

From Josefina's point of view, the practical problems of storing and gaining access to her possessions were almost overwhelming. For the first few months they stayed wrapped in a tarpaulin in an open garage at the back of the house. Wind, rain and damp affected her clothes, books, paintings and papers. Eventually, with the help of friends, Josefina managed to unearth what she needed and to find some of her much-loved belongings. The bare room began to feel like a typical Josefina room, full of wicker baskets, flowers, maquettes, interesting china and paintings. Visitors were constantly knocking at her door. And very soon she was back at work; a good sign for those who knew that Josefina was not happy if she was not making sculpture. She felt 'stripped for action' and concluded that 'what I have of work and ideas, designs for the future needs just this, and must be effective.'

Ann Taylforth came twice a week from Little Langdale to help with correspondence and other arrangements, often driving Josefina to appointments in other parts of the country or accompanying her to London. Josefina's diary filled up rapidly. She did not become involved with the other residents, or any of the activities of the home, which was something of a disappointment for them, as it was known that she had been very concerned to improve the lives of disabled people over the years. She knew in her heart that the energy she saved by living in Holehird could be used almost exclusively for her sculpture and for her charity work, and this was what mattered most.

During the year Josefina was much preoccupied with finding permanent homes for her work. Many of the larger pieces were in temporary locations, and some needed repair. Not all were displayed as Josefina would have liked. The search went on, involving a garden in Grasmere, and possible sites in Manchester and Edinburgh. After several years of deliberation the parish of St James the Great in Solihull, near Birmingham, agreed to place her *Lamb of God* on their east wall, and on 9 March 2000 Josefina drove down with Stephen Stalker to see it properly mounted. Many parishioners were there to greet her and found themselves working hard for most of the day in order to satisfy the artist's requirements. The Reverend Michael Caddy thought that 'she seemed to be transformed as soon as she started work – the years rolled away, it seemed, as did her aches and pains. Throughout she was alert and observant and full of ideas about the church and always, always full of reassurance and kind comments about the things we were trying to do for the re-ordering of the building.' The sculpture was blessed by the Bishop of Aston, John Austin, on Easter Day, 23 April 2000. Josefina the encourager, as always.

Old friends from the Society of Portrait Sculptors had been in touch before Christmas about arrangements for their 37th Exhibition, called 'Face 2000', to be held in London at the end of April. At the Private View on 26 April Josefina was presented with the Jean Masson Davidson Medal by the Acting Cultural Attaché from the Brazilian Embassy, and made a brilliant speech of thanks. This award was founded in 1962 and is made by the Society 'for distinguished services and outstanding achievement in the art of portrait sculpture.' Young sculptors who did not know Josefina were amazed to see this tiny, hunched figure, who had been sitting quietly at the door, wrapped in a black and white shawl, stand up and deliver such an amusing speech in a rich, deep voice. Her sculpture of Dame Edith Sitwell was on display. Not many of the original founders of the Society were still alive, and shortly after this event two of the original members died; Malcolm Fry, the administrator, and Franta Belsky, the sculptor.

An exhibition of portrait busts in a small gallery offers a curious experience to the viewer. Surrounded by strong and intense faces, staring with immobile eyes, the visitor can feel an uncanny sense of presence. The unique qualities of the portrait bust were discussed by Dr Penelope Curtis, Director of the Henry Moore Institute, in an essay printed as part of the catalogue for the exhibition. Dr Curtis was in the process of curating an exhibition on the portrait bust to be opened in Leeds later in 2000, and was aiming to focus attention on an art form that had become neglected in favour of the painted portrait or the photograph. She recognised that 'realistic figuration and modernism parted company after the war. The art of portraiture was thus separated from the dominant trend of artistic enquiry, and so divorced, has been forced to plough a narrow furrow.'[1] But she recognised that there was a period when the finest nineteenth and twentieth century sculptors engaged with the portrait bust, and she hoped that the Leeds exhibition would 're-introduce the bust to a public that has forgotten how to look at it; forgotten its place, its functions, and its means. It will sketch in something of its conventional heritage – its place in the library, the civic hall, as well as in the art gallery – but will concentrate upon the works themselves, on the bust, and on the face.'[2]

In fact the conventional placing of the portrait bust in gloomy municipal buildings can work against its recognition as a serious work of art. It is all too easy to sweep past a bust and pay no attention whatsoever to its quality. Yet there is still a demand for this art form, and there is still a fascination with the unique, three-dimensional aspect of the work. Very few painted portraits show the back of a head and the vulnerability of the relationship between the head and the neck, something that Josefina brought out very clearly in her bust of James Cameron.

Nearly fifty years earlier, the president of the newly-formed Society of Portrait Sculptors, Sir Charles Wheeler, wrote in his foreword to the catalogue for the Second Annual Exhibition that 'there is an additional power in the use of the third dimension.' He went on to say:

> It is the sculptor's business to emphasise those forms and lineaments which bring out the individuality of the subject. All views of the sitter are incorporated in a single thing so that a kind of composite person is represented rather than one aspect of him only. We trust that our exhibition will show how well sculpture can serve in perpetuating a likeness in a manner more complete, perhaps, and often more convincing than is possible by painting.

Perhaps the new century has lost the trust in the artist that allows for these unique qualities to be appreciated, and needs to be reminded of the special role the portrait sculptor can play, a role that was certainly known and understood by Josefina and her colleagues.

During the spring plans for the installation of a *Reconciliation* sculpture in Northern Ireland were being made by the International Ministry at Coventry, and Josefina was very happy that this should go ahead. Originally supported by Mo Mowlam when she was Secretary of State for Northern Ireland, the project was now in the hands of her successor, Peter Mandelson, and his advisors. Again the cost of casting in bronze would be met by Sir Richard Branson.

Naturally Josefina wanted to be involved in every aspect of the scheme, and was driven down to Coventry to meet a delegation from Northern Ireland. Many difficulties were aired but when the visiting party was shown around the Cathedral and brought to see Josefina's sculpture she was sure that the atmosphere changed. Agreement was reached to place the sculpture in the extensive, well-kept grounds of Stormont Castle outside Belfast, with the fervent hope that the Peace Process would hold firm in the meantime. An agreement in principle did not mean that all the problems were resolved, however, and an idealistic scheme to place melted-down weapons as a symbol of peace between the two kneeling figures immediately created conflict – whose weapons would be melted down? The idea was quickly brushed under the carpet and it was agreed that the sculpture should be cast without any further embellishment.

Josefina continued to worry about the site and the plinth, and was reluctant to allow responsibility for this to pass into the hands of other people. Eventually, as with coming to live at Holehird, she accepted that she must relinquish some control. Her role was to create, and to allow others to support her work, even though she knew that most of the practical details which were causing delays could at one time have been easily dealt with by her.

The frustrations of being distanced from day-to-day progress on the Stormont launch may have been irritating, but she was soon able to forget them when she was engulfed in a huge wave of love and appreciation from a wide-ranging group of friends and supporters. For several years the art historian Linda Clifford had been working on a pictorial appreciation of the sculptor and in spring 2000 she published her book *Sculptor: Josefina de Vasconcellos*. Hundreds of people attended an afternoon launch party at Rydal Hall on 30 April, and Josefina herself signed every book sold. It was a glorious, warm spring day and many people had travelled from all parts of the country to see their old friend and to give her their good wishes. Apart from one or two articles published in fine art journals many years previously, this was the only serious appreciation of her sculpture and Josefina was very pleased. So were many friends who felt that at last her achievements had been properly recognised.

Josefina exhibited at the Lake Artists Society show in the summer of 2000, and attended the Private View. She had new works to display, and was delighted to make some sales. Later in the year she also exhibited at the Cumbrian Sculptors show at Hutton in the Forest, and attended the Private View in her capacity as President of the Society.

Projects nurtured over several years were now becoming urgent in her mind, and she felt energised by the pressure to see results: 'Don't be concerned about my "watered-down condition" if too many things are undertaken. I am at my best in that situation,' she said. 'Think of it as plants set in the earth long ago – each now coming up and showing leaf. Each must be watered from time to time – but none quickly, or all at once.'

There was a general need to put things into place, such as returning the original wheel of the *Harriet* to the Maritime Museum at Fleetwood. Josefina visited the Museum in June and handed over the wheel and the ship's compass to Dorothy Westell, of Lancashire County Council. Josefina had made a cast of the wheel for the Team House at the Harriet Centre in Millom so that a link was maintained with her original scheme. She even managed to find the silver coin that had been placed under the mast for luck, and this has also gone to the educational display in Fleetwood.

Then there was the ancient altar that had been used at the chapel at Beckstones. Josefina was hoping that this could be transported to St Patrick's Church in Patterdale and be rededicated to all the airmen lost on the Fells during the Second World War. Eventually this was achieved, and another concern was laid to rest.

Meanwhile, she continued to worry about the installation of the Stormont *Reconciliation*. There were delays in the casting and promised stones had not materialised. She was sad that her old friend Professor Robert McKinlay, who had been so instrumental in bringing Josefina's sculpture to public notice as a symbol of peace, would not see the Stormont project come to fruition. He died at the beginning of October and Josefina lost another valued supporter who had shared a great deal with her over the years: 'I will always miss his gentle strength and wisdom,' she wrote after his death.

The Stormont sculpture was unveiled at a ceremony on 7 November 2000. Josefina had hoped to visit the site in advance, but her trusty blacksmith Stephen Stalker fell off a horse and broke his leg, so he was not able to drive her there as she had planned. She had to be content with the assurances of Canon White about the beauty of the site. When she saw the placing of the sculpture on the day of the unveiling, having flown over to Belfast that morning accompanied by

Rachel Polkinghorne, she was delighted. The sculpture was in the centre of a pool, fed by a small curving cascade. In spring, daffodils and cherry blossom surround it. The setting was designed by the Landscapes Section of the Department of the Environment's Construction Service, and the team involved did a splendid job.

Leaders of Northern Ireland used the occasion, and the sculpture, to pledge themselves again to the Peace Process, which Coventry Cathedral had referred to as 'a call for day to day commitment to the work of reconciliation.' Lord Alderdice, First Minister David Trimble and Deputy First Minister Seamus Mallon all spoke hopefully about the future. Canon White described the background to the sculpture and introduced Josefina to great applause. The prayer written for Josefina by Paul Oestreicher was slightly altered for the occasion to refer to the presence of representatives from four cities, and led to the ceremonial placing in the pool of stones from their countries by Amiram Magid, Minister Plenipotentiary from the Israeli Embassy, Kenjiro Monji, Political Minister from the Japanese Embassy, and Douglas Getty, Honorary Consul of the Federal Republic of Germany. Despite torrential rain, the occasion was warm and positive, although the local media took a typically dry approach to symbolic gestures as a solution to violence.

Josefina was invigorated by her trip to Northern Ireland and the appreciation that her work received there. After all her anxieties about the placing of the sculpture, she concluded that it was the most pleasingly sited of all the *Reconciliation* pieces. Unfortunately plans for another sculpture to go to Jerusalem may have to wait for some time.

Shortly afterwards a miniature *Reconciliation* was presented to Count Hans von Sponeck by the International Ministry at Coventry, the second such Peace Prize to be awarded. The *Reconciliation* image was taking on a presence and a significance that continued to reach throughout the world.

But despite this recognition, friends continued to be concerned about the legacy of Josefina's work in the face of an indifferent art establishment. At the end of November arrangements were made for Sarah Crellin and Jon Wood from the Henry Moore Institute in Leeds (part of the Henry Moore Foundation) to visit her and see her work. They were able to make a tape-recording of her for the British

Library 'Living Artists' series and have established an interest in placing a photographic record of her sculpture in their impressive archive.

More recognition came shortly afterwards when the Scottish film and television company Scope Picture Productions came down to make a film about Josefina as part of the Eikon series for Scottish Television. This half-hour film concentrated on Josefina's religious sculpture, which fitted Eikon's remit to deal with religious, moral, ethical and social issues. The film was given the Gold Award for the 'Best Christian Film 2001' by the Christian Broadcasting Council.

Much of Josefina's restlessness in Holehird was caused by the difficulties of working in her small room. By the autumn it was filled with maquettes and other pieces that had been gathered together and there was barely room to turn around. The willow cabin was about to burst at the seams. Fortunately the offer of studio space came from the helpful Head of nearby St Anne's School, a private school for girls with an excellent art department. Josefina was very relieved to have space to work on her new sculptures and to be in contact with talented girls who were interested in what she was doing. She worked on a fountain for a commission and, assisted by Stephen and Ann, managed to complete it in March 2001. She also made a start on another portrait bust of Richard Branson, feeling that she now understood more clearly what she needed to do.

Her affection for Ambleside never left her, and in December she cut the ribbon to reopen the refurbished Oxfam shop: 'We're old friends – some of my best clothes came from here,' she said at the event. She also gave the shop one of her sculptures, *Destination Unknown*, to auction for their funds.

Renewal of interest in her dancing mat for the blind gave Josefina a huge surge of energy. Connected to the carpet was a plan to make a braille trail with sculptures in the garden of Roundhill, a large house in Grasmere, with a fibreglass version of the carpet for outdoor use. In February she visited the Joseph Clarke School for the Visually Impaired in London and this involved the rail journey to London and being bounced down the long platform at Euston on a luggage trolley because no one had made arrangements for a wheelchair, but Josefina did not care. She was pushing ahead, and that was all that mattered. Somehow things would work out, and they invariably did.

But Josefina was becoming increasingly concerned about the cost of her residential care. Although Delmar had left her comfortably off financially, a great deal of money had been spent since his death, and property sales of Josefina's various houses, including a cottage in Somerset left to her by a step-aunt, had not produced the capital that they might have done. She was anxious not to be left penniless, and again she tried to find alternative accommodation nearby, even thinking about moving into a caravan. Then, suddenly, to the great consternation of her many friends, she decided to move to Porthmadog on the west coast of Wales. She had spent Christmas there with her old friends Jimmy Cassidy and Brian Walsh and she asked them if she could stay with them permanently. They agreed, and Josefina was swayed by the feeling that she would be looked after 'as one of the family', where the sound of the sea reminded her of her childhood.

Her mind was made up; the move could not come soon enough, and with the same kind of determination that saw her leave the Wash House with unreasonable haste, she packed up her belongings one more time. On 21 March 2001, a day when blizzards swept over the Welsh mountains, she climbed into the van hired by Stephen Stalker to transport her belongings and set off. Once more, her life was in plastic bags. She was to move four times in the next nine months.

Deciding to leave the Lake District after so many years amazed her circle of friends and left Ann Taylforth, who had been through good times and bad with Josefina, shocked and saddened. Even at the age of ninety-six she was still able to make her own decisions about her life. She made light of the distance between Cumbria and Wales and dismissed the practical problems that concerned those who had helped her in the past. Her indomitable spirit kept her forging ahead, full of optimism and plans for the future.

Unforeseen difficulties emerged, however, as many had predicted, and she found that she was too far from her caster and her blacksmith on whom she had come to rely. Four abstract works, never exhibited before, waited to be cast, and she wanted to be on hand. She returned to the Lake District, hoping to live on her own in a small cottage in Grasmere, but this was not achievable. Then she moved to a farm cottage near Kendal, where she continued to work on small pieces sitting in a chair, and to direct others to achieve larger works. Her health began to deteriorate and late in 2001, increasingly frail, she moved again to stay with friends in north Cumbria, near Wigton, in a handsome old farmhouse overlooking the Solway Firth. Since then she has returned to her favourite town, Ambleside, which holds so many memories for her.

Once more Josefina rallied her strength and was able to celebrate her ninety-seventh birthday with an exhibition of her work at the Stone Gallery in Kendal – 'quite the best birthday party one could have,' she said. Many friends came to the Private View on 27 October 2001, including her old friend Ian Davidson of the Friends of War Memorials.

Josefina de Vasconcellos continues to inspire others through her work and her very being. Sculpture has been her life and the evaluation of her achievement will demonstrate a career that began with huge talent and endured throughout a lifetime of much distress but much fulfilment. Josefina has always linked her work most immediately to ancient Chinese stone carving and Byzantine ivories. In the lines of *The Last Chimera*, with its deep planes and strong, surging forces, she does achieve these elemental qualities, as she does in *Escape to Light*, fifty years on. The powerful image of *Reconciliation* has become an international icon and will probably be her most enduring and best-known work.

Undoubtedly this line of sculpture reveals her greatest strengths. Much of the work produced after Delmar's death in 1983 has seemed sentimental and too close to her own emotional state during difficult years. Many of the sculptures done in this period could have been created by a different hand than the strong, inspired sculptor of *Escape to Light*, which is in another category altogether. This comes much closer to Josefina's own view of her sculpture: 'in my work I try to follow Wordsworth – speaking to people in their own language (communication) and in as direct and few words possible (art).' And what she communicates are fundamental ideas: the need for human love, for redemption, for reconciliation and for justice. Her sculpture was often at the centre of idealistic though seldom realised ambitions to right wrongs, particularly towards suffering children, so that the physical reality of a sculpture would become a focus for changing human behaviour.

She has always resisted the critical view that only abstraction can deal with the modern age because she sees abstraction throughout the history of sculpture:

> From the stone dolmens of Ireland and Cornwall, up to works in stone and bronze to the present day, the abstract goes its way through art in its natural and traditional way. The mistaken notion is to think it is *the* art, and 'new'.

She is not an isolated voice. Henry Moore stated in 1960 that 'all art is abstract in one sense. Not to like abstract qualities or not to like reality, is to misunderstand what sculpture and art are about.'[3] And it may be that the twenty-first century will see a change in direction for some serious sculptors. Antony Gormley, one of the most highly regarded British sculptors today, may seem very distanced from Josefina in terms of technique and design but he shares many of her preoccupations. He said recently that:

> Good sculpture can change the way things are, by conveying something of the way things feel. The body is capable of conveying emotion and feeling that no other form can. The history of 20th century art has been very much towards abstraction, followed by conceptualism. I feel this need to return to first-hand experience, concentrating on what it feels like to stand very still and feel the air passing over your skin.[4]

Many of the views he expresses are very near to Josefina's understanding of the art of sculpture, especially when he notes that 'One of the things that really excites me about making sculpture is the silence that hopefully can communicate anywhere,' and insists that 'there is no question that sculpture is archaic. It tries to inscribe within geological time some record of human experience.'[5] His acceptance of the human body (usually his own) as a basis for sculpture was shared recently by the young sculptor Mark Wallinger with his figure of Christ, *Ecce Homo*, that stood on the empty, fourth plinth in Trafalgar Square, and proved to be enormously popular with the public as well as the critics.

Gormley also finds common cause with Josefina in his view that 'the art of our time has failed us if it has to rely on the special conditions of the museum, of the private collection, of the commercial gallery. The neutrality of the white cube (any minimalist gallery space) has meant art has had to rely on rather clinical hospital conditions. It's not good for the culture that surrounds it.'[6] Josefina, when she was arranging exhibitions in the 1950s, was saying much the same thing, when she pleaded for sculpture to be seen 'in the arms of nature'.

The growing interest in outdoor sculpture has also been an invitation to a new audience for works of art. Helen Simpson, writing in the journal *Sculpture Matters*, feels that 'This incredible surge in public monuments encouraged artists to work fully in the round and forced people to look at work from all angles and in all changing conditions of light and atmosphere.'[7] She also defends the need for sculpture to be understood and valued in its own time and in the future: 'All the art placed in towns and cities today will be meaningless in 50 or 100 years time, as obsolete and incomprehensible as the monuments of the nineteenth century, if people are unable to comprehend its relevance and feel it is worth maintaining and preserving.'[8] Josefina's aim, to be the Wordsworth of sculpture, 'communicating in ordinary language to ordinary people,' is starting to be fashionable once more.

Sir Alan Bowness maintains in his book *Modern European Art* that sculpture is 'one of the great arts of the 20th century.'[9] It is certainly one of the arts that reaches out most directly to the public at large, causing pleasure or outrage, but always creating a response. A controversial painting may stay safely in a gallery but a public sculpture makes its presence felt day in and day out, and can often become a much cherished icon. Antony Gormley's *Angel of the North*, opening its arms to the busy traffic on the A1 at Gateshead, is a case in point. *Reconciliation*, which has touched many people throughout the world, is another.

In churches and cathedrals, in gardens and private homes in this country and abroad, the work of Josefina de Vasconcellos will keep her name alive. Many will remember her generosity; many will never forget the fierce determination with which she drove forward difficult projects that she believed in, such as Beckstones and the Harriet. Others will remember her gentler side, as she sat surrounded by flowers and birds in her Wash House studio, and the inspiration of her close relationship to the natural world. Christians will see someone who has a positive sense of healing love that is essential to her faith. She passes her own inspiration on to others, aware of the precious gift that inspiration represents, saying that 'the secret is that I am a spirit which, more than being alive, is inspired to be alive. And everything I make and feel is part of this spirit, even the most ordinary things. Maybe my eyes and my spirit are like windows without panes; not only do they see what is outside, they also let in the light of the sun.'

However she is remembered, the recollections will not be dull:

the broken wall
of a cattle shed,
where a babe cried,
the hole in his side –
the stained shroud –
are rents in the cloud,
through which we see,
'Lovest thou me?'

J de V, Christmas 1985

Chapter One

1   E Bradford Burns, *A History of Brazil*, p 232

2   F G Sturm, 'Religion', in *Modern Brazil*, p 248

3   Dewi Morgan, *They Became Christians*, p 152

Chapter Two

1   Penelope Curtis, *Sculpture 1900–1945*, p 89

2   Herbert Maryon, *Sculpture*, p 33

3   ibid, p 38

4   Philip Rawson, *Sculpture*, p 38

5   ibid, p 20

6   Julia Thorogood, *Margery Allingham, A Biography*, p 66

7   Margery Allingham, 'Green Corn'

8   John Milner, *The Studios of Paris*, p 226

9   ibid, p 3

10 James Lord, *Giacometti*, p 82

11 Milner, p 68

12 Richard Cork, *Cambridge Guide to the Arts in Britain*, p 174

13 Maryon, p 73

Chapter Three

1   Morgan, p 150

2   Delmar Banner, 'Memories of Beatrix Potter', p 230

3   ibid, p 231

4–8   Unpublished letters donated to the Victoria and Albert Museum by
    Mrs Banner: 28 February 1938, 7 October 1937, 14 September 1936,
    8 September 1936, 25 February 1938

Chapter Four

1   Robert Woof, *The Artist as Evacuee*, p 67

2   ibid, p 54

3   ibid, p 52

4   ibid, p 70

5 Sarah Wilson, 'Kurt Schwitters in England', p 16

6 Woof, p 14

7 Unpublished speech from Mary Burkett papers

8 Philip James, *Henry Moore on Sculpture*, p 79

9 Judy Taylor (ed), *Beatrix Potter's Letters*, p 430

10 Barbara Hepworth, *A Pictorial Autobiography*, p 20

11 ibid, p 39

12 ibid, p 39

13 ibid, p 35

14 Rupert Croft-Cooke, *The Dogs of Peace*, p 25

15 Robert Hewison, *Culture and Consensus*, p 23

16 ibid, p 23

Chapter Five

1 Hewison, p 61

2 W Heaton Cooper, *Mountain Painter*, p 123

3 G S Sandilands, 'Josefina de Vasconcellos', p 11

4 George Fearon, *You Owe Me Five Farthin's*, p 65

5 ibid, p 66

6 Unpublished letter from Norman Nicholson to Austen Williams

7 Fearon, p 71

8 Unpublished note from Mary Burkett papers

9 Unpublished note from Sheona Lodge papers

Chapter Six

1 Morgan, p 156

2 Edward Lucie-Smith and Elizabeth Frink, *Frink: A Portrait*, p 35

3 ibid, p 60

4 Rawson, p 15

5 Lucie-Smith and Frink, p 29

6 Hepworth, p 92

7 Lucie-Smith and Frink, p 92

8 James, p 58

Chapter Seven

1   Autumn Stanley, *Mothers and Daughters of Invention*, pp 181–82

Chapter Eight

1   Martin Israel, *Precarious Living*, p 23
2   ibid, p 23
3   ibid, p 31
4   Morgan, p 156

Chapter Nine

1   Mary Burkett papers
2   Berlin Wall Memorial Site and Exhibition Center Association, *Berlin Wall*,
    p 40
3   ibid, p 34

Chapter Ten

1   Penelope Curtis, 'Return to Life: A New Look at the Portrait Bust',
    Catalogue of the 37th Exhibition of the Society of Portrait Sculptors,
    April 2000
2   ibid, p 16
3   James, p 204
4–6 Antony Gormley, 'Why the Body Needs to be set in Stone', *The Independent*,
    25 February 2001, p 10
7   Helen Simpson, 'Sculpture Parks 2000: Quality or Quantity?', p 7
8   ibid, p 8
9   Alan Bowness, *Modern European Art*, p 194

BIBLIOGRAPHY

Allingham, Margery, 'Green Corn', unpublished manuscript

Berlin Wall Memorial Site and Exhibition Center Association, *Berlin Wall*, Jaron Verlag GmbH, Berlin, 1999

Bowness, Alan, *Modern European Art*, Thames and Hudson, London, 1972

Burns, E Bradford, *A History of Brazil*, 3rd edition, Columbia University Press, New York, 1993

Bushnell, D and N Macaulay (eds), *Latin America in the Nineteenth Century*, OUP, Oxford, 1994

Chevalier, Denys, *Maillot*, Ufficio Press, Lugano, 1970

Clifford, Linda, *Sculptor: Josefina de Vasconcellos*, Linda Clifford, Southampton, 2000

Conniff, M L and F McCann (eds), *Modern Brazil-Elite and Masses in Historical Perspective*, University of Nebraska Press, Lincoln, USA, 1991

Cork, Richard, 'The Visual Arts', in *The Cambridge Guide to the Arts in Britain*, vol 8, CUP, Cambridge, 1989

Croft-Cooke, Rupert, *The Dogs of Peace*, W H Allen, London, 1973

Curtis, Penelope, *Sculpture 1900–1945*, OUP, Oxford, 1999

Fearon, George, *You Owe Me Five Farthin's*, Skeffington, London, 1961

Gombrich, E H, *The Story of Art*, Phaidon, Oxford, 1972

Gormley, Antony, *Exhibition Catalogue* for Malmö Konstall (1993), Tate Gallery, Liverpool (1993–94), Irish Museum of Modern Art (1994)

Hall, Marshall, *The Artists of Cumbria*, Marshall Hall Associates, Newcastle upon Tyne, 1979

Haring, C H, *Empire in Brazil*, Harvard University Press, Cambridge, Mass, 1958

Heaton Cooper, W, *Mountain Painter*, Frank Peters, Kendal, 1984

Hepworth, Barbara, *A Pictorial Autobiography*, Adams and Dart, Bath, 1970

Hewison, Robert, *Culture and Consensus: England, Art and Politics since 1940*, Methuen, London, 1995

Israel, Martin, *Precarious Living*, Mowbray, Oxford, 1982

James, Philip, *Henry Moore on Sculpture*, Macdonald, London, 1966

Lane, Margaret, *The Tale of Beatrix Potter*, Frederick Warne, London, 1946

Lord, James, *Giacometti: A Biography*, Farrar Straus Giroux, New York, 1983

Lucie-Smith, Edward and Elizabeth Frink, *Frink: A Portrait*, Bloomsbury, London, 1994

Maryon, Herbert, *Modern Sculpture: Its Methods and Ideals*, Sir Isaac Pitman and Sons, London, 1933

McKinlay, Robert, *The University of Bradford: the Early Years*, Bradford, 1998

Milner, John, *The Studios of Paris*, Yale University Press, London and New Haven, 1988

Morgan, Dewi (ed), *They Became Christians*, Mowbray, London, 1966

Rawson, Philip, *Sculpture*, University of Pennsylvania Press, Philadelphia, 1997

Sandilands, G S, 'Josefina de Vasconcellos', in *The Studio*, vol 151, no 754, January 1956

Simpson, Helen, 'Sculpture Parks 2000: Quality or Quantity?' in *Sculpture Matters*, Scottish Sculpture Trust, Edinburgh, September 2000

Stanley, Autumn, *Mothers and Daughters of Invention*, Rutgers University Press, New Brunswick, NJ, 1995

Taylor, Judy, *Beatrix Potter, Artist, Storyteller and Countrywoman*, Frederick Warne, Harmondsworth, 1986

Taylor, Judy (ed), *Beatrix Potter's Letters*, Frederick Warne, Harmondsworth, 1989

Thorogood, Julia, *Margery Allingham*, Heinemann, London, 1991

Wearing, J P, *American and British Theatrical Biography*, Scarecrow Press, NJ, 1979

Wilson, Sarah, 'Kurt Schwitters in England', Baltic Newsletter No.4, Gateshead

Woof, Robert, *The Artist as Evacuee: The Royal College of Art in the Lake District 1940–1945*, The Wordsworth Trust, 1987

REPRESENTATION IN MAJOR EXHIBITIONS

Royal Academy Summer Exhibitions, regularly from 1926 to 1966

'Sculpture by Josefina de Vasconcellos and Paintings by Delmar Banner',
Royal Watercolour Society Galleries, London, 1946–47

'The Famous in Sculpture', Imperial Institute, South Kensington, London,
1953, under the auspices of the Society of Portrait Sculptors, and annual
exhibitions of the Society from 1954 onwards

'Paintings by Delmar Banner and Sculpture by Josefina de Vasconcellos',
Royal Watercolour Society Galleries, London, 1955

'Sculpture in the Open Air', Battersea Park, London, 1960

'Intercession: Photographs and Sculpture on the theme of World Need',
St Paul's Cathedral, London, 1963

'Call to the Fells and Perchance to Dream' (Works by Delmar Banner
and Josefina de Vasconcellos), Bradford Art Galleries and Museums
in collaboration with the University of Bradford, 1987–88

One Man Show, Manchester Cathedral, 1991

'Art in the Garden', Oddfellows Gallery, Kendal, 1994

'Retrospective Exhibition', Oddfellows Gallery, Kendal, 1995

'The Tarns and Waterfalls of Cumbria', Oddfellows Contemporary Art Gallery,
Kendal, 1996

Recent Works, Stone Gallery, Kendal, 2001

ACKNOWLEDGEMENTS

Many of Josefina's friends have shared their recollections with me. Indeed, her circle is so wide that it has not been possible to consult everyone whose life has been touched by her unique qualities. I would like to thank in particular Dr Anne Mathieson for her sensitive insights, Mary Burkett for her clear and informed view of Cumbrian artists, and Dr Robert Woof and Pamela Woof for their interest and support. Among the many others whose advice has been most valuable are Maggie Berkovitch, Sir Richard Branson, Professor Andrew Burton, Eva Castle, Julian Cooper, Muriel Cuppage, Dr Penelope Curtis, Dr Ayliffe Edwards, Hugh Ellison, Meryll Evans, Margaret Eve, Gloria Greci, Jennifer Hales, Dr Theo Harman, Lady Jardine, Fenwick Lawson, Sheila Lemoine, Peter Lewis, Tamzin Lewis, Sarah Loveday, Leslie Meurant, Professor John Milner, Mary Neeson, Dr David Pearson, Rachel Polkinghorne, Leslie Randall, Dr Frances Spalding, Ann Taylforth, Helen Taylor Thompson, Julia Thorogood, Chris Wadsworth, Hugh Walter, Brenda Weedon, Canon Andrew White, and Derwent Wise. In creating a biography of a living person, the contribution of friends is crucial, and I am grateful for the material they have added to this book.

I would also like to thank the staff of both the Fine Art Library at the University of Newcastle and the Lit and Phil Library of Newcastle upon Tyne for their assistance. Helpful advice and information has also been provided by Abbot Hall, Coventry Cathedral, the John Rylands University Library, the Margery Allingham Estate, the Royal Academy of Arts, the Royal Geographical Society, the Royal Liverpool Philharmonic Society, the Royal Society of British Sculptors, the Royal Watercolour Society, the Society of Portrait Sculptors, the Theatre Museum, the University of Bradford, the University of Westminster, and the V&A Museum.

The extract from 'Green Corn' is published by kind permission of the Margery Allingham Estate. Unpublished letters to Mrs Banner from Beatrix Potter are published by kind permission of the V&A Museum, who received them as a gift from Mrs Banner. Direct quotations from Josefina came from interviews conducted by the author and private correspondence as this book was being written. Josefina herself has been unfailingly responsive during our discussions and has taken a great interest in this book, offering me access to a lifetime of personal memorabilia.

My thanks also go to Gainford Design Associates (Eddie, Ken, Freda and Amy) whose expertise has contributed a great deal to the appearance of this book.

Photographs

Photographs have been sourced mainly from Josefina's private collection. Particular thanks are due to B Broadway (68), Mary Burkett (69), Bernard Kunicki (back cover), Dermot MacGreevy (79), Dr David Pearson (63, 70, 71, 74, 75, 76, 77), Leslie Randall (57, 58), S Redman (42, 44, 48), University of Bradford Photographic Unit (67). Bryan Horner photographed much of the work of the Banners, and should be acknowledged for the front cover photograph, as well as 32, 33, 36, 38, 47, 49.

We regret that we have failed in our best attempts to trace the following photographers and agencies from the 1940s and 1950s, but wish to acknowledge their work and value the contribution they have made to this pictorial record of Josefina's career: Elsam, Mann and Cooper Ltd (51), Keystone Press Agency Ltd (46, 50), London News Agency Photos Ltd (54), Zichy at Baron Studios (52).

Credit to other photographers whom we have been unable to identify is given with gratitude.

End Pieces

The small illustrations placed at the end of some chapters are by Josefina, as are the motifs, and are taken from her unpublished book of poems, 'Words and Woodcuts'.

Abbot Hall, 78, 115, 160, 167

Académie de la Grande Chaumière, 32–35

Aldershot, Heroes' Shrine, 96–97, 188–189

Allingham, Marjorie, 22–25

Andreotti, Libero, 41–42

Art Bronze Foundry, 123

Balfour, Ronald, 56, 71, 85–86

Banner, Billy, 71, 90, 162–163

Banner, Brian, 71, 90, 135, 162, 198

Banner, Delmar, birth, 29; family, 30–31, 58; marriage, 51 ff; painting style, 61–62, 77–78; Lay Reader, 80; influence on Josefina, 93–94, 101, 168; Public Lecture, 99; unpublished book, 131–132, 145–146; death, 158

Battersea Park Exhibition, 122

Beckstones, *see* Outpost Emmaus

Belsky, Franta, 104, 109

Blackhall, David Scott, 120

Borrelli, Mario, 31, 115, 128

Branson, Sir Richard, 183–187, 203, 207

Brownsword, Howard, 22, 31

Butler, Fanny (Mrs Alfred Coleman), 5, 7, 58 (death)

Butler, Frank Hedges, 7–8

Burkett, Mary, 78, 118–119, 147, 158, 160, 168–170, 187

Calore, Guido, 31

Cameron, James, 110, 123, 144, 203

Castle, Eva, 106–107, 109, 192

Chacaro (Brown), Geoffrey, 57, 166, 170

Coleman, Dr Alfred, 3, 5–8, 150

Coleman, Freda (Mrs H de Vasconcellos), 2, 5, 27–39, 43, 63, 74, 96, 110, 125–127 (death)

Cooper, Julian, 103, 148

Coventry Cathedral (International Centre for Reconciliation), 183–186, 203–206

Cumbrian Sculptors, 204

da Fonseca, Marechal Deodoro, 3, 168

Delago, Giovanni, 43

Denning, Lord, 129, 157, 173, 175, 180

de Vasconcellos, Hippolyto, 2, 4–5, 8 ff, 25–27, 37–40, 43, 62–63 (death)

de Vasconcellos, Josefina (Mrs Banner), birth 2; school 10–14; visits to Brazil 15–17, 43–46, 168; Regent Street Polytechnic, 19–30; study in Paris 32–35; Florence, 31–32, 41–43; Varengeville commission, 35–37, 46–47; marriage, 49 ff; The Bield, 69–70; adopted children, 71–74; London studios, 91; 1947 Joint Exhibition with Delmar, 91–93; 1955 Joint Exhibition, 107–108; Outpost Emmaus, 129–134; buys farm, 135; inventions, 135–137, 148–150, 207; Harriet Trust, 150 ff; death of Delmar, 158; MBE, 161–162; Ambleside friends, 160–161; *Major Works*: Aldershot Memorial, 60–61, 96–97, 188–189; Last Chimera, 83–88, 92, 182; Boys Wrestling, 86–87, 122–123; Reunion, 107; Vision of Bega, 109; Mary and Child, 110; St Michael, 171–172; The Family of Man, 172; Joyous Mary and Babe, 174–175; Weight of Our Sins, 194–195; Reconciliation sculptures, 183–186, 196–198, 203–206; Escape to Light, 181–182, 194

Edinburgh Festival, 105

Edwards, Professor Ted, 144, 152, 155

Epstein, Jacob, 20, 47, 98, 104, 106

Evans, Meryll, 166, 173, 187

Festival of Britain, 97–98

Festival of the City of London, 124

Fiske, Robert and Elizabeth, 118

Frink, Elizabeth, 2, 139–141

Giacometti, Alberto, 34

Gormley, Antony, 210–211

Guild of Lakeland Craftsmen, 154

Hales family, 73

Hamilton, Richard, 77

Harman, Dr Theo, 146

Harriet Trust, 150–153, 157–158, 179–181, 193–194, 205

Hart, Barry, 19
Heaton Cooper, Ophelia, 102–104, 147–148
Heaton Cooper, William, 102–104
Henry Moore Institute, 206–207
Hepworth, Barbara, 2, 19–20, 31, 47, 59,
    87, 140–141
Herrmann, Zeugheer, 29–30
Hervey, Dr Ayliffe, 137–138, 152
Holy Trinity Church, 159, 174–175
Huyton Hill School, 72, 136

Israel, Dr Martin, 163–164

Kunicki, Bernard, 94–95

Lake Artists Society, 103, 204
Liverpool Cathedral, 128
Lodge family: Dr Oliver, 119–121; Sheona,
    119–121, 165, 170–173, 187, 189, 191;
    Fiona, 157; Anne (*see* Mathieson)

MacBride, Sean, 154–155
McKinlay, Dr Robert, 144–145, 205 (death)
Maillot, Aristide, 33
Manchester School of Art, 17, 19
Mathieson, Dr Anne, 157, 198
Mestrovic, Ivan, 33
Meurant, Leslie, 174, 178, 187
Moore, Henry, 19–20, 31, 47, 59, 78, 123,
    141, 210
Morgan, P H, 23, 35
Mowatt, Geoffrey, 119–120
Myerstein, E H W, 85

National Trust, 130, 154, 175–177
Nicholson, Norman, 111, 113, 118, 124,
    129, 156, 173

Oestreicher, Canon Paul, 183–185, 206
Outpost Emmaus (Beckstones), 129,
    130–135, 153–154, 205

Parbury, Kate, 98, 104
Park Lane Festival, 99
Pearson, Dr David, 190–191
Potter, Beatrix (Mrs Heelis), 63–68, 78–79,
    80–81

Randall, Leslie, 119, 133
Rawnsley, Canon Hardwicke, 90, 176
Rawnsley, Mrs Eleanor, 90–91
Regent Street Polytechnic, 19, 22–25, 91
Rodin, Auguste, 34, 195
Royal Academy, 39–41, 60–61, 85, 93, 103,
    123–124
Royal Academy Schools, 48–49
Royal College of Art, 19, 74–78 (in Ambleside)
Royal Society of British Sculptors (RBS),
    82, 93, 175
Royal Watercolour Society, 91, 107

St Bartholemew the Great, 124
St Martin in the Fields, 111–116, 125,
    128–129, 131
St Paul's Cathedral, 91, 109–110, 124–125,
    129
Schwitters, Kurt, 76–77, 129, 170
Sitwell, Edith, 99–100, 202
Society of Friends (Quakers), 143–144
Society of Portrait Sculptors, 96, 104–105,
    202–203
Spencer, Gilbert and family, 75–77
Spencer, Stanley, 76
Stalker, Stephen, 170–172, 194–195, 201,
    205, 208

Taylforth, Ann, 157–161, 175, 192, 201,
    207–208
Thurston, Christian, 191, 193, 198
Tristram, Professor E W, 75

University of Bradford, 108, 143–145,
    154–155, 160, 167, 182–183
Unknown Political Prisoner Competition, 100

Varengeville sur Mer, 36, 46–47

Walker, Hugh, 58, 71
Wheeler, Sir Charles, 70, 99, 104, 107, 203
Wilde, Andrew, 179, 195
Williams, The Reverend Austen, 111–114,
    129–133
Williamson, Shaun, 161, 173, 191
Woof, Dr Robert, 75–77
Wordsworth, Jonathan, 164–165